D0744544

# Work–Life Balance in the 21st Century

*The Future of Work Series*

Series Editor: **Peter Nolan**, Director of the ESRC Future of Work Programme and the Montague Burton Professor of Industrial Relations at Leeds University Business School in the UK.

Few subjects could be judged more vital to current policy and academic debates than the prospects for work and employment. *The Future of Work* series provides the much needed evidence and theoretical advances to enhance our understanding of the critical developments most likely to impact on people's working lives.

*Titles include:*

Julia Brannen, Peter Moss and Ann Mooney
WORKING AND CARING OVER THE TWENTIETH CENTURY
Change and Continuity in Four Generation Families

Geraldine Healy, Edmund Herry, Phil Taylor and William Brown (*editors*)
THE FUTURE OF WORKER REPRESENTATION

Diane M. Houston (*editor*)
WORK–LIFE BALANCE IN THE 21st CENTURY

Paul Stewart (*editor*)
GLOBALISATION, THE CHANGING NATURE OF EMPLOYMENT AND THE FUTURE OF WORK
The Experience of Work and Organisational Change

Michael White, Stephen Hill, Colin Mills and Deborah Smeaton
MANAGING TO CHANGE?
British Workplaces and the Future of Work

---

**The Future of Work Series**
**Series Standing Order ISBN 1–4039–1477–X**

You can receive future titles in this series as they are published by placing a standing order. Please contact your bookseller or, in case of difficulty, write to us at the address below with your name and address, the title of the series and one of the ISBNs quoted above.

Customer Services Department, Macmillan Distribution Ltd, Houndmills, Basingstoke, Hampshire RG21 6XS, England

---

# Work–Life Balance in the 21st Century

Diane M. Houston

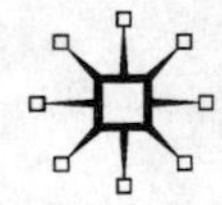



First published 2005 by
PALGRAVE MACMILLAN
Houndmills, Basingstoke, Hampshire RG21 6XS and
175 Fifth Avenue, New York, N. Y. 10010
Companies and representatives throughout the world

PALGRAVE MACMILLAN is the global academic imprint of the Palgrave Macmillan division of St. Martin's Press, LLC and of Palgrave Macmillan Ltd. Macmillan® is a registered trademark in the United States, United Kingdom and other countries. Palgrave is a registered trademark in the European Union and other countries.

ISBN-13: 978–1–4039–2062–1 hardback
ISBN-10: 1–4039–2062–1 hardback

This book is printed on paper suitable for recycling and made from fully managed and sustained forest sources.

A catalogue record for this book is available from the British Library.

Library of Congress Cataloging-in-Publication Data
Work–life balance in the 21st century / edited by Diane M. Houston.
p. cm. – (The future of work)
Includes bibliographical references and index.
ISBN 1–4039–2062–1
1. Work and family–Great Britain. 2. Work and family–Government policy–Great Britain. 3. Hours of labor, Flexible–Great Britain. 4. Personnel management–Great Britain. I. Title: Work–life balance in the twenty-first century. II. Houston, Diane M. III. Future of work (Series)

HD4904.25.W737 2005
306.3′6′0947–dc22 2004051400

10 9 8 7 6 5 4 3
14 13 12 11 10 09 08 07 06 05

Printed and bound in Great Britain by
Antony Rowe Ltd, Chippenham and Eastbourne

# Contents

# Acknowledgements

This book was planned quite some time ago, indeed the idea for the book was conceived before much of the data described in the chapters was even collected. Since this time the life events of many of the contributors would be sufficient to fill an entirely different kind of volume! I am grateful to all those who have contributed for their continued commitment and good humour. On behalf of all the authors I would like to acknowledge the Economic and Social Research Council's funding for the projects from which all the chapters are drawn. Particular thanks must also go to Peter Nolan for his support to us all throughout the Future of Work Programme. Here at the University of Kent, Jennifer Degnan Smith did an excellent job of supporting me in her role as editorial assistant and in producing the index for the book. Finally, I am grateful to my children, Ben, Zoe and Alice, for their part in enhancing my work–life balance in the 21st Century!

# Foreword

The boundaries between paid employment, unpaid domestic labour and leisure are blurring. The rhythms and patterns of employment are changing, many commentators argue, to accommodate the realities of global competition. There is clear evidence of new patterns of working – in hotels, catering, retail, and other services such as hairdressing. But the widely cited twenty-four hour seven days a week economy has been a reality for many workers in, for example, the health service and manufacturing for decades.

In the early years of the twenty first century, there is evidence that the strains on households and parents are becoming more taxing. What are the implications of home-working and how have new management practices impacted on working lives? This important new book explores the complex dynamics that are reshaping the domestic and employment experiences of people in the UK. It reveals that global competition is one dynamic affecting working patterns, but there are other determining factors constraining and constructing the choices that people are making with respect to work and family life.

The most authoritative research on this subject, this collection of essays draws upon the projects conducted under the ESRC Future of Work Programme. Based in 22 UK Universities since 1998, the researchers involved in the Future of Work Programme have explored the impact of new management practices on the employment prospects of women with young children, the impact of human resource management on working time, and the factors that shape the choices that women make with respect to employment. Other projects have investigated historically the changing boundaries of paid and unpaid work, and, with an international focus, the effects on work of different systems of care provision for the elderly in Europe and beyond.

Bringing together leading sociologists, psychologists and economists in the UK, this important new book demonstrates the knowledge benefits of constructive collaboration between social scientists that form different disciplines. The results of this collaboration will shape the policy and academic agenda for the next decade.

Peter Nolan
Director
ESRC Future of Work Programme

# List of Tables

# List of Figures

# List of Contributors

**Chris Baldry** is Professor of Human Resource Management in the Department of Management and Organisation at the University of Stirling. His research interests have included technological change in the workplace, occupational health, changes and continuities in the experience of work, and the social construction of workspace. He is also Editor of the journal *New Technology, Work and Employment.*

**Alison L. Booth** is Professor of Economics at the Australian National University and also at the University of Essex. She is a Research Fellow of the Centre for Economic Policy Research (CEPR), London (since 1993) and of the IZA Bonn (since 1996). She was appointed as Fellow of the Royal Society of Arts (FRSA) in 1999. She is known for her work on trade unions, gender issues and human capital formation, and has written and edited books in these fields in addition to international refereed journal articles. She has received research grants from the Economic and Social Research Council (ESRC), the Leverhulme Trust, the Nuffield Foundation and the Australian Research Council.

**Harriet Bradley** is Professor of Sociology and Dean of the School of Social Science and Law, University of Bristol. Professor Bradley is an acknowledged expert on the sociology of gender, ethnicity and work.

**Irene Bruegel** is joint leader of the Employment and Education element of the ESRC programme of research on Families and Social Capital at London South Bank University. She previously directed the Local Economy Policy Unit at South Bank. The main body of her research relates to the gendered construction of labour markets in Western Economies.

**Nickie Charles** is Professor of Sociology in the School of Social Sciences and International Development at the University of Wales Swansea. She is currently working on an ESRC-funded project, 'Social change, family formation and kin relations', and has recently published a book, *Gender in Modern Britain* (Oxford University Press, 2002).

**Angela Dale** is Professor of Quantitative Social Research at the Centre for Census and Survey Research (CCSR) at the University of Manchester. She became Director of the ESRC Research Methods Programme in 2002 and was formerly Director of CCSR. Her current research extends analysis of Pakistani and Bangladeshi women's labour market experiences to draw comparison across a wider range of ethnic groups. She is also heading one of the 'value-added' arms of the new Economic and Social Data Service that is responsible for large-scale government surveys and leads the CCSR team providing academic access and support for microdata samples (Samples of Anonymised Records) from the Census.

**Andy Danford** is Reader in Employment Relations. He has published widely in the areas of trade union renewal and critical studies of lean production in the aerospace and automotive sectors.

**Jeff Frank** is Professor of Economics at Royal Holloway College, University of London. He was previously Reader in Economics at the University of Essex, and has been Visiting Professor at the University of Callfornia (Berkeley) and the Kennedy School of Government, Harvard University. Frank's primary research topics include the interaction of labour and financial markets with macroeconomic fluctuations; incentive systems (including performance related pay and the use of promotions) in labour markets; and the unequal experiences of different groups (by ethnicity, gender and sexuality) in the labour market.

**Anne Gray** is a Senior Researh Fellow in the Families and Social Capital Research Group, London South Bank University. Working on time use and care, she has written a number of papers on the division of childcare responsibilities between fathers, mothers, grandparents and other carers. She is also the author of several publications on labour market issues, including most recently 'Unsocial Europe; Social Protection or Flexploitation?' (Pluto, 2004).

**Catherine Hakim** is Senior Research Fellow in the Sociology Department, London School of Economics in London, England. Her research covers women's employment and work orientations, occupational segregation, and changing patterns of employment. Publications include *Key Issues in Women's Work* (2004), *Work-Lifestyle Choices in the 21st Century* (2000), *Models of the Family in Modern Societies: Ideals and Realities* (2003), *Social Change and Innovation in the Labour Market* (1998), and over 70 papers in academic journals and books.

**Geraldine Healy** is Professor of Employment Relations, Centre for Business Management, Queen Mary, University of London. Professor Healy has published widely on gender, ethnicity, career and employment.

**Diane M. Houston** is Professor of Psychology at the University of Kent, where she directs the Work–Life Research Group. Her research interests are within applied social psychology and its interface with sociology, particularly in the areas of work, health and education. She has been a research advisor to The Women and Equality Unit in the Department of Trade and Industry, The Equal Opportunities Commission and Chartered Institute of Personnel Development.

**Jeff Hyman** is Professor of Human Resource Management in the Department of Management Studies at the University of Aberdeen Business School. His main research interests include the future of work, work–life balance and industrial democracy.

**Emma James** is a Research Fellow in the National Centre for Public Policy, also at the University of Wales Swansea, where she works in areas of public policy and health and pursues her interests in rural Welsh community studies. She has authored a chapter on Welsh rural communities in an edited book, *Welsh Communities: New Ethnographic Perspectives* (University of Wales Press, 2003).

**Gillian Marks** is Lecturer in psychology at Leeds Metropolitan University. Her research interests are in social and health psychology.

**Nupur Mukherjee** was a Research Officer at the University of Bristol, she then worked as a researcher on a qualitative evaluation of the Connexions programme funded by Dfes.

**Mike Richardson** is a Senior Researcher in Industrial Relations. He is co-author with Andy Danford and Martin Upchurch of *New Unions, New Workplaces*.

**Michael Rose** is Professorial Research Fellow at the University of Bath and Editor in chief of *Work, Employment & Society*. During his long career, which began as a research officer for the classic Luton Studies in the 1960s, he has taught and researched mainly at Bath University, and also at several French universities, where he wrote *Servants of Post-Industrial Power?* (1979). His publications in English include 10 single author or joint author books, notably *Reworking the Work Ethic* (1985) and *Sill and Occupational Change* (1994, edited jointly with R. Penn and J. Rubery) and numerous articles or chapters. He directed research projects for large-scale ESRC programmes such as SCELI in the 1980s, the *Future of Work* in the early 2000s, and currently the *e-Society*, and made OU films related to employment. In the last 10 years he has specialised in secondary analysis of large employee data-sets to develop a longer-term concern with relations between work attitudes and skills.

**Dora Scholarios** is a Reader in Organisational Behaviour at the Department of Human Resource Management in the University of Strathclyde, Glasgow,

Scotland. She received her PhD in Industrial/Organizational Psychology from The George Washington University in Washington, D.C. (1990). Her research interests are in the areas of personnel selection and classification, social process perspectives of selection, and the effects of emerging forms of work on career patterns and employee well being.

**Maria Sigala** is a researcher in the Department of Social Policy and Social Work at the University of Oxford. Her educational background is in social and economic psychology and she has researched the psychology of taxation, women's decisions about work and childcare, and poverty.

**Paul Stewart** is Professor of the Sociology of Work and Employment. He has published widely in the areas of employment relations and labour processes in the automotive industry and the new lean politics of partnership at work.

**Stephanie Tailby** is Principal Lecturer in Employment Relations. Her recent research focuses on 'partnership at work' in the UK, and contingent employment in the European healthcare and financial services sectors.

**Clare Ungerson** was Professor of Social Policy at the University of Southampton from 1993–2004. She has recently retired from that post and is now an Honorary Professor of Social Policy in the School of Social Policy, Sociology and Social Research at the University of Kent where she continues to research and write. She has published widely in the field of gender and social policy in general, and on the topic of gender and care in particular and is the author of many books and articles across a wide range of disciplines, including social policy, sociology, gerontology, and women's studies.

**Martin Upchurch** is Reader in International Employment Relations. His research focuses on trade union strategies and comparative industrial relations.

**Sue Yeandle** is Professor of Sociology at Sheffield Hallam University, where until recently she was Head of Social Policy Research in the Centre for Regional Economic and Social Research (CRESR); she is now Director of the Centre for Social Inclusion at Sheffield Hallam. She has published widely particularly in the field of gender and employment, on work/life balance, and on domestic and care work in the European Union. She is currently engaged in work on gender mainstreaming in relation to local government service delivery.

# 1

# Work–Life Balance in the 21st Century

*Diane M. Houston*

> Working longer and longer hours is not good for business – or for you. Worrying about childcare or eldercare will only add to your stress levels. Returning to work too soon after a major life event such as birth, death or illness is likely to take its toll in the end.
>
> But if you work with your employer (or with your staff if you're an employer or manager yourself), together you can find ways to be more flexible about working arrangements. And there'll be benefits all round.
>
> Work–life balance isn't only about families and childcare. Nor is it about working less. It's about working 'smart'. About being fresh enough to give you all you need for both work and home, without jeopardising one for the other. And it's a necessity for everyone, at whatever stage you are in your life. (Department for Trade and Industry, UK, 2001)

In March 2000, the UK Prime Minister, Tony Blair, launched the Government's campaign to promote a better work–life balance at a business breakfast at 10 Downing Street. The ongoing government campaign aims to encourage employers to introduce flexible working practices and stresses the need for work–life balance for all workers, not just those with caring responsibilities. In April 2003, a legislative measure was introduced giving parents with children aged under six, or disabled children under 18, the right to request a flexible working pattern and their employers the duty to consider their applications seriously. In order to monitor attitudes, demand and uptake of work–life balance policies and to examine the impact of such policies on business, a baseline study of both employers and employees was conducted in 2000 (WLB1, Hogarth *et al.*, 2000) and this was followed up in 2003 (WLB2, Woodland *et al.*, 2003; Stevens *et al.*, 2004).

## Why work–life balance?

The current promotion of work–life balance in the UK reflects changes in the economic and political climate as well as social changes. The drive for change in employment practices is, to some extent, related to changes in families and family life. The gap in economic activity rates between women and men has declined from 22 per cent in 1984 to 12 per cent in 2001. This reflects increasing employment rates among women in the 1980s, and decreasing labour market participation among men in the 1990s. (Dench *et al.*, 2002). One key aspect of women's increasing economic participation has been the employment rates of women with preschool children which almost doubled from 28 per cent in 1980 to 53 per cent in 1999 (McRae, 2003). Decreasing numbers of families now assume the traditional model of fathers who work and mothers who remain at home to care for children and/or the elderly. In addition there has been dramatic growth in the number of one-parent households from 9 per cent in 1971 to 25 per cent in 2001. Lone parents are predominantly mothers (22%), rather than fathers (3%) (Dench *et al.*, 2002).

Political pressure for legislation to promote work–life balance has come from the European Commission as part of the European Employment Strategy, which aims to modernise and reform EU labour markets. With European Social Funding (ESF) funding, key priorities in the first six years of the 21st century are to prevent the drift into long-term unemployment, reintegrate marginalised groups into the economy and society, and help in the transition towards the knowledge-based economy. In the UK, the 2001 Labour Party Manifesto made commitments to 'fair and flexible work' and to increase maternity leave and introduce statutory paternity pay. As a consequence, rights to flexible working for parents and additional maternity leave for mothers, as well as a new right for fathers, were implemented in 2003.[1]

Despite political and social pressure for work–life balance, the drive for more flexible working is strongly related to the needs of employers. Within business, globalisation and the new economy have resulted in changes in customer demands and expectations for access to goods and services 24 hours a day. Increasingly this means that organisations must operate outside the traditional nine to five structure. Therefore organisations have to employ people who are prepared to work flexibly outside traditional working hours. Flexible working is popularly viewed as a means of increasing work–life balance for the individual, however, from an organisational perspective the benefits of flexible working may be related to non-standard contracts and the elimination of overtime payments, rather than greater work–life balance for employees. Purcell *et al.* (1999) found that contract flexibility did facilitate labour market participation for certain groups, such as students. However for many employees flexible working resulted in greater job insecurity and poor conditions of employment.

The tensions between the individual's desire for work–life balance and employers' need for greater flexibility are reflected in employees' attitudes and work behaviour. Employees in the United Kingdom work the longest hours of any European country (Eurostat, 1997). Long hours are particularly common amongst men who have partners and children. Dual earner couples have become the norm, but women's participation in the workforce continues to be limited by the presence and age of a dependent child. The birth of children continues to perpetuate traditional divisions of work and caring roles in most couples, despite an expressed desire to share these roles more equally (Houston and Marks, 2002, 2005; Houston and Waumsley, 2003). Most women with children move into part-time work, but part-time working and career breaks negatively impact upon women's lifetime earnings and the gender pay gap (Anderson, Forth, Metcalf and Kirby, 2001; Walby and Olsen, 2002; Manning and Petrongolo, 2004).

The WLB2 survey (Woodland *et al.*, 2003; Stevens *et al.*, 2004) reported a high level of support for the principle of work–life balance, with 94 per cent of employers and 95 per cent of employees agreeing that 'people work best when they can balance their work and other aspects of their lives'. However the employee survey revealed clear anxiety about the impact of flexible working on job security and career prospects. Men were more likely than women to agree that flexible working patterns would damage their career prospects and job security. Fifty-one percent of employees agreed that working reduced hours would negatively affect their career – and only 38 per cent disagreed. Not being able to work beyond their contracted hours was seen as having a negative effect on career by 42 per cent, as were leaving to look after a child (37%) and working from home (25%). Similar findings were reported by Houston and Waumsley (2003), whose survey of electrical and engineering workers, highlighted the tension between desire for flexible working and success at work.

## The chapters

This edited book presents work from 12 projects within the ESRC's Future of Work Research Programme, launched in 1998. Across the 12 projects there are analyses of large-scale national surveys, in-depth studies of individual workers and carers, and comparative studies of organisations. The qualitative and quantitative research reflects the breadth of UK social science – economics, sociology, social policy, psychology, industrial relations and human resource management. These different methodologies, disciplinary and theoretical perspectives, are linked in their analysis of work–life balance in the UK and Europe.

Booth and Frank begin by providing a helpful analysis of how labour market flexibility can have very different outcomes for employees as well as the ways in which non-standard jobs can vary dramatically in their format.

Drawing on the results of a series of papers from their Future of Work project, Booth and Frank consider evidence about the prevalence of non-standard jobs in the British economy, their rates of pay, and the gender balance of non-standard jobs. They go on to discuss how different policies, such as equal pay rules, might result in greater equality in pay and opportunity for men and women in the workplace. They argue that their research does not support the policies of stipulating equal pay and conditions for different types of contracts (temporary vs permanent, and full-time vs part-time). Instead, they suggest extending greater flexibility (particularly with respect to career breaks) throughout the economy, for all workers. In recognition of the fact that a major factor behind non-standard work flexibility is child-rearing, Booth and Frank also suggest that, as children represent an externality for society as a whole, parents could be subsidised for raising children.

Rose's chapter examines career outlook (the readiness to state that one has a career), its growth since the 1980s, and its consequences for success at work and personal well-being. Rose demonstrates that almost two-thirds of British employees now regard themselves as having a career, compared to only half in 1985. By contrast career commitment or 'careerism' has not increased substantially, however those who show high levels of career commitment get rapid promotion and pay increases. Careerists work longer hours, but they do not appear to suffer negative consequences of this in terms of their own work–life balance and its impact on health and relationships.

Hakim examines national survey data in the context of Preference Theory (Hakim, 2000). She demonstrates that substantial sex differences persist in the propensity to adopt a primary or secondary earner identity and that these cut across levels of education, income and social class. However she argues that differences between three lifestyle preference groups (work-centred, adaptive and home-centred) are more important than sex differences in work orientations and job values. Further, that policies that are aimed at those who seek a balance between work and family life will be of little interest to those who are work-centred and therefore prioritise work over family in the pursuit of their careers. Hakim concludes that 'employers and national governments need to recognise the diversity of lifestyle preferences among women *and* men, and devise policies that are neutral between the three lifestyle preference groups' (Hakim, 2005).

Houston and Marks report evidence from a longitudinal survey of first-time mother's intentions in relation to work and childcare, and their experiences during the three years after the birth of their child. The attitudes, beliefs and experiences of those who worked full-time, part-time or did no paid work were compared and examined in the context of the debate around women's work orientation (e.g. Crompton and Harris, 1998; Hakim, 2000; McRae, 2003). The findings from this study revealed a high level of satisfaction amongst women who had given up work to care for their child, particularly in relation to the impact of this decision on their child. Women who were combining paid work with motherhood expressed concerns about the impact this was having on their child, whilst recognising that their own work participation was important for both income and their career progression. While the majority of women in the survey sought a balance between work and family, they had to overcome both psychological and practical barriers in order to work. The majority of women wanted a more equal balance of work and caring between themselves and their partner and wanted very young children to be cared for within their own families. This chapter also highlights women's frustration at not being able to find rewarding part-time work that reflected their own experience and aspirations.

Difficulties with part-time work are echoed in Sigala's chapter which describes a qualitative study of 16 mothers of preschool children who worked part-time. Sigala describes women's frustration with organisational cultures, their inability to fashion an identity for themselves as legitimate members of their organisation and the career costs of part-time employment. As part-time work is a key component of flexible working in many organisations, this and previous chapters challenge the extent to which part-time work (in its current form) is a useful stepping-stone in working life.

The importance of family support in balancing work and caring is a dominant theme in the chapter by Hyman, Scholarios and Baldry. They conducted a study of call centre workers, a fast growing area of service work, typified by shift and seven-day working and populated by high proportions of women. Despite the flexibility required to staff call centres, the researchers found little evidence of employer policies which supported families or helped employees to manage their working time. Most of the call centre workers relied upon their partner and grandparents to balance the demands of work and caring, alongside informal support by work colleagues in balancing shifts and work cover. The authors argue that organisational flexibility in reality means imposing temporal flexibility onto workers to meet service demands, rather than providing flexible but predictable working times suited to the needs of employees.

Using national survey data, Bruegel and Gray explore the ways in which work culture and family factors may influence fathers' care of their children. They found that fathers work longer hours, for higher pay, in more male dominated work environments than other men; by contrast mothers work shorter hours, for lower pay in more feminised environments than other women. The chapter examines the complex relationship between working environments, working time, maternal employment and fathers' participation in care. Bruegel and Gray conclude that the interaction between family relationships and economic pressures result in a complex picture of the division of childcare between parents, which highlights the contradiction between the persistent dominance of the role of male breadwinner with increased salience of the role of carer in modern fatherhood.

Charles and James describe an interview study with employees in three different workplaces. They explore the gendering of work–life balance and whether or not it is affected by experiences of job insecurity, family-friendly policies and flexible working. The three different workplaces were associated with different ways of reconciling paid employment and unpaid care work. In retail work the availability of part-time hours of work enabled women to care for their children while their partners retained a provider role. In the public sector the availability of maternity leave and chilcare facilities enabled women to combine motherhood with full-time employment. In the manufacturing organisation both women and men tended to work full-time, many of them on shifts, and informal arrangements were used for reconciling paid work and childcare. In manufacturing there was a view that job insecurity was as bad for women as it was for men as women were just as likely to be their families' main providers; in the other two workplaces the view that it was worse for men because of their provider role was more widespread. The authors suggest that family-friendly policies can have the effect of reproducing a gendered work–life balance.

Tailby, Richardson, Danford, Stewart and Upchurch consider the potential for partnership between employers and trade unions for working together on work–life balance issues. Their chapter reports evidence amassed from a case study of one local authority that illustrates some of the tensions and contradictions of such partnership. Tailby *et al.* found that work–life balance was not the most salient of issues for employees. Whilst there was support amongst employees for work–life balance in principle, issues of pay were more salient and the authors argue that many of those who took part in the survey could not afford to consider alternative working patterns as they needed to work long hours or multiple contracts to gain an adequate income. In organisational terms there were clear tensions between the need to obtain cost savings and efficiency gains and the implementation of work–life policies. Tailby *et al.* highlight the contradiction between work intensification and work–life balance in the 21st century.

Bradley, Healy and Mukherjee broaden the analysis of work–life balance, beyond paid work to voluntary, political and community work. Their focus is on black and minority ethnic women and their experience of trade union activism. They found that, whilst struggling to handle the demands of family and work, black and Asian women also suffered the multiple effects of racism and sexism. This experience shaped their willingness to get involved in trade unions and struggle for social justice in the workplace and in their local communities. Thus the attachment of these women to voluntary work, especially within ethnic communities, was a key issue emerging from the study. The authors argue that it was commitment and passion for racial harmony and justice that fuelled these women activists' ability to handle their multiple burdens.

Pakistani and Bangladeshi women have tended to have much lower levels of labour force participation by comparison with other ethnic groups, but those with higher educational qualifications are much more likely to be economically active than those without such qualifications. Angela Dale's chapter explores how family formation influences labour market participation amongst women with different levels of qualifications and what changes we can expect amongst younger Pakistani and Bangladeshi women who have grown up in the UK. Dale finds very clear evidence of change across generations. By contrast with their mothers' generation, where family took priority and there were few opportunities for paid work outside the home, younger women who had been educated in the UK saw paid work as a means to independence and self-esteem. Despite this, all the women interviewed expected to get married and have children, and accepted that this would require some adjustments to their working lives. Women with higher-level qualifications also showed considerable determination in wanting to combine paid work and childcare. Dale argues that, by comparison with their white counterparts, Pakistani and Bangladeshi women face many more difficulties in reconciling work and family.

The final chapter in this volume, by Ungerson and Yeandle, presents a unique perspective on care of the elderly and work–life balance. They use empirical data generated by a cross-national study, conducted in five European countries, of elderly care users and their care workers who were employed directly by them. The care users were enabled to employ their own care workers through the operation of cash supplements paid to them by their respective welfare states. The chapter outlines the way in which the dichotomous concept of 'work–life balance' can be divided into three types of time: work time, care time and personal time. This threefold distinction is then used as the underpinning concept for an analysis of the way in which the payment of care workers and caregivers impacts on their ability to maintain a balance between these various types of time. Ungerson and Yeandle suggest that different schemes, and the way they are regulated, determine the way in which the care workers can balance their work time, care time and personal time, and finds that while some schemes are organised in such a way that the workers gain in self-esteem and in personal time, others, in the less regulated schemes, lose autonomy altogether.

## Implications for employment practice and policy

The chapters in this book demonstrate that work–life balance is very much a theme for the 21st century. However, the research described paints a picture of imbalance, rather than balance, in terms of the interplay between work and the rest of life. Changes in social attitudes and increases in material aspirations and consumer debt (Schor, 1991) have resulted in the growth of the dual earner family. However the impact of childbirth and care responsibilities across the lifespan continues to perpetuate traditional divisions of labour between the majority of men and women. Flexible working may provide an opportunity for women who have children to participate in the labour market, but their participation is constrained by the poor opportunities offered by part-time and non-standard work. Work intensification and the growth of a 24/7 economy have also provided even greater opportunities for men to engage in more work, particularly in order to compensate for reductions in their partner's employment. Across this book there is a great deal of evidence that men are seeking to have greater input into family life, and that both men and women want to share work and care more equally. However this desire is constrained by the need for reliable income and/or aspirations for careers which, currently require long hours, either to make ends meet in low paid work, or to demonstrate 'commitment' in career positions. Family-friendly or flexible working has the potential to either deepen, or eliminate, the gender differences in work participation. Unless flexible working and other work–life balance policies become synonymous with high levels of performance and ethical work practices they will not be used by those who perceive themselves to be either breadwinners or careerists. Unless rights to flexible working become universal, for all employees, there may be division within workforces and discrimination against those groups who have the right to periods of leave or flexibility. Moreover, for those working for low pay, where long hours are the only means of reaching a basic standard of living, work–life balance will only be achieved by further improvements in the minimum wage and in contractual conditions for non-standard and part-time workers.

For both employees and employers, there are already strong reasons for organisations to challenge the long hours culture and create working environments that facilitate work–life balance across the life-course: the impending pensions crisis (Ginn, 2003) and the prospect of longer, healthier lives means that it is likely that people will work longer, and thus seek more flexibility at different periods in their working lives. A great deal of research has shown that working long hours has wide ranging negative effects on family life (e.g. Dex, 2003; White, Hill, McGovern, Mills and Smeaton, 2003). More generally, there are established physical and psychological costs of work-related stress (e.g. Michie and Williams, 2003). Psychological research has also investigated the causes of errors in a wide variety of jobs and demonstrated that error-proneness is increased by continuous long periods of task performance, as well as by time pressure (e.g. Reason, 1990). Despite a considerable body of research that examines the impact of work on outcomes for the individual, there is a need for more research which specifically measures the relationship between productivity and hours of work. Kodz (2003) conducted a comprehensive review of long hours working for the Department of Trade and Industry. Whilst this highlights methodological difficulties with the research base, the evidence reviewed gives absolutely no indication that long hours are beneficial in terms of productivity. This review, combined with the very substantial evidence of the impact of long hours on individual's health, well-being and performance, indicates that there can be no good business case for the perpetuation of a long hours culture. Working more flexibly, daily or across the life-course, will require radical assessment of the individual's role within organisations as well as the way in which work tasks are allocated and performance managed. However, this may create entirely new possibilities for productivity and innovation, as well as gender equity and work–life balance.

## Note

1. From April 2003 a statutory right to maternity leave of 26 weeks was introduced, 6 weeks at 90 per cent of pay and 20 weeks at £100 per week. For fathers the right to two weeks leave, paid at £100 a week was introduced.

## References


Anderson, T., Forth, J., Metcalf, H. and Kirby, S. (2001) *The Gender Pay Gap*, Women and Equality Unit, London.

Crompton, R. and Harris, F. (1998) Explaining women's employment patterns: orientations to work revisited, *British Journal of Sociology, 30*, 425–27.

Dench, S., Aston, J., Evans, C., Meager, N., Williams, M. and Willison, R. (2002) *Key Indicators of Women's Position in Britain*, Women and Equality Unit, London.

Dex, S. (2003) *Families and Work in the Twenty-First Century*, JRF, The Policy Press.

Eurostat (1997) *Labour Force Survey Results, 1996*, Luxembourg, Office for Official Publications for European Communities.

Ginn, J. (2003) *Gender, Pensions and the Lifecourse*, Bristol, The Policy Press.

Hakim, C. (2000) *Work-lifestyle Choices in the 21st Century: Preference Theory*, Oxford: Oxford University Press.

Hakim, C. (2005) Sex differences in work-life balance goals, in Houston D.M. (ed.), *Work life Balance in the Twenty First Century*, Palgrave.

Hogarth, T., Hasluck, C., Pierre, G., Winterbottom, M. and Vivan, D. (2000) *Work-life Balance 2000: Baseline study of work-life balance practices in Great Britain*, Institute of Employment Research, DfEE.

Houston, D.M. and Marks, G. (2002) *Paid and unpaid work in early parenthood*, End of Award Report to the Economic and Social Research Council.

Houston, D.M. and Marks, G. (2005) Working, caring and sharing: Work-life dilemmas in early motherhood, in Houston D.M. (ed.), *Work-life Balance in the Twenty-First Century*, Palgrave.

Houston, D.M. and Waumsley, J.A. (2003) *Attitudes to flexible working and family life*, JRF, The Policy Press.

Kodz, J. (2003) *Working Long Hours: A review of the evidence*, Employment Relations Research Series, DTI, London.

Manning, A. and Petrongolo, B. (2004) *The Part Time Pay Penalty*, Women and Equality Unit, London.

McRae, S. (2003) Constraints and choices in mothers' employment careers: a consideration of Hakim's Preference Theory, *British Journal of Sociology, 54*, 317–38.

Michie, S. and Williams, S. (2003) Reducing work related psychological ill health and sickness absence: a systematic literature review, *Occupational and Environmental Medicine, 60(1)*, 3–9.

Purcell, K., Hogarth, T. and Simm, C. (1999) *Whose Flexibility? The Costs and Benefits of 'Non-Standard' Working Arrangements and Contractual Relations*, JRF.

Reason, J. (1990) *Human Error*, Cambridge University Press.

Schor, J. (1991) *The Overworked American: The Unexpected Decline of Leisure*, New York: Basic Books.

Stevens, J., Brown, J. and Lee, C. (2004) *The Second Work-life Balance Study: Results from the Employees' Survey*, DTI.

Walby, S. and Olsen, W. (2002) *The Impact of Women's Position in the Labour Market on Pay and Implications for UK Productivity*, Women and Equality Unit, London.

White, M., Hill, S., McGovern, P., Mills, C. and Smeaton, D. (2003) High performance management practices, working house and work-life balance. *British Journal of Industrial Relations, 41*, 175–95.

Woodland, S., Simmonds, N., Thornby, M., Fitzgerald, R. and McGee, A. (2003) *The Second Work-life Balance Study: Results from the Employers Survey*, National Centre for Social Research, DTI.

# 2

# Gender and Work–Life Flexibility in the Labour Market

*Alison L. Booth and Jeff Frank*

A friend had a job playing in *The Mousetrap* in London. It was a one-year contract (with no chance of renewal), involved 8 shows a week (6 evenings and 2 matinees), and contained a gratuity clause where he would be penalised £50 (from the end-of-contract gratuity) for every show he missed, even if due to illness. This contract reflects the sort of labour market flexibility desired by some employers, with no employment protection, with effectively no sick pay, and with unsocial hours. Employers would argue that this flexibility serves a clear functional purpose. The unsocial hours are necessary since not many people would go to see a performance at 9 in the morning. The one year limit on employment is necessary since a regular turnover of cast is important to keep the show fresh. Absences – even due to illness – need to be discouraged since it is undesirable to have understudies rather than cast members perform. Employers would also argue that workers receive the appropriate compensation for this flexibility. While this particular contract can be extremely attractive to some individuals – and indeed there is no difficulty in recruiting new cast members – it would also be extremely inconvenient to others. In a competitive labour market, the rate of pay would contain 'compensating differentials' – by which is meant that wages must be higher if a job is unattractive to compensate for the disutility of working there and lower if a job is attractive. Depending upon supply and demand, the equilibrium compensating differential might be positive (if there are few individuals who wish to work these inflexible hours) or negative (if individuals take advantage of the late hours of performances to take on a day job as well as the *Mousetrap* contract).

The *Mousetrap* contract contains flexibility in the sense that the terms and conditions of the contract differ from the standard ones in the economy, and are designed largely for the benefit of the employer. A very different sort of flexibility might benefit workers. Employees might wish to have greater flexibility in their job in terms of hours worked (both number of hours and times during the week) or the possibility of taking extended leave from work, perhaps to raise children. One way of obtaining this sort of flexibility is to have a 'spot' market for labour. Just as you can draw on your electricity supply – and, in some areas, return your home-generated electricity into the mains system – whenever you wish (although, in some systems, at different pricing depending upon the time of day), you could show up for work as you wish, choosing your hours and days, and even taking months or years off to raise children or travel the world. While the market could have different wages for different times of days – for example, higher wages during lunchtime hours and over the weekends – it would not penalise part-time working or other forms of flexitime.

It is not realistic to expect there to be spot markets of this sort. One reason is that labour is not – unlike electricity – a homogeneous good. If someone teaches financial economics, and someone else teaches development economics, the second lecturer cannot bid to show up to teach a lecture on option pricing. The quality of output is not easily measured, and as a result firms need to offer complex incentives – including promotion systems – to induce worker effort and consequent high productivity. There needs to be investment on both sides in both general training and in job-specific training. Unions and individual workers will also wish to bargain with employers to ensure a split (between the employer and the workers) of the gains to an employment relationship, rather than – as might happen in a flexible labour market – leaving the employer with all the gains to trade.

In practice, individuals wanting flexibility in their jobs – for example, for child-rearing – often face a limited menu of choices. They may have to choose occupations where the hours and terms of work meet their personal interests, and employers that are prepared to accommodate requests for flexitime. The research we report in this paper confirms that jobs with non-standard hours of work are often otherwise unattractive jobs, with low training, low job satisfaction, and low pay. Women – particularly those who are rearing children – may have to take these jobs to gain the necessary work–life flexibility. As a result, there is an apparent gender bias in wages and conditions of work that raises fairness issues. Interestingly, though, we find that the disadvantages faced by women in the workforce are not uniform. There is evidence that women do not suffer in promotions relative to men, although they do suffer in the wage rises received consequent upon promotion. Women do not suffer the same scarring effect from part-time and temporary jobs that men suffer from taking such jobs. It is important in evaluating policy to understand these nuances of differential outcomes in the economy. It is also vital to try to understand the mechanisms that sustain unequal outcomes. For example, in our research we find that outside offers, and employers' responses to outside offers, is significant in explaining the existence of the gender pay gap.

After exploring our findings about the nature of non-standard jobs and the nature of the gender gap relating to non-standard jobs, we turn to policy. We begin by considering policies such as equal wages. It is not clear that equal wage rates across different types of jobs and contracts are either fair or efficient. Productivity may well differ across numbers of hours worked, or the particular hours in a day. Further, the main beneficiaries of equal wage rates may well be men. This is in part because men in non-standard jobs suffer a significant penalty compared to men in standard jobs. The same does not apply to women. Further, equal wages may well primarily benefit men in conventional relationships where the male married partner specialises in market activities and the female married partner in household activities. Equal wages for part-time work, for example, may primarily benefit conventional marriages with this specialisation in activities. We therefore consider policies to level the playing field by raising job flexibility for all participants. Further, if there is a policy desire to support child-rearing, this should be done by an explicit subsidy and not indirectly by workplace regulations.

## The evidence on gender, pay, and flexible employment contracts

European directives have led the UK government to require firms to offer equal pay and conditions to fixed-term and part-time workers, compared to full-time permanent workers. In the near future, this will be extended to agency workers (workers who go on short-term assignments from an employment agency) as well. The primary motivation given for these policy shifts is to address issues of gender pay disparity. In fact, our research shows that these policies are not well-aimed at equalising pay. Indeed, they may make matters worse by removing current market mechanisms for dealing with the desire of individuals – particularly women – to have job flexibility.

Booth, Francesconi and Frank (2003b) report cross-tabulations, reproduced in Table 2.1, from the British Household Panel Survey, a large representative sample of households throughout Britain.

It is certainly the case that women are less likely than men to find themselves in permanent jobs. These jobs include seasonal/casual work, fixed-term contracts, and employment through an agency. However, the percentage in these jobs is relatively small for both men and women. Even though women are 50 per cent more likely to hold non-permanent jobs than men, this only represents 8.4 per cent of the female workforce. The much more significant difference between the genders resides in part-time work. Few men (4.8%) hold part-time jobs, while 26.7 per cent of women hold part-time jobs. This is the primary way that women gain flexibility in the labour market.

In terms of pay, women are paid significantly less than men in permanent, full-time jobs. What is interesting, however, is that women suffer a much smaller pay loss for holding a flexible job than do men. As seen in the table, women in seasonal/casual, fixed-term and agency jobs actually

*Table 2.1* Worker distribution (%) and gross hourly wages (£) by gender, BHPS data

| | Men | | Women | |
|---|---|---|---|---|
| | % | Hourly pay | % | Hourly pay |
| **Contract** | | | | |
| Permanent | 94.1 | 9.557 | 91.6 | 7.465 |
| Seasonal/casual | 2.2 | 6.095 | 3.3 | 7.610 |
| Fixed-term contract | 2.0 | 7.770 | 2.7 | 8.434 |
| Agency temping | 1.7 | 5.962 | 2.5 | 6.061 |
| Number of observations | 3715 | | 4224 | |
| **Employment status** | | | | |
| Part-time | 4.8 | 6.179 | 26.7 | 5.802 |
| Full-time | 95.2 | 9.069 | 73.3 | 7.519 |
| Number of observations | 18,389 | | 21,273 | |

*Note*: Figures for 'Contract' are from person-year observations from Waves 9 and 10 (1999 and 2000) of the British Household Panel Survey. Figures for 'Employment status' are calculated from person-year observations from Waves 1 through 10 (1991 to 2000). Gross hourly wages are in constant (2000) prices. Reproduced from Table 3.3, Booth, Francesconi and Frank (2003b).

earn more than men in those jobs, and there is only a small negative gender gap in part-time work. Further empirical evidence from regression analysis (where we control for a large range of personal and workplace characteristics) appears in Booth, Francesconi and Frank (2002). There, we exploit the panel nature of the British Household Panel Survey (BHPS) data to consider career dynamics rather than just static pay levels at one point in time, and we report the estimates from panel earnings equations as well as duration analyses, in which we control for experience and employment type. The most important finding in the current context is that women who start their careers in temporary jobs eventually catch up – in terms of their earnings – with those women who started in permanent jobs. For men, however, the pattern is very different. Even ten years into their careers, men who started on temporary jobs earn less than those who began their career in permanent jobs.

Booth, Francesconi and Frank (2003a) look at career dynamics from a different perspective – in terms of who gets promoted and what effect promotion has on wages. In that study, we used data from the first five waves of the BHPS, which provides information on the timing and type of job changes including changes at the same employer as well as across firms. Information about reasons for job change – including promotion – was elicited. This study used regression analysis, that allowed us to control for a host of factors including experience, education and occupation, estimated over a sample of full-time individuals – 2449 men and 1374 women. We found that, contrary to common belief, women are promoted just as often as men, ceteris paribus. However, our estimates revealed that women gain significantly smaller wage increases consequent upon promotion than do men, so wage differentials persist and indeed widen.

Our conclusion from these studies is that the nature of jobs held by women – disproportionately temporary and part-time – and the nature of the promotions process is not the problem. Indeed, temporary and part-time contracts represent the major way for women to gain flexibility in their employment to allow, for example, for child-rearing responsibilities. The gender pay gap problem is that women in permanent jobs, and women who receive promotions, do not gain the same wage rewards as men. In that sense, regulations that severely limit the existence of temporary jobs (by providing employment protection comparable to workers hired on permanent contracts) and part-time jobs (by requiring terms and conditions comparable to full-time jobs) may actually limit the job market flexibility facing women without significantly improving their income status. Indeed, men – who currently face large wage and career penalties from starting employment in temporary and part-time jobs – may well be the beneficiaries from the new European directives. We return in a later section to the issues of why women in good jobs do not receive the same pay as men.

## Types of flexibility

In fact, the discussion in the previous section understates the degree of employment flexibility in the economy. In this section, we distinguish between the following aspects of flexible work arrangements, the first of which has been discussed in the preceding section. These are:

1. *Temporary work*, which may be either seasonal or casual work, or work done under contract or for a fixed period of time.
2. *Place-of-work flexibility*, which distinguishes between those working at home, those who work driving and travelling, and those working in more than one place (for a single job).
3. *Working times*, which separately identifies those who work mornings only, those who work either afternoons, or evenings, or nights or both lunch and evening ('other parts of the day'), those who have varying patterns and those who work in rotating shifts.
4. *Number of hours of work*. We distinguish between those who work 1 to 15 hours per week ('mini-jobs'), those who work between 16 and 29 hours per week and those who work more than 48 hours per week.[1]

Given these definitions of the various forms of non-standard work, notice that workers in 'standard' jobs are on a permanent contract, work at the employer's premises during the day, and for a number of hours ranging between 30 and 48 per week. If we define a 'standard' job as one where individuals work at the employer's premises during the day and for 30–48 hours a week, only 41 per cent of men and 40 per cent of women hold 'standard' jobs.

Table 2.2 presents the distribution of workers across various forms of non-standard employment for the entire workforce and by gender, repro-

*Table 2.2* Distribution of flexible forms of employment and union coverage by gender

| | All | Men | Women | Gender gap |
|---|---|---|---|---|
| **Non-standard contract** | | | | |
| Seasonal/casual | 0.052 | 0.039 | 0.063 | –0.024***<br>*–8.497* |
| Fixed-term contract | 0.031 | 0.029 | 0.033 | –0.004<br>*–1.630* |
| **Standard contract** | | | | |
| (permanent contract) | 0.917 | 0.932 | 0.904 | 0.028***<br>*7.844* |
| Non-standard place | | | | |
| Working at home | 0.009 | 0.008 | 0.011 | –0.003***<br>*–2.777* |
| Driving/travelling | 0.073 | 0.124 | 0.028 | 0.095***<br>*28.838* |
| More than one place | 0.065 | 0.090 | 0.043 | 0.047***<br>*14.847* |
| **Standard place** | | | | |
| (employer's premises) | 0.853 | 0.778 | 0.918 | –0.139***<br>*30.900* |
| Non-standard time | | | | |
| Mornings only | 0.056 | 0.016 | 0.091 | –0.074***<br>*–25.233* |
| Other parts of the day | 0.073 | 0.039 | 0.103 | –0.064***<br>*–19.173* |
| Varying patterns | 0.079 | 0.081 | 0.078 | 0.003<br>*0.902* |
| Rotating shifts | 0.095 | 0.130 | 0.064 | 0.065***<br>*17.333* |
| **Standard time** | | | | |
| (during the day) | 0.697 | 0.734 | 0.664 | 0.070***<br>*11.771* |
| Non-standard hours | | | | |
| < 16 a week | 0.093 | 0.028 | 0.150 | –0.123***<br>*–33.370* |
| 16–29 a week | 0.131 | 0.018 | 0.228 | –0.210***<br>*–50.740* |
| > 48 a week | 0.172 | 0.288 | 0.071 | 0.216*** |

*Table 2.2* Distribution of flexible forms of employment and union coverage by gender – *continued*

| | All | Men | Women | Gender gap |
|---|---|---|---|---|
| Non-standard hours | | | | |
| < 16 a week | 0.093 | 0.028 | 0.150 | –0.123*** *–33.370* |
| 16–29 a week | 0.131 | 0.018 | 0.228 | –0.210*** *–50.740* |
| > 48 a week | 0.172 | 0.288 | 0.071 | 0.216*** *46.252* |
| **Standard hours** | | | | |
| (30–48 a week) | 0.604 | 0.666 | 0.550 | 0.116*** *18.527* |
| **Any non-standard employment** | 0.598 | 0.593 | 0.604 | –0.011* *1.772* |
| **Union coverage** | | | | |
| Unweighted | 0.526 | 0.547 | 0.507 | 0.040*** *6.206* |
| Weighted | 0.524 | 0.546 | 0.504 | 0.042*** *6.594* |
| Union-covered standard workers as a proportion of all workers | 0.219 | 0.222 | 0.217 | 0.005 *0.907* |
| Union-covered standard workers as a proportion of total standard workers | 0.546 | 0.547 | 0.544 | 0.003 *0.754* |
| Union-covered non-standard workers as a proportion of all workers | 0.307 | 0.326 | 0.291 | 0.035*** *5.906* |
| Union-covered non-standard workers as a proportion of all non-standard workers | 0.513 | 0.550 | 0.481 | 0.069*** *8.213* |
| Number of person-wave observations | 24,007 | 11,186 | 12,821 | |

*Note*: Figures may not add up to one due to rounding. 'Gender gap' is the difference in average male rates and average female rates. The value of the *t*-test for the significance of the difference is reported in italics.
*** significant at 0.01 level, * significant at 0.10 level.
*Source*: Table 1 in Booth and Francesconi (2003).

duced from Booth and Francesconi (2003). Table 2.2 shows that, over the period 1991–1997, approximately 59 per cent of men and 60 per cent of women are in non-standard employment. About 8 per cent of all workers are in jobs involving non-standard contracts and almost 15 per cent are in jobs with some form of non-standard place of work (working at home, driving/travelling, or more than one place of work). A larger fraction of the workforce is involved in jobs with non-standard times (30%) and an even larger fraction has jobs with non-standard hours (40%). Gender differences are shown in the last column of Table 2.2: with only two exceptions (fixed-term contracts and varying patterns), all gender differences are significant.

Men are more likely to be found in jobs that involve rotating shifts, driving/travelling, working in more than one place, and long working hours. Women are more concentrated in seasonal/casual jobs, working fewer than 30 hours a week, working at home, working mornings only or in other parts of the day.

Traditionally, being covered by a trade union was viewed as part of a standard job. However, the table shows that only 22 per cent of all workers are in standard jobs *and* union covered, which means 55 per cent of all standard workers are union covered – there is no significant gender difference in union coverage among standard workers. For men, union coverage is just as high among non-standard workers. This does not hold for women in non-standard jobs; they have significantly lower union coverage by about 7 percentage points.

While these results are perhaps not surprising, they make the point that flexibility goes beyond the nature of the job contract (whether or not it is full-time and permanent), and involves the details of the job. The characteristics of non-standard work undertaken by men reflect flexibility in place of work and hours of work that largely benefits the employer. In contrast, the flexibility in jobs typically held by women potentially reflects a need to organise employment around household responsibilities such as child-rearing. Regulations on equal pay and conditions between part-time and full-time work, and between temporary and permanent jobs – while they may be desirable in their own right – are not designed to directly and fully address the needs for job flexibility. This holds particularly for individuals – usually women – who are engaged in child-rearing responsibilities.[2] The results on unions and gender in non-standard jobs are important insofar as unions continue to serve an important role in protecting workers and in raising wages. If unions, due to relatively low coverage, cannot negotiate the details of job contracts that make them sufficiently flexible for women, there may be a greater need for government intervention.

## The limits of equal pay

The standard policy approach to job flexibility – as in the recent new European directives – is to impose equal pay and conditions between flexible jobs and standard jobs. There are of course serious issues of enforceability, even in exactly comparable jobs. Despite long-standing equal pay laws with respect to race and gender, studies consistently show that – in comparable jobs – women earn less than men. In Blackaby and Frank (2000) and Blackaby, Booth and Frank (2002), we found that ethnic minority and female academic economists were paid less than comparable male economists. This was the case despite our controlling for personal characteristics such as age, workplace characteristics, and productivity measures such as quality of publications. But leaving aside issues of enforceability, there are other problems with the implementation of equal pay for work of equal value across flexible and standard jobs.

An example of the simplest sort of job is strawberry picking. A team of pickers goes out collecting strawberries, with each doing the same, independent task. The productivity of each worker is readily measured by the amount of strawberries produced. Typically, such workers would be paid on a piece rate system. Weigh the strawberries picked, and use that as the basis for reward. If there is different productivity among men and women, incomes will differ. If full-time workers develop better skills, they will gain higher incomes per hour than part-time workers. There may be positive or negative returns to scale – a strawberry picker may collect more strawberries in the second hour than the first, as he or she gets into a routine, or less, as the worker gets tired. It is possible that productivity is higher during the early morning, when it is cool, rather than in the heat of the afternoon sun. For all these reasons, productivity and pay will differ and this unequal outcome seems fair and efficient. It rewards workers for their effort and for their skill acquisition. If it transpires that the average woman is paid less than the average man, this can be ascribable to productivity and – insofar as this is affected by flexible working – to the choices made about hours of work. A woman with child-raising obligations who can only work for a few hours during the afternoon may have lower average hourly production than a man (or woman) who can work throughout the day.

To what extent can or should government policy seek to over-rule actual productivity differences in applying equal pay across jobs and workers? As economists, we would tend to argue that basing pay upon productivity is a fair and efficient approach. If some individuals wish to work flexible hours due to child-raising commitments, or because they have artistic interests they wish to pursue for part of the day, or indeed because they wish to race cars on long weekends, it is not appropriate to impose conditions on employers to facilitate these other activities. As we will discuss in a later section, the appropriate approach is to provide direct subsidies to desired activities such as child-raising. Trying to equalise pay and require flexible working arrangements can lead companies to avoid hiring those workers with lower productivity who would take advantage of these policies. Rather than lessening inequality, the policy can create unemployment or force individuals into low-skilled, low-paid jobs where the flexibility is less costly to the employer.

There are of course very good reasons to support equal pay for work of equal value in the sense of equal productivity. We will not get into the discussion about whether equal value should be understood entirely in the economist's sense of market valuations, or whether it can be understood in a broader sense. But even within the economist's definition, there are market failures that support intervention. There can be an interaction between individual workers' need for flexibility and these market failures that can call for particular focus upon non-standard jobs and their wage and conditions in comparison to standard jobs at the same employer.

The main potential problem is a 'taste for discrimination'. As noted, our research shows that – for very comparable workers in British universities – women and ethnic minorities are paid less than white males, even after controlling for measured productivity. This may be due to a 'taste for discrimination'. Further, a 'taste for discrimination' can be self-fulfilling in that workers may receive assignments that lower their productivity in ways that can then be used to justify lower wages. For example, if strawberry pickers are assigned to different parts of the strawberry field, overseers might allocate the most productive areas according to their prejudices. Female workers might be allocated less support or indeed might suffer harassment that affects their work performance. In universities, for example, female academics may be given more administrative tasks than comparable males and therefore have lower research productivity. While the effects of 'taste for discrimination' may have a relationship with non-standard work (such as part-time work), they are unlikely to be limited to that. It is unlikely that an employer or manager who wishes to discriminate against women will only do so with respect to women in part-time jobs. In that sense, equal pay and conditions for part-time and other non-standard jobs, compared to standard jobs, is only a partial way of addressing inefficient outcomes due to a 'taste for discrimination'.

A situation where rewards follow hours of work in an inefficient way is described in Landers *et al.* (1996). They develop the argument that, in the early stages of a law career, junior lawyers put in a large number of hours to signal to senior partners of the firm that they are likely to continue to put in effort at work, even when promoted. Even though most of the additional hours are wasted rather than productive, this effort serves a signalling function. If individuals with household responsibilities – typically women – do not put in these wasted hours, they are inefficiently punished with lower wages or lower possibilities of promotion. Indeed, in a model where effort can be observed, Booth, Francesconi and Frank (2003a) show that women should be promoted just as often as men to induce the right level of effort. Booth, Francesconi and Frank (2003a) find that this theoretical result is confirmed by the data from the BHPS, which finds that women – while receiving lower wages – are promoted just as often as men, as we noted in an earlier section.

Another argument for government intervention to equalise pay across part-time (and other non-standard jobs) and standard jobs is provided by the role of market power in determining wages. Wages do not generally equal marginal productivity – as in simple economic theory – since workers and firms bargain over wages, splitting the gains to the employment relationship. It is here that women in general, but in particular those women holding part-time posts, may suffer. In Blackaby, Booth, and Frank (2002), we look at academic labour markets, using regression techniques applied to a cross-sectional data set.[3] One of our purposes in that analysis is to try to understand how wage differences unrelated to productivity can persist in a competitive market. Our main finding concerns the relationship of outside offers to pay, and the gender differences in the outside offer process. We find that women, taking account of productivity and other characteristics such as age, are still less likely than men to receive outside offers of jobs. Further, when women do receive outside offers, they are not matched by salary rises at their current employer. Men who receive outside offers gain significant wage increases at their current employer. These observations are consistent with the 'loyal servant' hypothesis. If employers believe that most women have low job mobility due to household responsibilities, women are unlikely to receive job offers since the potential new employer is sceptical that the woman will accept the job. If she does receive an offer, her current employer is sceptical that she will accept the new job, and therefore does not feel the need to respond with a competing offer. Here there is no productivity reason for differential wages between men and women. It is only market power that leads to different outcomes, and government intervention is appropriate and efficient. There is reason to believe that individuals in part-time or other non-standard jobs will have particularly weak market power, and therefore suffer in their wages and conditions of employment.

The overall message from the discussion so far in this section is that there are good economic reasons for government intervention in equalising pay across non-standard and standard jobs, but that this does not solve gender disparities due to tastes for discrimination and weak bargaining power. The gender pay gap – as discussed earlier in this paper – is not primarily about women in non-standard jobs receiving lower pay, but about women in good standard jobs receiving lower pay than comparable men. We now argue that there are also problems with trying to enforce equal pay across jobs. We focus in particular upon regulation that in effect reinforces conventional relationships and provides a double reward to people in those relationships.

In Booth and Frank (2003) we use a new data source that was reported in AUT (2001). These data cover university employees in the UK based upon a survey that asked a number of questions about personal circumstances – including child-raising responsibilities, partnership and sexual orientation – that are only rarely explored in standard surveys. While it must be kept in mind that the university sector offers particular opportunities for flexible working, it is nonetheless interesting that child-raising responsibilities have no impact upon pay. What is found in these data – as in the literature in general – is that married males receive a large premium over the pay of single or partnered males, or married/single/partnered females. In our research, we try to shed light on the causes of this married male premium.

There are three explanations typically given in the literature: more able males typically get married, so the wage premium just reflects the higher average ability within this group; within the conventional married household, responsibilities are divided so that the male devotes more effort to market activities (and obtains a higher income as a consequence) and the female to household activities; and finally, that there is discrimination favouring married males. In our research, we argue that – if marriage selects more able individuals on the basis of their ability to maintain a committed social partnership – the same effect should hold for partnered gay males, compared to non-partnered gay males. We find no such effect, which suggests that the married male premium is either due to discrimination or to the allocation of tasks within the household in a conventional framework. The latter explanation, introduced into the economics literature by Becker (1965) considers a household traditionally organised along gender lines, with the male spouse freed from most household and childcare responsibilities and the female spouse (even if she is also working in a full-time job, but *a fortiori* if she is working part-time) undertaking the bulk of these responsibilities. The importance of the basis of the married male premium for the current analysis is that the extension of equal pay provisions to non-standard jobs may in practice be predominantly a further subsidy to conventional families. We argue later that, if it is desired to have a subsidy for child-raising, then the subsidy should be directed in a non-distorting way at child-raising.

## Levelling the playing field

In our study of the academic labour market – Blackaby, Booth and Frank (2002) – we find that career breaks – defined as time out of the labour market – have no direct impact on future income. One explanation for the lack of a direct career break effect on income is that the academic labour market offers particular flexibility. There are limited specific requirements to the job, most of the obligation being – in addition to the typically small teaching component – to do research at a time scheduled by the individual. All staff normally have the opportunity to take breaks on sabbatical or to visit other universities. The losses suffered by women in this market – and we do find that females suffer significant wage penalties and glass ceilings – are therefore not associated with career breaks. Indeed, from other regressions in this paper and in Booth and Frank (2003), we find that marriage and child-raising have no direct effect on female academic incomes. The question we pose in this section is whether this general flexibility of the academic job can be extended more generally in the labour market, and the implications of this for gender equality.

Under current regulations, statutory maternity pay is 90 per cent of average pay for six weeks, and then £102.80 or (if less) 90 per cent of average pay per week for 20 weeks. Fathers are entitled to choose one or two weeks paid leave at the same rate as statutory maternity pay. Although employers can claim back most or all of the statutory maternity pay, there are other obligations including the right to return to work. These can be costly to the employer, and further extension of paternity leave – even if they were at a significantly higher level – would not level the playing field throughout the job market. We therefore consider the implications of a broader levelling of the playing field, where all workers become entitled to sabbaticals and can use them for any purpose: child-rearing, study, travel, or alternative work. The idea is that, with a levelling of the playing field in this way, firms no longer have a reason to discriminate against women in the anticipation that they may take career breaks to raise children.

One of the reasons to consider greater flexibility – and career breaks – during the working life is the decline in pension provision and the likely response in extending the retirement age. One of the most dramatic shifts in recent years has been the decline in final salary pensions and associated growth in defined contributions pensions. Further, company contribution rates have been cut as part of this shift, in an environment where realistic investment returns over the next decade are much lower than those in the recent past. There is no clear economic rationale for this shift away from pension provision, although there is clearly a lack of political action designed to limit the decline in pension saving. There is reason to think that it may be more politically viable to introduce regulated sabbaticals than the restoration of adequate pension contribution levels, particularly if the labour market continues to weaken. If individuals are going to work to age 70, it may be more important to take career breaks to maintain human capital and to provide the extended relaxation periods previously concentrated in retirement.

The idea of mid-career sabbaticals is well-established in the managerial career structure, with workers encouraged and funded to undertake mid-career MBA studies. These breaks can allow individuals – after exposure to applied problems – to go back to university and gain a greater understanding of the theoretical framework that can be applied to business problems. Further, these breaks can take individuals out of a routine, and allow them to develop new ways of viewing things, particularly since they are certain to be reassigned to a different job when they return.

In practice, if workers are required to take a significant period of time – 6 months or a year – off from their employment, what activities would they engage in? Some women would continue to take maternity leave and devote their activities to child-rearing. Some men, in the spirit of the recent extension of leave to paternity, might do the same. Other women and men would spend the time traveling, building or renovating a house, caring for elderly relatives, or in learning new skills or developing new interests.

To what extent would this increase or decrease productivity in the economy? Turnover in the economy has increased, but this is generally a shifting across jobs, rather than breaks for the acquisition of human capital. Rises in turnover have both positive and negative effects. Other than the correct reallocation of labour, they also have the effects of 'creative destruction'. Specific human capital is lost, but also lost are the negative effects of inefficient allocation of time to workplace politics. Merrett and Seltzer (2000) describe how, in Australian banks in the early 1900's, there was deliberate shifting of workers across branches to discourage the possibility of dishonest behaviour. The diplomatic corps also adopts the same principal in order to align incentives and prevent key personnel identifying more strongly with the destination country than with the home country.

While levelling the playing field in this way will remove some of the reason to distinguish between women and men in the labour market, there remains a residual effect. Men may well spend their sabbatical period, not on child-rearing, but on gaining additional human capital, thereby exacerbating male/female wage differentials. We argue in the following section, however, that the appropriate way to deal with this is to provide more direct subsidies for child-rearing.

## Direct support for child-rearing

Evidence from time use studies establishes that women with children – especially small children – work very long hours when both market production and domestic production are taken into account (Apps, 2002). Home production typically involves two outputs – substitutes for market production (caring for small children, DIY and dinners) and complements to market production (children, who cannot be produced in the market sector – surrogate mothers apart). Home carers – typically women – are supported financially in domestic production through transfers from the breadwinning partner, both in traditional households where women do not participate and in households where women work part-time.[4] Such a division of domestic labour is justified by many economists on the basis of comparative advantage of men and women in market and home production respectively. Not only is it sometimes held that the division of domestic labour satisfies women's exogenous preferences for maternity and domesticity,[5] but it also allows the household to specialise. Such specialisation allows one partner to engage in domestic production and the other partner consequently to spend more time in market production, and therefore win more bread to bring home to share with the family.

Such a model seems dated from the perspective of the early 21st century, when fertility is a choice variable, when cohabitation – and separation and divorce – are commonplace, and when there is evidence that poverty has become feminised as a consequence (Akerlof, 1998). Some governments, concerned by declining fertility rates and ballooning future pension liabilities, have suggested that women are being selfish in choosing to have fewer children than their mothers and grandmothers before them. In short, they are trying to restore the cultural values that ensured that women preferred domesticity and altruistic transfers from their husbands, despite the changes in the objective environment.

One perspective is that this argument is about externalities. Consider a simple 2-period overlapping generations model. In period 1 individuals produce either domestic output (children who will be the labour input into period 2) or market output (some of which will be saved as capital), and in period 2 they retire and live off their investments. People are not paid for producing children but they are paid for their market production, including the capital good. While the production of children in earlier generations might be viewed as biologically determined – although there is some dispute even over this – the prevalence of contraception has made fertility a choice decision.[6] If in fact women choose to have fewer children in period 1, then pensioners will have less to live on in period 2, since production depends upon both labour and capital. And with fewer workers the returns to capital will decline, affecting savings. Thus fertility is associated with an externality that individuals do not take into account in making their decisions about whether or not to have children.

How can we internalise this externality? One answer is simple: pay couples to have children, either as a lump-sum or as an annuity. The parents could then choose to spend this on childcare while they work in the market sector, or on either parent foregoing market production in order to look after the child. Parents would have to be given this choice, because there is heterogeneity of preferences and talents for market and home production. In fact, this proposal is not all that distant from the child benefit system currently in force in the UK. The major difference, though, is in magnitude. A system that provided a sufficient period of absence from market production would need to involve much larger sums than the current tax and benefit system does for child-rearing.

## Conclusions

In this chapter, we drew on the results of our papers from our Future of Work project, plus related work by other authors. We considered evidence from a number of sources about the prevalence of non-standard jobs in the British economy, their rates of pay, and the gender balance of these non-standard jobs. We also discussed the impact of standard policies, such as equal pay rules, and considered two alternative ways to seek to level the playing field. One alternative is to extend greater flexibility (particularly with respect to career breaks) throughout the economy, for all workers. The other is to recognise that the major factor behind non-standard work flexibility is child-raising. Insofar as children represent an externality for society as a whole, parents should be subsidised (or taxed, if it is a negative externality) in raising children.

In general, our research does not support the policies of stipulating equal pay and conditions for different types of contracts (temporary vs permanent, and full-time vs part-time). The market matching of workers seeking different types of employment into different types of jobs can be an efficient one, and productivity in different types of contracts need not be the same. This is the fundamental difference between equal pay laws covering discrimination within a particular job, and seeking to set the same wages across contracts and jobs. Pay gaps are consistently found in the data, for a given type of job and contract, based upon gender and ethnicity. It is clearly fair and efficient to equalise wages across these characteristics. The same does not necessarily hold for different types of jobs and contracts. A part-time worker may be more or less productive per hour than a full-time worker. The particular hours worked may be more or less valuable to the firm than the standard hours worked by a full-time worker.

Further, it is not clear that the major beneficiaries of this pay equalisation would be the intended ones. Our research has shown that the main beneficiaries of the equalisation of pay and conditions for non-standard work would be male, and not female. Male workers on non-standard contracts suffer an immediate pay penalty, and a long-term career penalty, compared to males on standard contracts. The same immediate pay loss and long-term scarring effect does not occur for women. Further, the major effect could be to reward and sustain conventional relationships – where the female takes an unequal role with respect to the market economy – rather than promote greater equality within the home.

We argue that the better approach is to encourage flexibility throughout the economy, with equal opportunities for men and women, for married, partnered and single individuals, for individuals of different ages, and for workers of different sexual orientations. All workers should have the opportunity to take sabbaticals, whether to have children or to take up art or philosophy. If the policy is to encourage childbearing, then there should be a direct subsidy for having children, that can be applied to childcare allowing both parents to work full-time, or to allow one or the other of the parents to lessen their time commitment to market activity.

## Acknowledgements

This chapter presents an overview of our recent research, much of which was undertaken as part of our ESRC Grant *The Future of Work: Flexible Employment, Part-time Work and Career Development in Britain*, Award No. L212252007. We are also grateful to the Royal Economic Society and the Association of University Teachers for providing data used in some of the analysis.

## Notes

1. Reasons for the choice of cut-offs are as follows. Workers in mini-jobs (and low income) are potentially eligible for the Income Support and Jobseeker's Allowance benefits, which cut off at 15 hours. Those working between 16 and 29 hours are part-timers. Those working long hours are the target of recent EU policy initiatives (such as the 1998 European Working Time Directive) that aim to reduce the number of hours worked in a week to below 48.
2. Our published studies summarised in this Chapter all employ regression analysis using large data sets, and our discussion consequently refers to average behaviour. Since on average women bear most of the responsibility for childcare, as time use studies also show, in the text we refer to women typically assuming responsibility for childcare. However, this is not intended to imply that no men assume responsibility but simply reflects our focus on average behaviour.
3. This was the postal survey of academic economists conducted in 1999 by the Royal Economic Society Working Party on the Representation of Ethnic and Other Minorities in the Economic Profession. The survey – sent to Heads of Economics Departments in the United Kingdom, who were asked to distribute the forms to full-time academic economics staff – achieved 516 responses. Our results summarised here were based on regression analysis of these data. Note that approximately 83 per cent of this sample was male.
4. These transfers are sometimes termed by economists as 'altruistic'; see for example the research surveyed in Weiss (1997: 91). The family head controls family resources and can make transfers as he sees fit. 'Altruism' in such a context reduces the need for bargaining. Of course, other economists see bargaining within the household as being a more appropriate modelling framework, a notion that dates at least from the work on Manser and Brown (1980).
5. For a sociological perspective on this, see Hakim (2002).
6. Although reproduction is of course biological, the form it takes is heavily influenced by culture, as can be seen from evidence about the number and timing of children in societies unaffected by the contraception revolution. We are grateful to an anonymous referee for this point.

## References

Akerlof, G.A. (1998) Men without Children. *The Economic Journal, 108*, 287–309.

Apps, P.F. (2002) Gender, Time Use and Models of the Household. *World Bank Discussion Paper.*

AUT (Association of University Teachers) (2001) *Lesbian, Gay and Bisexual Participation in UK Universities.*

Becker, G.S. (1965) A Theory of the Allocation of Time. *The Economic Journal*, 1965, *75*, 493–517.

Blackaby, D., Booth, A.L., and Frank, J. (2002) Outside Offers and the Gender Pay Gap: Empirical Evidence from the UK Academic Labour Market. *CEPR Discussion Paper No. 3549*. Forthcoming *The Economic Journal*, February, 2005.

Blackaby, D. and Frank, J. (2000) Ethnic and Other Minority Representation in Economics. *The Economic Journal, 110*, F293–311.

Booth, A.L. and Francesconi, M. (2003) Union Coverage and Non-Standard Work in Britain. *Oxford Economic Papers, 55,* 383–416.

Booth, A.L., Francesconi, M. and Frank, J. (2002) Temporary jobs: stepping stones or dead ends? *The Economic Journal, 112,* F189–213.

Booth, A.L., Francesconi, M. and Frank, J. (2003a) A sticky floors model of promotion, pay, and gender. *European Economic Review, 47,* 295–322.

Booth, A.L., Francesconi, M. and Frank, J. (2003b) Labour as a Buffer: Do Temporary Workers Suffer? Chapter 3 in Fagan, G., Mongelli, F.P. and Morgan, J. (eds), *Institutions and Wage Formation in the New Europe.* Cheltenham: Edward Elgar Publishing.

Booth, A.L. and Frank, J. (2003) What Can Single and Gay Men Tell Us About The Marriage Premium? *Royal Holloway College, University of London Discussion Paper.*

Hakim, C. (2002) Lifestyle Preferences as Determinants of Women's Differentiated Labor Market Careers. *Work and Occupations, 29,* 428–59.

Landers, R., Rebitzer, J. and Taylor, L. (1996) Rat Race Reux: Adverse Selection in the Determination of Work Hours in Law Firms. *American Economic Review,* June, 329–48.

Manser, M. and Brown, M. (1980) Marriage and household decision making: a bargaining analysis, *International Economic Review, 21,* 31–44.

Merrett, D. and Seltzer, A. (2000) The Nature of Bank Work and Worker Monitoring: a Study of the Union Bank of Australia in the 1920s. *Business History, 42,* 133–52.

Weiss, Y. (1997) The Formation and Dissolution of Families: Why Marry? Who Marries Whom? And What Happens Upon Divorce? Chapter 3 in Rosenzweig, M.R. and Stark, O. (eds), *Handbook of Population and Family Economics,* 1A, Amsterdam: Elsevier.

# 3

# The Costs of a Career in Minutes and Morbidity

*Michael Rose*

## The career pattern in employment

A *career pursuit pattern* in employment attitudes and behaviour is identifiable both at the aggregate level and that of the individual worker. The following examination first establishes the principal features of this pattern. It will then be shown that people with a career pursuit orientation to the labour market are likely to work significantly longer hours, especially if they are women. The consequences for individual well-being will then be examined.

It will be argued that a career pursuit pattern reflects planned decisions shaped by consciously-held preferences, and by intentions that are premeditated and well-structured. To this extent, career patterning is seen here as a product of rationality. It implies a deliberate effort by a labour market actor to impose a higher degree of planning and control upon a personal work-history than many other actors succeed in imposing. The degree of planning, the amount of effort, and the relative success actors have, no doubt reflect individual attributes (*idiosyncrasy*) such as accidents of personality, peculiarities of family background, and educational experiences. Such attributes are, however, also socially distributed, and conditioned to some extent by structural realities such as class and occupational group.

In Sociology in particular, the term *career* has had several distinct senses. Most can safely be disregarded here. For example, in the mid-20th century USA, Everett C. Hughes (1958) and his sociological collaborators at Chicago deployed career as a concept to show underlying similarities in social process between diverse situations. The Hughes school went about their work in a decidedly non-judgmental spirit: the work-history patterns of lawyers or other professionals might be compared directly with those of the drug dealers they represented in court. Illuminating as this procedure is for understanding process, it may lead to conceptual devaluation: to use the same term to cover the work-histories of scientists, footballers, and plumbers creates the same kind of tension as using the term *profession* and *professionalisation* to embrace general practitioners and routine car-assembly workers (Barley, 1989).

Recent social class theory (Erikson and Goldthorpe, 1992) embodies a different notion of career, through its emphasis on employment relationships. Until recently employment contracts differed mainly between a *service relationship* pattern for professional and managerial occupations and a more limited *labour only* model typical of blue-collar and some routine white-collar jobs. A service relationship aims to secure a long-term commitment to the organisation on the part of its highest qualified employees by offering *prospective* advantages such as regular salary increments, promotion opportunities, and a secure retirement pension, thus providing internal career opportunities to compete with those offered by job mobility. The present treatment will be somewhat closer to this approach.

It does not discount the importance, well attested in recent research (Li *et al.*, 2002), that career may have as an organising concept for some blue-collar workers. In the present examination, however, a distinction will be made between: a) *career outlook*, as a broad attitude towards paid work aiming at continuity of employment, together with some planning of career development; b) *career commitment* as the prioritisation of career aims against others; and c) *career pursuit* as an empirical pattern manifesting such commitment. Career outlook is evidently essential for stronger types of career commitment to appear, but it is not a sufficient condition for this. Neither career commitment nor career pursuit are particularly frequent, empirically, as will be shown shortly.

Yet thinking of oneself as having a career is widespread; thus for some employees it may imply little more than the aspiration to avoid lengthy withdrawals from the labour market or to resist constrained switches of occupation; to others it may imply something more like contingency planning for future employment, with an effort to foresee difficulties and a readiness to take opportunities, but no setting of specific targets (Li *et al.*, 2002). Finally, having career can have a strict connotation of setting targets for one's own employment and striving to attain them through carefully calculated, unsentimental action in work organisations and the labour market – something close to the *careerism* of everyday speech. Seeing oneself as having a career in all these senses can have implications for time-budgeting and the balance between work and non-work life. The chapter will put some bench-mark figures on those relating to career commitment.

## Career outlook

Career outlook, as the readiness to state one has a career, has been growing steadily and quite fast in Britain over the last 20 years (Rose, 2004 forthcoming). Between one-quarter and one-third more British employees and self-employed people in 2001 thought of themselves as having a career than had done so in 1985. As a proportion of the total employed and self-employed workforce, the rise was from around half in 1985 to close to two-thirds in 2001. A large majority of all full-time employees now have such a perspective, and the minority of part-time employees having it has increased too, although it remains a minority. There are clear sex differences in the rate of change. At the time of the SCELI Work Histories and Attitudes survey (1985) three-fifths of British male employees already thought they had a work career, and a bare majority of full-time women employees also said this. ONS data (2001) show that large majorities of full-time employees (72 per cent of men and 67 per cent of women) now think they have a career.

Only 22 per cent of part-time employees in the SCELI sample in 1985 said they thought they had a career, but even this rose to 37 per cent in the ONS sample. As the vast majority of part-time workers remain women, the spread of career outlook among such women employees is remarkable and seems significant in terms of changing attitudes toward employment. This is shown further by a control for age. Though already quite strong among older men in 1985, career outlook was rare for older women; by 2001, older women employees were far more likely to have such an outlook too; in the youngest age-group (under 25), women had a career outlook almost as often as men.

Table 3.1 shows that career outlook and career commitment remain closely associated with occupation. Career holding in managerial-professional groups (the service class in the Goldthorpe three-class model) was always high and has been consolidated: over nine out of ten teachers, lawyers, and medical practitioners say they think of themselves as having a career. Proportionately speaking, however, craft skilled and personal service occupations have moved ahead very rapidly, with between one-third and one-half more employees reporting career holding than 20 years ago.

Still, and surprisingly perhaps, it is the blue-collar semi-skilled worker groups that show the most spectacular proportionate growth, with around 60 per cent growth since the mid-1980s. Even the unskilled occupations have experienced significant growth in career outlook, though it remains a decidedly minority view among the unskilled. There is only one highly visible crack in this picture of growth, and it may be of theoretical importance for sociology. Clerical and secretarial occupations have experienced no overall growth in career outlook; more interestingly, male clerical workers now they say they have careers less often than women colleagues; 20 years ago, the situation was exactly the reverse.

## Career commitment

Table 3.1 shows that positive career commitment is much less widespread than career outlook. Overall, fewer than 1 in 6 employees chose 'follow my

*Table 3.1* Career outlook and career commitment by SOC major groups and sex

| | Has career | | | 'Follow career' important reason for working* | | |
|---|---|---|---|---|---|---|
| | All | Male | Female | All | Male | Female |
| | % | % | % | % | % | % |
| 1 Managers & administrators | **84** | 87 | 78 | **25** | 28 | 22 |
| 2 Professional occupations | **92** | 93 | 90 | **36** | 43 | 27 |
| 3 Associate professional & technical occupations | **80** | 78 | 79 | **19** | 22 | 18 |
| 4 Clerical & secretarial occupations | **50** | 53 | 49 | **13** | 17 | 12 |
| 5 Craft & related occupations | **59** | 67 | ** | **10** | 11 | ** |
| 6 Personal & protective service occupations | **52** | 50 | 52 | **6** | 19 | 3 |
| 7 Sales occupations | **40** | 56 | 34 | **6** | 25 | 0 |
| 8 Plant & machine operatives | **38** | 47 | 6 | **5** | 5 | 12 |
| 9 Other occupations | **20** | 24 | 12 | **0** | 0 | 0 |
| All employees | **61** | 67 | 54 | **16** | 20 | 11 |

* First choice or second choice of 8 major reasons for having paid work.
** Fewer than 10 cases.
*Source*: ONS Omnibus Survey, March 2001.
Weighted n = 840

career' as first or second from a list of eight possible reasons for having a job in the ONS sample used for Table 3.1. The association with occupational level is even sharper than for career outlook; even so, only just over one in three of the most career committed occupational category (professionals) gave following career as a principal reason for having paid work. Career committed people appear to form a minority even in occupational contexts that favour career following employment strategies. Attitudinally speaking, they have every appearance of being a highly self-selected group.

In passing, it is worth commenting on the possible link between career commitment and *expressive* reasons for having paid work as predicted by post-industrial theory (Bell, 1976; Inglehart, 1997; Kumar, 1978, 1995). Just like career outlook, expressiveness is closely associated with higher education levels. Developing a career, in a post-industrial perspective, is related to having and responding to expressive, self-actualising values: higher educated employees would choose such reasons for working as 'I enjoy working', 'To use my abilities to the full', or 'To feel I'm doing something worthwhile' more often. At the time (1985) of SCELI this seemed clearly correct; now it does not. In SCELI, 34 per cent of all reasons for working were such expressive reasons among employee groups with the highest educated and strongest career outlook; in another 2001 ONS sample examined by the writer this had fallen to 27 per cent of all the reasons given. The self-actualising component of career commitment may well be in retreat.

## A measure of career commitment

An option 'To follow my career' was first offered in the list of reasons for having paid work used by Martin and Roberts (1984) in their landmark *Women and Employment* enquiry of 1980. Methodologically speaking, an option worded in such terms is open to some objection, because only those people thinking they *do* have a career are able to select it as a priority. (None of the other options used by Martin and Roberts were restrictive and conditional.) Furthermore, it is so worded as to create a certain presumption for some employees that they *should* have careers. Non-career workers are thus excluded and might feel that in some sense their own work activity mattered less. (Rewording the question 'To build a career for myself' would easily fix this problem.)

The designers of the newly launched *Living in Britain* survey undertaken yearly with the British Household Panel (BHPS) sample decided to include the Martin and Roberts career option in its first wave of interviews (1991–2), and repeated the questions in its ninth wave (1999–2000). People currently active in the labour market (the employed, self-employed, unemployed) or potentially so (those taking time off work for courses, on training schemes, full-time students, and people of working age engaged on full-time family care) could choose 'Follow my career', among seven specific options, as either their main or as their second-most important reason for having paid work. BHPS also asked employees about their *job-facet priorities* at both these waves; that is, about those features of a job (pay, security, using initiative, etc.) they would put first and second when looking for a job or appraising a job move. The option 'Promotion opportunities' figured among the seven job-facets listed; choosing promotion opportunities first or second also suggests the respondent has career building aims.

For the present analysis, responses to these questions were used to create a simple and, it will be argued, effective measure of degree of career commitment. Using the COUNT command in SPSS, *Follow career* or *Promotion opportunities* scored double each when chosen first, and one point each when chosen second. People who had chosen neither the career following reason, nor the job promotion priority, scored zero. To simplify analysis and presentation, the small number of scores for 4 will be merged here with those for 3.

For the present, Table 3.2 shows the distribution of scores by sex and, for women employees, type of contract (full-time/part-time) for the ninth annual wave of BHPS (1999–2000), for 4282 (weighted) current employee cases,

*Table 3.2* Career commitment score by sex and employment status

| | Male, All % | Female | | Female, All % | All Employees % |
|---|---|---|---|---|---|
| | | Full time % | Part time % | | |
| Nil | 78 | 74 | 92 | 80 | 79 |
| Low | 13 | 12 | 5 | 10 | 11 |
| Moderate | 7 | 12 | 3 | 9 | 8 |
| High | 2 | 2 | * | 2 | 2 |

* Less than 10 cases.
*Source*: BHPS Wave 9.
Weight: Cross-sectional respondent at Wave 9 (IXRWGHT)
Weighted n = 4282

broken down by sex and type of contract. The headline distribution in the last column, applying to all employees, shows just over one-fifth (21%) expressed some degree of career commitment. There are some interesting minor differences between the sub-groups, perhaps the most important being the slightly (but statistically significant) higher proportion of women full-time employees with moderate levels of career commitment. However, the underlying pattern is clear and more uniform than might be expected. The validity of the resulting scale of career commitment is assessed in the next section.

## Career pursuit patterns

How valid is this measure of career commitment? Career commitment probably, and the term *careerism* certainly, imply an orientation towards *success* at work through upward mobility in terms of rewards, power, status, sense of achievement, and (for a few) self-actualisation, within the context of an organisation, that of a professional community, or both. Scores should therefore correlate well with indicators for these forms of success.

*Mobility aspiration*. First, however, a strong drive towards mobility as an element of work orientation can be confirmed. Mobility aspiration takes two main forms: a) a wish for a better job with the same employer or with a different employer; b) a wish for work-related training which enhances human capital and bargaining power in the jobs market. Table 3.3 shows the proportions seeking these goals in each score-band of the career commitment measure. Clearly, desire for promotion with the current employer is very strongly associated with career commitment, though the association with wish to change employer is, perhaps surprisingly, barely significant. Wish for further training is very strongly associated with commitment scores. So is adherence to a work ethic, in the sense of wishing to keep working for a living. Table 3.3 provides some evidence, then, for the validity of the measure. The influence of sex in shaping these aspirations is weak and not shown. Those women who have similar levels of career commitment to men as measured here have very similar aspirations for success at work as defined here.

*Achieved job mobility*. BHPS enables several more powerful tests of career commitment, based upon behavioural and work-history outcomes. It is now possible to examine what happened over the next decade to those people who answered the career commitment questions at Wave 1 of BHPS in 1991–2. Only people who were employees at Wave 1, gave interviews in person as employees at Wave 10 (2000–01), and were employees in all other waves, will be considered here; because of retirements, other reasons for leaving the labour-force temporarily (unemployment, family care) or permanently (long-term sickness or disability), and panel drop-outs, the employee sample at Wave 10 is much smaller (1580) than at Wave 1 (4974) but still adequate for present purposes. The first question to ask is whether career commitment is behaviourally associated with greater job mobility.

Thanks to work-history data collected for all BHPS respondents of working age who are not permanently disabled, it is relatively easy to tally all significant job-moves. These may have taken the form either of an internal promotion, a lateral movement to another employer (or workplace) without promotion, or such a move plus a promotion. The raw association between number of job-moves over the 10-year period is associated with career commitment, and quite spectacularly so. As noted, Table 3.4 shows data for a balanced employee panel, i.e. those people appearing as employees at all waves. There is a linear increase in the mean number of posts reported. Even people with weak career commitment scores reported almost 40 per cent more changes, and the strong commitment group reported almost 140 per cent more. In terms of mean number of moves, the difference between people with a score of 1 or more for career commitment

*Table 3.3* Aspirations for work and employment by level of career commitment

| | Better job, same employer % | Better job, different employer % | Work-related training % | Give up paid work % |
|---|---|---|---|---|
| Nil | 35 | 27 | 47 | 29 |
| Low | 55 | 31 | 67 | 21 |
| Moderate | 54 | 29 | 70 | 17 |
| High | 75 | 31 | 86 | 9 |
| All | 40 | 27 | 52 | 27 |

*Source*: BHPS Wave 9 data.
Weight: Cross-sectional respondent at Wave 1 (AXRWGHT)
Weighted n = 4282

*Table 3.4* Mean number of job changes Wave 1–Wave 10 by career commitment level of employee at Wave 1

| | Male | Female | All |
|---|---|---|---|
| Nil | 1.7 | 1.8 | 1.8 |
| Low | 2.4 | 2.5 | 2.5 |
| Moderate | 3.0 | 2.5 | 2.8 |
| High | 4.6 | 3.6 | 4.3 |
| n | 863 | 717 | 1580 |

*Source*: BHPS.
Selection: People who were employees at every wave
Weight: Cross-sectional respondent at Wave 1 (AXRWGHT)

and the non-career majority is highly significant ($t = 9.45$); it is not quite significant ($t = 1.73$) for the difference between persons with low and moderate career commitment scores, but is very significant ($t = 4.04$) for the difference between moderate and high scoring cases. This pattern holds, as does the significance of differences, with sex controlled.

Simple mobility data (number of job moves) do not provide any evidence of the practical *effectiveness* of career commitment; that is, by themselves they do not show whether extra job-mobility brings accomplishment in career terms; after all, the data might simply show a rather footloose approach to the jobs market. Other evidence, however, confirms that mobility is typically successful for career pursuers in terms of promotion and pay.

Firstly, the job changes of the career committed are associated with more upward mobility in occupational terms. One rough way of assessing such movement is by comparing occupational level at Wave 10 with that at Wave 1. The UK Standard Occupational Classification (SOC, 2000), and its fore-runner SOC 90, grade occupations in terms of skill level and specialisation of skills. Occupations are aggregated at several levels from the most detailed (the several hundred recognised *unit occupations*) to the most general (the 9 *major occupational groups*) that vary from Unskilled occupations (Major group 9) to Managerial and Administrative occupations (Major group 1). A simple way of gauging occupational movement is to compare (by simple arithmetic) major group membership at $t_1$ with major group membership at $t_2$. (This requires some preliminary recoding, since numbering of Major groups follows the convention that the highest group is scored 1.) Scores for a measure created on this basis can vary from +8 (spectacular upward mobility) via 0 (no vertical mobility, and the most common situation by far) to –8 (calamitous downward mobility).

A complication must be dealt with. Career commitment score, as suggested in Table 3.1, is positively associated with occupation, with disproportionate numbers of the career committed entering employment at a relatively high initial level, in one of the three highest rated major groups (*Managers and Administrators, Professional Occupations, Associate Professional and Technical Occupations*) which largely form the Service Class group in the Goldthorpe three-class model (Erickson and Goldthorpe, 1992). Inclusion of persons already having reached these occupational levels – and they tend not to move down from them unless they are managers – must result in under-estimation of the association of career commitment with occupational mobility effects. To obviate this problem, only those employees at Wave 1 who were *not* already in a service class occupation will be considered first.

Thanks to the effects of work experience, age, and seniority, more employees of all kinds, career committed or not, must be expected to move up than move down. Table 3.5 shows the results for the *lower starters* in the balanced employee panel, i.e. those whose initial position was in Major groups 4 or above. (As noted, these are *lower* ranked major groups.) Stronger career commitment should be clearly associated with a higher likelihood of moving upwards, and moving *further* upwards. Table 3.5 shows that the data strongly support the first part of this proposition; 67 per cent of employees with high scores for career commitment, against only 28 per cent for nil score cases, experienced upward occupational mobility. It is worth noting that the patterns for the sexes differ only in detail; fewer women than men with moderate commitment moved up, although exactly the same proportion with high commitment as men did so. Thus the data suggest that while highly ambitious women do as well as men in terms of this measure at least, those who have moderate ambitions do somewhat worse than their male counterparts, while women with low career commitment do very much better than their male counterparts.

*Table 3.5* Career commitment and upward job mobility
Proportion of 'Lower Starters'* Experiencing Upward Occupational Mobility between Wave 1 and Wave 10.

| | Male % | Female % | All % |
|---|---|---|---|
| Nil | 27 | 29 | 28 |
| Low | 39 | 50 | 43 |
| Moderate | 58 | 52 | 56 |
| High | 67 | 67 | 67 |
| n | 541 | 488 | 1029 |

* Lower starters were employees in occupations forming part of Major Groups 4 to 9 of SOC 1990.
*Source*: BHPS
Selection: Cases which appeared as employees at both Wave 1 and Wave 10 in BHPS, and were *not* in occupations at Wave 1 falling in Major Groups 1 (Managerial & Administrative), 2 (Professional), or 3 (Associate Professional/Technical) of SOC 90 at Wave 1
Weight: Cross-sectional respondent at Wave 1 (AXRWGHT)

As to the *scale* of upward mobility, 23 per cent of the highly committed had moved up at least three ranks in the major group hierarchy, compared to 17 per cent of the moderately committed, and 11 per cent of the low committed. However, 14 per cent of nil commitment group also moved up three ranks or more. Among the high starters (those who were already in one of the top three major occupation groups) there is a rather weak link between career commitment score and moving into a higher group, presumably accounted for largely by employees classified initially as either professionals (Major group 2) or as associate professional and technical employees (Major group 2) moving into management positions. However, other indicators than that of occupational upward mobility are required to show success in career striving for the high starters. Changes in pay do this well.

Figures 3.1a, 3.1b, and 3.1c show the association between average monthly gross pay in pounds sterling and career commitment score for men, for women full-time employees, and for women part-time employees, for the 2031 (weighted N) of BHPS individual respondents who were employees at both Wave 1 and Wave 11. Allowance must be made for inflationary effects, which were relatively severe in the earlier 1990s, following the Lawson Boom. In money terms, gross average monthly pay rose almost exactly 60 per cent between Wave 1 and Wave 11 in money terms; in real terms, the rise was around half that. Between the two waves, the shape of the distributions alters dramatically; initially, strength of career commitment is apparently not associated with pay; at Wave 11 (2001–02) in all three figures a sharp differentiation is apparent, with employees expressing even low career commitment at Wave 1 enjoying a pay advantage over those who had not. For males and full-time female employees, there was a clearly stepped set of differentials at Wave 11 related to career commitment, and a less clear version of it can even be seen for the Wave 11 women part-time employees.

The full-time women earned less than their male counterparts, as would be expected from all research on the pay gap between the sexes, but the proportionate changes for each level of commitment are fairly similar. Returning to the *high starters* who were already members of Major groups 1, 2, or 3 in SOC 90, their performance in terms of enhanced pay rewards is overall higher for the period than the sample as a whole, especially for males. For example, *high starter* males expressing high career commitment at Wave 1 were earning an average of £1391 at Wave 1; by Wave 11 this had risen to £3503, an increase of about 150 per cent. Women high starters did less well, though only 6 women fall in the high commitment group once the *high starter* selection criteria are applied.

## Costs of a career to work–life balance

People with career commitment are more active in developing their employment opportunities, more successful in achieving upward job mobility, and

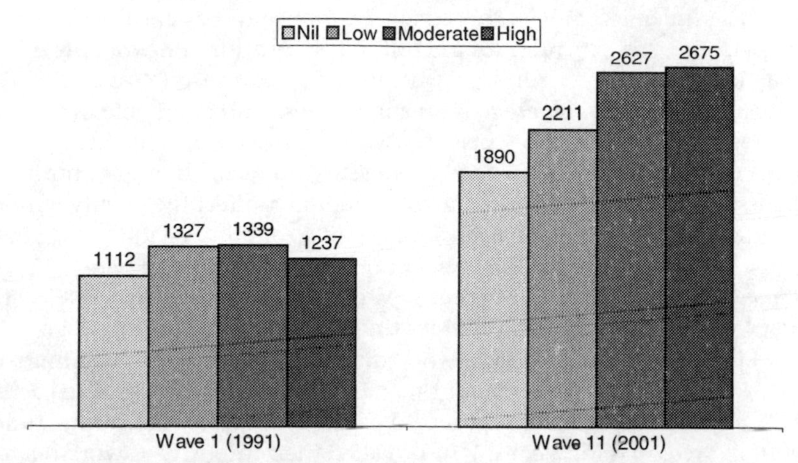


*Figure 3.1a* Male employees

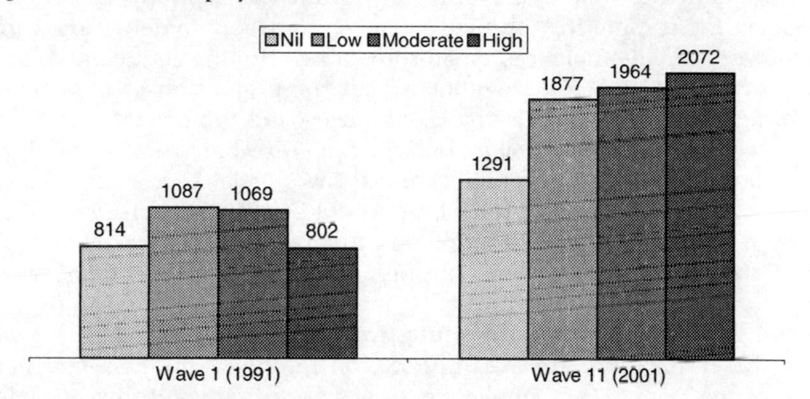


*Figure 3.1b* Female full-time employees

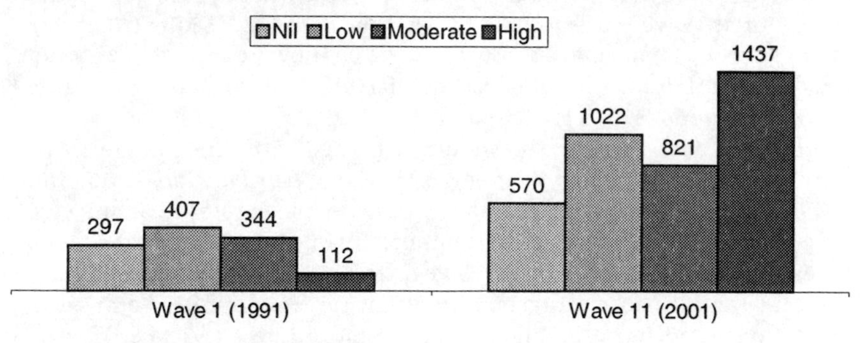


*Figure 3.1c* Female part-time employees

*Figure 3.1* Career commitment and earnings growth over 10 years
Monthly Net Pay of Employees at Wave 1 and Wave 11
*Source*: BHPS.
Selection: Employee at Wave 1 and at Wave 11
Weight: Cross-sectional respondent at Wave 1 (AXRWGHT)
Weighted n: 2031

earn higher incomes. Surely, there must be a price to pay for this objective career success? The expansion of interest in the costs for non-work life of the demands of employment has grown rapidly since the publication of the Brannen (1994) review of research on employment and family life in the UK. More recent research on the area as a whole is discussed elsewhere in this volume (see Chapter 1). Despite the overall surge in research output, however, the question of how *types* of work involvement may affect the quality of non-work life, first raised by the *Employment in Britain* enquiry (Gallie *et al.*, 1998: chapter 8), requires further development of the kind attempted here.

*Temporal costs*. The most obvious cost of career commitment is a longer average working week. BHPS provides time data for: a) a current job; b) any second job; c) overtime regularly worked; and d) time taken to commute to work. No estimate can be made for time taken up in such work-related activities as phone-calls or document reading at home. Again, commuting times cannot be weighted for what might be called their intensity as work-related periods; numerous employees work on documents, lap-top PCs, or the phone during commuting journeys by public transport. Whether they are worriers or not, all employees spend some time thinking about workplace questions when outside the workplace, but the proportion of their non-work time spent on such reflection is unknown. Thus the estimates for total time spent on work-related activities are certainly somewhat on the low side. If it was possible to create fully corrected work-related time accounting systems, it seems likely that work time would be still more clearly longer and more intensive for career committed employees, whose plans and calculations about work extend further ahead and seek to be better calibrated.

Figures 3.2a and 3.2b show, for male and female employees respectively, the smoothed mean times in minutes from Wave 1 to Wave 11, for all employees in the relevant wave of BHPS, controlling for different levels of career commitment. The sample at each wave consists of all those people who: a) personally answered the career-related work attitude questions at Wave 1 or at Wave 9 irrespective of whether they held a job at that time, and b) *did* have a job at any subsequent wave. They are weighted as recommended by BHPS for such analysis as that undertaken here; unweighted data in fact produce closely comparable results.

These time commitment data should be treated with care as there are two significant sources of error in them: differential *panel attrition*, and *attitudinal revision*. Attrition occurs because some people employed at any given wave will have left employment (temporarily or permanently) at the next wave, cannot be contacted by BHPS field staff, or withdraw altogether from the BHPS sample. It might be expected that career committed employees, being busier and more mobile, would be more likely to leave the BHPS panel. In fact, the reverse is true; from Wave 1 to Wave 8 the proportion of career pursuers increases slightly, by about two percentage points, from 22 per cent to 24 per cent, but the change is barely significant statistically.

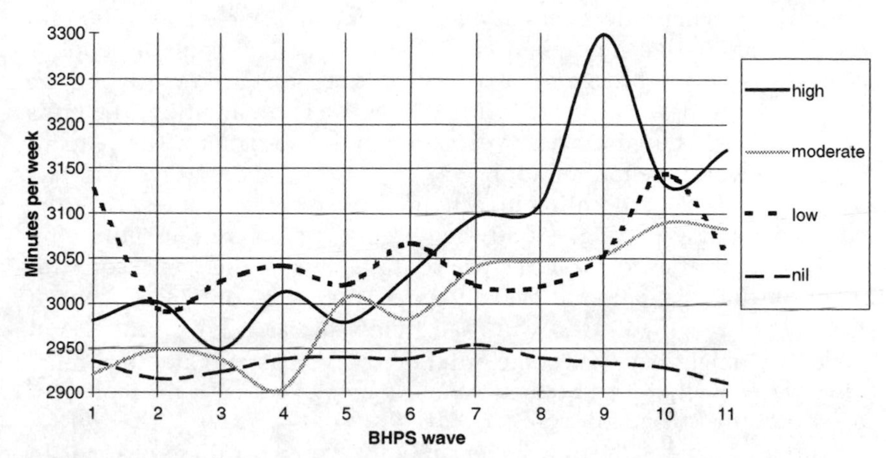


*Figure 3.2a* Male employees

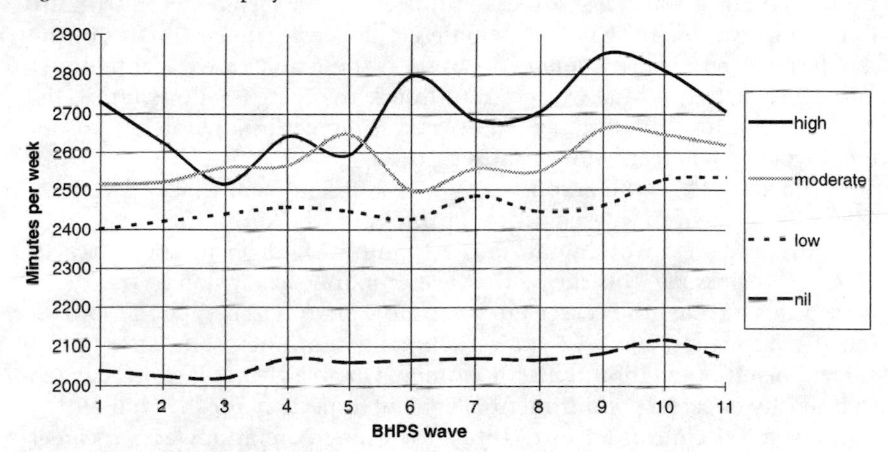


*Figure 3.2b* Female employees

*Figure 3.2* Career commitment and minutes of work-related* time per week in the 1990s

* Basis: Time main job + overtime main job + time any second job + travel–to–work time.

*Source*: BHPS.

Selection: Employee at Wave 1

Weights: Cross-sectional respondent weight (AXRWGHT) at Wave 1, then longitudinal respondent weight (WLRWGHT) for subsequent waves

Weighted n: Varies by wave, with substantial attrition; 4953 at Wave 1, reducing to 2337 at Wave 11

Revision of work attitudes is a possibly more worrying problem, but should not be exaggerated. Some revision is to be expected as most people expressing career aims have relatively modest goals, and as these objectives are achieved some people will adopt new preferences. Others, in response to changed circumstances, will develop career ambitions. Analysis is automatically limited in the present case to a comparable group of people – all those asked the BHPS work orientation questions at Wave 1 (for the Waves 1–8 results) or at Wave 9 (for Waves 9–11). In addition, the cross sectional weights used in these years are applied to data for the years in which the work orientation apply. (As noted earlier, the weights in fact make surprisingly little difference to most percentage values.) For the balanced employee panel (1580 weighted cases) of respondents who had held a job at every wave, 73 per cent had *exactly* the same scores for career pursuit orientation at Wave 9 as at Wave 1; so did 73 per cent of those (2240 weighted cases) who had held a job at Wave 1 and also at Wave 9 but might have had some other employment status at one or more other waves. Fully 89 per cent of Wave 1 employees with nil scores for career pursuit also had nil scores at Wave 9.

Figures 3.2a and 3.2b show a clear picture even with these provisos in mind. Having at least *some* career commitment is associated with working longer hours for both male and female employees. (Time estimates in the charts are given as mean *minutes per week*, as these totals are easier to digest and compare than a total expressed in hours involving fractions.) In statistical terms (*t*-test) the difference between careerists as a whole and other employees is significant at every wave.

At the same time, the graph for men is different from that for women. Male career pursuers worked more minutes per week from the early 1990s onwards, and were working around 130 minutes longer in 2001 than in 1991; quite possibly, this shows that the economic expansion in the UK in these years affected the career pursuers more sharply. There are fewer systematic differences between males in time commitment and strength of career pursuit orientation than for women, where a clearer layering related to intensity of career commitment is evident, especially for the later 1990s.

Above all, the mean minutes totals for women are all lower; for career pursuing women they are around 400 minutes less per week than for career pursuer men; the differences between non-career pursuer men and non-career pursuer women is even greater, around 900 minutes per week. It must be remembered at this point that a large minority of women work part-time by necessity or by choice. Relatively few (between 15–20%) of career pursuer women were classified as part-time employees at any given wave of BHPS, compared with 40 per cent of non-career pursuer women. If women classified as part-time are excluded, the difference in minutes worked per week by career pursuer women rises to around 2750 – much closer to the mean for career pursuer men.

The relevance of these data for women to the debate about women's orientations to work (Crompton and Harris, 1998; Ginn *et al.*, 1996; Hakim, 1995, 1996, 2001) is evident. Very clear objective behavioural differences can be linked to work orientation. In terms of overall patterns, there is support for *preference theory*, at least insofar as it refers to differences of work orientation and labour market behaviour. At the same time, of course, it provides no evidence either for or against a central claim in preference theory, i.e. that women's work orientations essentially reflect a choice made during adolescence. Other points at issue in this debate for which the present data may be relevant must also left to others to take up. The present treatment is essentially a discussion of commonalities in the work attitudes and behaviour of people with career pursuit orientations, irrespective of sex. What matters most here is that both men and women career pursuers tend to work significantly longer each week than other employees. We now examine other costs related to career pursuit.

## Other costs of career pursuit

How do the career committed experience these extra time pressures on their work–life balance? The BHPS data suggest that the career committed typically accept them with equanimity. The pattern of satisfaction with hours worked among them is almost identical to that among other employees, though it is marginally lower among career committed women; overall, large majorities of them express some degree of satisfaction with hours worked at each wave of BHPS. The employment questionnaire also asks whether employees wish to work fewer, more, or the same hours as at present; here too, there is almost no discernible association with career commitment, except that a slightly higher proportion (just over 15 per cent as opposed 10 per cent for other women employees) of career committed women do express dissatisfaction with hours worked combined with the wish for fewer hours. Thus some discontent exists in this sub-group but it is slight and not statistically significant.

Again, the higher time demands experienced by some career committed people are not associated, overall, with greater morbidity among this group, and this finding holds for both men and women career pursuers separately. Measures for no fewer than seven aspects of psychological and somatic well-being, six being specially created for the research, were created for the BHPS Wave 9 employee data (4282 weighted cases). Findings for them are summarised in Table 3.6. (The measures are described in the Methodological Appendix.)

First, the apparent bad news: subjective experience of work-related stress *is* higher among the career committed. A set of four questions about work-related stress were asked at Wave 9, referring to worrying about work, failure to unwind after return home, and a sense of feeling drained or exhausted after work. The questions did not focus upon stress specifically from *time* pressures at work, though evidently time famine may exacerbate an experience of stress. The data show an association of experience of higher stress and having some career commitment, for both sexes; but this

*Table 3.6* Health indicators and career committed employees, by sex

| Health dimension | Male career pursuer | Female career pursuer |
|---|---|---|
| Work-related stress score | Higher (ns) | Higher*** |
| GHQ Likert | Lower*** | Lower (ns) |
| Symptoms | Fewer* | Fewer* |
| Disability score | Lower** | Lower** |
| Recent physical energy | Higher** | Higher (ns) |
| Recent mental attitude | More positive * | More positive (ns) |
| Health optimism | Higher*** | Higher (ns) |

Reference group: Employees nil commitment score of zero
Data: BHPS Wave 9
N = 4282 weighted cases
* p<.05; ** p<.01; ***p<.001 (*t*-test, equal variances assumed)
Variable construction: see Methodological Appendix

was not statistically significant for the career committed males, among whom experienced stress actually falls back for the high commitment subgroup. On the other hand, stress experience scores rise in a more or less linear way with level of career commitment among women: thus 25 per cent of high commitment women had elevated stress scores (above 1 standard deviation) as against 12 per cent of high commitment men.

The good news is that the higher experienced stress of the career committed does not result in higher scores for incipient psychological ill-health or a rise in somatic stress symptoms among the career committed of either sex. On the Likert Scale version of the General Health Questionnaire (Goldberg and Williams, 1988), which *does* aim to detect the onset of psychological ill-health, career pursuers of both sexes emerged with lower average scores than other employees: for women, the difference was not large enough to reach statistical significance, but for men it was highly significant.

BHPS permits an examination of how experience of somatic stress symptoms or actual disease (such as migraine, elevated blood pressure, digestive disorders, substance-abuse, or strokes) distribute between career commitment levels. One in 15 employees reported at least one such symptom, but risk *fell* significantly among career commitment employees; and, for both sexes, the highly committed actually had the *lowest* scores. Smoking was not included among the somatic amber lights used to construct this scale, and results for it should be noted separately: around 40 per cent of the highly committed, compared to just over 25 per cent of all other groups, admitted they were smokers, and the difference is significant. Possibly this might reflect individual idiosyncrasy (in particular, distribution of Type A personality types) rather than reflecting experienced stress. It might signal future health problems, but hardly an imminent health catastrophe, though clearly it would be better for the people concerned if they could simply stop doing it.

Results for four further measures of health and well-being are reported in Table 3.5. The *disability* measure reports actual physical problems, recent *physical energy* summarises statements about sense of vitality and vigour, recent *mental attitude* reflects a position on a spectrum of states of positive to negative consciousness, and *health optimism* registers beliefs about one's own physical and mental well-being. It might be expected that performance on each of these measures might be significantly *worse* for the career committed. On all of them, nevertheless, mean scores for the career committed indicated higher well-being: scores for women failed to reach statistical significance on three of the measures, but were in every case better than for the non-committed, as they were for men. Overall, then, evidence for an ill-health offset for higher commitment to career pursuit is conspicuously absent in this sample.

Nor does commitment to career aims lead to personal relationships that are conspicuously and systematically less successful, though at first sight it seems that career builders fail to create domestic partnerships. The average age of people committed to a career, when first appearing at Wave 1, was lower (33) overall and fell to 26 for the highly committed: distributions were identical for the sexes. For other employees the average age was 41; thus they were likely to have reached somewhat different positions on the life and family cycles.

In particular, career pursuers should be less likely to have established partners or to be married, and without an age control this is clearly the case. Once age is controlled, however, any 'loner' effect largely evaporates, though it does not do so completely. Restricting comparison to people in their 20s, the proportion (just under one-quarter) cohabiting but not married is to all intents and purposes identical; however, the proportion of the career committed as a whole who have married is 16 per cent (only 8 per cent for the highly committed) against 24 per cent for all other employees. Once again, there is little sex-related difference. However, planned deferment of marriage may be the underlying process rather than the expression of lifestyle options or the existence of a serious 'no one to play with' problem (Jenkins and Osburg, 2002).

Moreover, there is no sign that rates of separation and divorce are higher for the career committed who have married, except possibly for women with high career commitment, where small numbers make the finding very provisional and statistically non-significant. However, the proportion of high career commitment women expressing positive satisfaction with a partner (30%) *is* much lower than the proportion (53%) of highly committed men, and both are rather lower than the proportions of both men and women not expressing career commitment (over 70% in each case): in terms of the *t* statistic, there is a highly significant difference here between the career committed as a whole and other employees.

Yet while the committed may be, for whatever reason, less successful in finding partners that suit them, or are more exigent in their expectations of partnership because of their own career ambitions, they do not appear to have a general disposition towards conscious unease and dissatisfaction with their lives. Their satisfaction with life overall, whether measured by a single item seven-point rating scale or by a summed total of life-facet scores, is marginally though not significantly *higher* than that of other employees at Wave 9. Satisfaction is slightly lower with specific facets such as amount of leisure time and use of leisure time, where one might anticipate some disappointment, but the differences are not statistically significant. Satisfaction with a current partner or spouse is much lower, as noted; and in statistical terms this relative disappointment is equally significant for the sexes. Apart from this, the lack of difference is striking.

Moreover, there is one area of life satisfaction where the career committed emerge as very significantly more content with their lives. This is in terms of current satisfaction seen in relation to the previous year. Figure 3.3 suggests a near-linear association between degree of career commitment and rising satisfaction with the way the respondent's life had been moving relative to the previous year, and by implication, with personal achievement. Though the proportionate differences (13 percentage points for men, only 7 for women) for the low commitment employees are not significant for female employees on a two-tail basis, the overall form of the

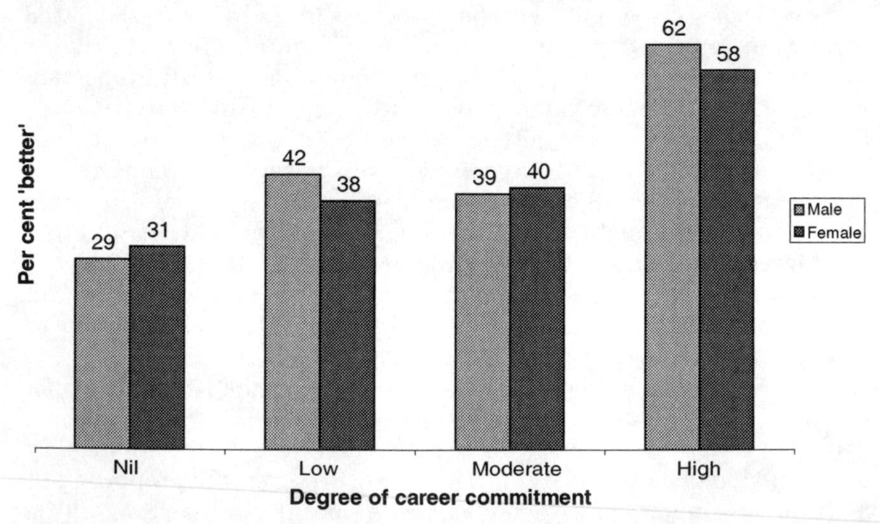


*Figure 3.3* Satisfaction with life as a whole this year compared to last year, by career commitment and sex of employee
*Data*: BHPS Wave 9.
N = 4282 weighted cases
Weight: IXRWGHT

graph suggests that a one-tail test is appropriate in this case, and such a test is significant. For the high commitment employees, the proportionate differences are in each case highly significant on a two-tail basis.

The chart also has a feature to which attention has been repeatedly drawn in the foregoing analysis: the considerable similarity of the response patterns for the two sexes. While there are certainly important differences between the sexes within the career committed as a category, but they are often of degree rather than kind. This suggests that the somewhat rough and ready measure of career commitment does succeed in tapping attitude configurations which, within structures of opportunity and constraint imposed on ambitious women that vary from those on ambitious men in many ways, do tend to produce similar kinds of behaviour, experience, and consequential attitudes.

## Conclusion

Career builders, then, seem able to perceive a higher degree of achievement in their own lives in terms of their core employment values. In one sense, this should hardly be surprising since, as we saw earlier, in terms of salary increases and job mobility the career committed *do* achieve disproportionate success. These are not goals shared with equal intensity, or at all, by most other workers; and it may be that the commitment of career builders to their present aims is sometimes higher than is good for them. Yet career builders do not report more such problems, except for some partnership difficulties; indeed, they often report fewer.

It is possible that temporal pressures are moderated for at least some career committed people because they are more likely to have jobs in occupations, or in work organisations, where flexible time arrangements such as flexitime, annualised hours, job sharing, etc. are offered. This possibility is supported, after a fashion, by the data for both Waves 9 and 11 in BHPS, where seven possible flexitime arrangements were examined, enabling a count of total flexitime arrangements enjoyed. Overall, only one in four employees reported at least one such arrangement at Wave 11, but there was a difference for career pursuers as a whole: against 24 per cent for non-career employees, 28 per cent for low commitment, 29 per cent for moderate commitment, while 31 per cent for high career commitment employees reported such an arrangement. The finding is significant in terms of the $t$ statistic, and reassuring for policy expectations. But it fails to provide a sufficient explanation for the apparent ability of career builders to manage work-related stress: there was no significant relationship between having such friendlier time arrangements and subjective stress.

Despite the relative immunity of career pursuers to stress related and other illnesses, it is possible that the sense of subjective well-being characteristic of them may amount to an adrenalin powered delusion. Clearly, the higher number of hours per week worked by career builders may be undesirable in knock-on terms, becoming manifest in health effects, strained relationships, and sense of well-being among their partners and/or dependents. However, the data to hand simply fail to disclose any signs of such ticking time-bomb effects, except for that related to smoking – which in any case affects only a minority. In the absence of other and more negative evidence it is hard to find a way of fashioning a general warning from the few troublesome effects detected.

Should this be so surprising? Career builders are, by definition, more highly involved in work as a daily activity. Gallie *et al.* (1998: 228–231), while documenting in great detail the effect on non-work life of work-related strain and stress as shown in the *Employment in Britain* survey, also found that any impact on general psychological health appeared to be moderated by a higher degree of work involvement. The present results confirm these findings.

Thus, an alternative interpretation of what might seem the failure of the career committed to register the costs of a longer work week, and of its possible knock-on effects in the other areas of private life over the longer term, is available: career committed employees do not suffer the effects that might be predicted for them because the disutilities they experience have already been priced into their work strategies. Although survey data can give only a highly condensed and schematic pointer to work values, there is reason to believe that when employees report on their reasons for having paid work, and on their priorities when seeking and choosing between jobs, they do their level best to provide accurate information. Those reporting some commitment to career building will attempt to pursue development strategies for their personal employment that achieve their goals, having accepted beforehand certain costs in doing so. A degree of work–life imbalance in terms of time commitment that an observer might find worrying is accepted by them as an inescapable condition of pursuing valued aims.

It is not appropriate for a social researcher to object to such a premeditated choice by a responsible adult, which in any case may well be modified as aims are achieved. An objection must have other grounds. Other knock-on effects may arise. For example, the longer hours willingly put in by a group of employees with high career commitment in a given workplace may become established as an informal social norm to which the performance of less ambitious workers is referred. (Case studies in work organisations should be better adapted to examining this possibility.)

The risk to the well-being of others, of positive harm to partners or dependent children, may also be higher. Some BHPS data relevant to the question is available but a quick review of it fails to provide any clear evidence of such higher risks for the partners of the career committed. However, a fuller examination taking in possible lags in the appearance of harmful effects needs to be undertaken. Thus, from the viewpoint of social policy, as from that of commonsense, there exists a case for keeping the hidden costs of career striving under vigilant review.

**Acknowledgements**

The findings reported result from analysis undertaken for the ESRC project R000223499 *Labour Market Trajectories and Rationales of Work.*

**References**

Barley, S.R. (1989) 'Career, identities, and institutions: the legacy of the Chicago School of Sociology', in M.B. Arthur, D.T. Hall, and B.S. Lawrence (eds), *Handbook of Career Theory*, Cambridge University Press.

Bell, D. (1976) *The Cultural Contradictions of Capitalism*, London: Heinemann.

Brannen, J. (1994) 'Employment and Family Life: A Review of Research in the UK 1980–1994', Department of Employment.

Crompton, R. and Harris, F. (1998) 'Explaining women's employment patterns: 'Orientations to work' revisited', *British Journal of Sociology*, 49, 1: 118–136.

Erikson, R. and Goldthorpe, J.H. (1992) *The Constant Flux*, Oxford: Clarendon Press.

Freed Taylor, M., Brice, J., Buck, N. and Prentice-Lane, E. (2003) *British Household Panel Survey User Manual Volume A: Introduction, Technical Report and Appendices*, Colchester, Essex: Institute of Social and Economic Research.

Gallie, D., White, M., Cheng, Y., and Tomlinson, M. (1998) *Restructuring the Employment Relationship*, Oxford University Press.

Ginn, J., Arber, S., Brannen, J., Dale, A., Dex, S., Elias, P., Moss, P., Pahl, J., Roberts, C., and Rubery, J. (1996) 'Feminist fallacies: A reply to Hakim on women's employment', *British Journal of Sociology*, 47, 1: 175–77.

Goldberg, D.P. and Williams, P. (1988) *A User's Guide to the General Health Questionnaire*, Windsor: NFER-Nelson.

Hakim, C. (1995) 'Five Feminist myths about women's employment', *British Journal of Sociology*, 46, 3: 429–455.

Hakim, C. (1996) *Key Issues in Women's Work: Female Heterogeneity and the Polarisation of Women's Employment*, Athlone Press.

Hakim, C. (2001) *Work-Lifestyle Choices in the 21st Century: Preference Theory*, Oxford University Press.

Hughes, E.C. (1958) *Men and their Work*, Glencoe, Illinois: Free Press.

Inglehart, R. (1997) Modernization and Postmodernization: Cultural, Economic, and Political Change in 43 Societies, Princeton, N.J.: Princeton University Press.

Jenkins, S. and Osburg, L. (2002) 'Nobody to play with? The implications of leisure coordination', Paper for BHPS Users' Conference, Colchester, Essex: Institute of Social and Economic Research.

Kumar, K. (1978) Prophecy and Progress: The Sociology of Industrial and Post-Industrial Society, Allen Lane.

Kumar, K. (1995) *From Post-Industrial to Post-Modern Society: New Theories of the Contemporary World*, Blackwell, Oxford.

Li, Y., Bechhofer, F., Stewart, R., McCrone, D., Anderson, M. and Jamieson, L. (2002) 'A divided working class? Planning and career perception in the service and working classes', *Work, Employment, and Society*, 16, 4: 599–616.

Martin, J. and Roberts, C. (1984) *Women and Employment – A Lifetime Perspective*, Department of Employment: OPCS.

Penn, R., Rose, M. and Rubery, J. (eds) (1994) *Skill and Occupational Change*, Oxford University Press.

Rose, M. (2004, forthcoming) 'Shaping a CV? Career perceptions and career pursuit in the UK, 1986–2002' in P. Stewart (ed.), *The Experience of Work and Organisational Change*, Macmillan.

## Data sets used

Economic and Social Research Council Research Centre on Micro-Social Change. British Household Panel Survey (computer file). Colchester, Essex: The Data Archive (distributor), 2003. SN4340.

Office For National Statistics, Omnibus Surveys, January, March, and April 2001. Colchester, Essex: The Data Archive (distributor), 2003; SN4533, SN4534, SN4535.

# Methodological Appendix

## SURVEY DETAILS

1. SCELI (ESRC Social Change and Economic Life Initiative, Work Histories and Attitudes)
*Date of main wave fieldwork*: 1985
*Sample Type*: Purposive choice of six British travel-to-work localities, random sampling of individuals within each locality
*Sample size, current employees (weighted N in parentheses):* 3650 (3241)
*Comments*: The SCELI employee survey required personal interviews by professional fieldworkers lasting on average 75 minutes with current employees aged 20–60 years. Many SCELI questions have been included in later British employee surveys and its main findings are often considered benchmarks for establishing longer term trends in the British workforce. The employee sample has been shown to approximate very closely to a true national random sample.
*Further information*: Penn, Rose and Rubery 1994, Methodological Appendix.
*UK Data Archive Study Number*: SN3273

2. *Living in Britain*/BHPS; British Household Panel Survey Waves 1 to 11
*Dates of main wave fieldwork*: Annual waves since September 1991, most interviews completed in autumn.
*Sample Type*: National random sample of households in mainland Britain, all employed individuals in household.
Sample sizes, current employees, (weighted N in parentheses): Vary from Wave 1, 1991 = 4974 (4849) to Wave 11 = 8737 (4184)
*Comments*: BHPS examines key employment related variables as part of its main purpose – showing micro social changes over time in Britain. It uses a complex national random sample of households, but individually interviews all currently employed people within a selected household. Households are revisited each year, and many individuals are thus re-interviewed in two or more years. Correctly applied, weightings allow creation of samples that approximate closely to annual national cross-sectional samples of individuals. However, correct weighting is not in fact essential to assess the overall effect of theoretically oriented explanatory variables of the kind examined here; in fact results are very similar for unweighted data. However, weighting is important for tests of significance.
*Further information*: Freed Taylor, M. *et al.*, 2003.
*UK Data Archive study number*: SN4340

3. ONS (Office for National Statistics Omnibus Survey)
*Dates of main wave fieldwork*: 2002 (January, March, April)
*Sample Type*: Three UK national random samples of individuals
*Sample size, current employees (weighted N in parentheses)*: January 751 (816); March 776 (840); April 882 (821)
*Comments*: The ONS Omnibus Survey is a general purpose survey available to not-for-profit researchers and policy makers. A core list of variables (sex, age, education, housing, employment status, etc.) is provided by ONS; users pay a standard fee to add questions covering the topic of interest to them, receiving methodological advice from specialists on the ONS staff. Around 1800 adults are interviewed at each data collection, which occur approximately 8 times per year.
*Further information*: http:// www.statistics.gov.uk
UK Data Archive study numbers: SN4533, SN4534, SN4535.

## HEALTH INDICATOR VARIABLES CREATED FOR THE ANALYSIS.

### *Work Related Stress*

Variable name: STRESSUM
Additive scale formed from BHPS items: *ijbstrna* (Worry about problems after work) *ijbstrnb* (Difficult to unwind after work) *ijbstrnc* (Feel used up after work) *ijbstrnd* (Feel exhausted after work)
Coding
1 NEVER
2 OCCASIONALLY
3 SOME OF THE TIME
4 MUCH OF THE TIME
5 MOST OF THE TIME
6 ALL OF THE TIME.
Cronbach's Alpha 0.828

### *Disability*

Variable name: H_DISAB
Additive scale formed from BHPS items with stem 'My health limits...' *ihlsf3a* (vigorous activities) *ihlsf3b* (moderate activities) *ihlsf3c* (carrying groceries) *ihlsf3d* (several flights of stair) *ihlsf3e* (one flight of stairs) *ihlsf3f* (bending/kneeling) *ihlsf3g* (walking a mile or further) *ihlsf3h* (walking half a mile) *ihlsf3i* (walking 100 yards) *ihlsf3j* (bathing/dressing).
Coding
0 YES, LIMITED A LOT
1 YES, LIMITED A LITTLE
2 NO, NOT LIMITED AT ALL
Cronbach's Alpha 0.842

### Health Outlook

Variable name: H_OUTLK
Additive scale formed from BHPS items *ihlsf10a* (I get ill more easily than others), *ihlsf10b* (I am as healthy as others), *ihlsf10c* (I expect health to worsen), *ihlsf10d* (My health is excellent)
Coding
1 DEFINITELY TRUE
2 MOSTLY TRUE
3 NOT SURE
4 MOSTLY FALSE
5 DEFINITELY FALSE
Cronbach's Alpha 0.718

### Recent physical energy

Variable name: H_VIGBOD
Additive scale from items retained: '(In the past month) *ihlsf9a* (Felt full of life) *ihlsf9e* (Had lots of energy) *ihlsf9g* (Felt worn out) *ihlsf9i* (Felt tired). The BHPS item *ihlsf9j* (Health limited my social activity) was dropped following the scale reliability test.
Coding
0 NONE OF THE TIME
1 A LITTLE OF THE TIME
2 SOME OF THE TIME
3 A GOOD BIT OF THE TIME
4 MOST OF THE TIME
5 ALL OF THE TIME
Items *ihlsf9g* and *ihlsf9i* were reverse coded
Cronbach's Alpha 0.827

### Recent mental attitude

Variable name: H_VIGMEN
Additive scale from items '(In the past month) *ihlsf9b* (Been very nervy) *ihlsf9c* (Felt down in the dumps) *ihlsf9d* (Felt calm and cheerful) *ihlsf9f* (Felt downhearted and low) ihlsf9h (Been a happy person). Items *ihlsf9d* and *ihlsf9h* were reverse coded.
Coding
0 NONE OF THE TIME
1 A LITTLE OF THE TIME
2 SOME OF THE TIME
3 A GOOD BIT OF THE TIME
4 MOST OF THE TIME
5 ALL OF THE TIME
Cronbach's Alpha 0.827

### *Stress symptoms*

Variable name: SYMPTOM
Count data, 1 for 'YES' on *ihlprbf* (Heart and blood pressure) *ihlprbg* (Stomach or digestive) *ihlprbi* (Anxiety, depression) *ihlprbj* (Alcohol, drugs) *ihlprbl* (Migraine) *ihlprbm* (Other symptoms).

# 4
# Sex Differences in Work–Life Balance Goals

*Catherine Hakim*

Are we heading for a unisex workplace in the future? Or will differences between men and women continue to shape their lifestyle choices and work histories? Answers to these questions matter, because they inform, explicitly or implicitly, perspectives on work–life balance, the employment policies of central governments, and the personnel policies of employers. This chapter argues that differences between men and women in work orientations will persist to some extent in the 21st century – in their attitudes, values, life goals and behaviour. Policy-makers should recognise and accept this fact, and devise realistic, evidence-based policies, rather than relying on wishful thinking to develop utopian unisex policies that will necessarily fail.

The European Commission's current goal of a single, dominant model of the family, and a single model of women's role in it, which will provide the basis for convergence on a single set of social and fiscal policies in the European Union (EU) ignores relevant research evidence and is unrealistic. Policy development in the British government follows the Commission's lead on this topic.

The European Commission's assumption is that, once women have genuine access to the labour market and employment careers, they will invariably choose the male pattern of full-time continuous employment throughout life, with only the briefest of pauses for childbearing or the care of elderly relatives (European Commission, 1997a). The assumption is that no woman voluntarily chooses to be a homemaker, either full-time or part-time, in preference to employment in the market economy. No reason is given for this assumption, but it seems to rest on the feminist idea that financial dependence on a husband or partner is demeaning for a woman – although financial dependence on the state is not considered to be equally demeaning. Another factor is the idea that women's lesser involvement in the labour market is due exclusively to sex discrimination, and that after such discrimination is abolished, sex differences in labour market behaviour will disappear completely. If the Commission is right, there will be convergence on a single model of the family, and of women's role in society, without prompting or pushing by policy-makers. This would then provide a conveniently uniform basis for social and fiscal policy within the EU.

## Ideal models of the family

Models of the family concern the allocation of roles and responsibilities, role specialisation and the division of labour among adult members. By the 1990s, the common feminist assumption, adopted also by the European Commission, was that women preferred employment careers to being unpaid homemakers.[1] It was assumed that, given the choice, women would willingly swap a domestic role in the home for waged work in the market economy, and that it was patriarchal male strategies of exclusion and segregation that kept women out of jobs, not choice (Walby, 1990: 53–6). Put simply, women were expected to prefer the authority of an employer (or the control of market forces) to the patriarchal power of a husband.[2] As a result, all families would eventually consist of dual-earner couples, with or without children, and some of these would be genuine dual-career couples.[3] The Commission's preferred model of the family is the Scandinavian model: all able-bodied adults work throughout life with only the briefest of interruptions for childbearing, and childcare is delegated to public agencies. In practice, public sector care work is staffed almost exclusively by women, and occupational segregation is higher in Scandinavia than in other European countries (Anker, 1998; Hakim, 2004b: 170–3). In practice, the Scandinavian model replaces individualised care in private homes by collective care under public control, without changing women's activities and occupations. Studies of the family, and of women's employment, usually look for convergence across western Europe at least, and even across the whole of Europe. Generally, they have failed to find it (Boh *et al.*, 1989; European Commission, 1991). Furthermore, studies done by, and for, the European Commission routinely find no sign of convergence even within countries. On the contrary, there is widespread evidence of the polarisation of attitudes and lifestyles in modern societies (Hakim, 2000a, 2004b).

The Eurobarometer question[4] reported in Table 4.1 is unusual in that it asks people about their personal choice or preference regarding ideal family model and family roles. In contrast, most social attitude surveys collect data on social beliefs, generalised attitudes on what is good for society in general. This crucial distinction between choice and approval, between personal preference and the public good, is routinely overlooked in analyses of attitude data (Hakim, 2000a: 72–82, 2003a: 47, 2003b, 2004a: 73–4). For example, people may accept that it is a good idea for everyone to use public transport, yet still prefer to use a car themself.

Social attitude data on public beliefs and public goods do not necessarily tell us about personal choices.

The EU survey shows that one-quarter of European adults still prefer the complete separation of roles in the family, with the wife financially dependent on a breadwinner husband. Rejection of this model does not necessarily mean that people accept completely equal sharing of income-earning and family work. One-third of adults only accept a compromise arrangement, in which the wife does some paid work as a secondary earner, for example in a part-time job. Only two-fifths of the EU population prefers the fully symmetrical roles family model.[5] This model attracted most support in Denmark, followed by Spain, the UK and Portugal. These results suggest that the so-called 'modern' symmetrical family is really a reversion to a pre-industrial model. As several scholars have pointed out, it is the dual-earner family that is traditional; the single breadwinner model of the family is a *modern* invention, and it remained the popular ideal for a relatively short time (Bernard, 1981; Davis, 1984; Seccombe, 1993: 202–9; Hakim, 1996: 82).[6]

The social desirability bias in responses to interview surveys (Turner and Martin, 1984; Marín and Marín, 1991; Hakim, 2003a: 62–8) may currently boost support for the symmetrical roles model of the family. For example, Spain has the very lowest female workrate in the EU: only 34 per cent of women of working age have a job, compared to 37 per cent in Italy, 40 per cent in Greece and 59 per cent in Portugal (Hakim, 2000a: Table 3.3, 2004b: Table 3.2). Nonetheless, Spanish people express remarkably high levels of support for the model of the family with fully symmetrical roles, one of the highest in the EU in 1987 (Table 4.1). By 1999, support had grown even further, to over two-thirds of people of working age (Hakim, 2003a: 51). It seems likely that these results are influenced by the social desirability bias that affects responses to all social attitude surveys to some degree.[7]

The complete separation of roles attracts most support in Luxembourg, Germany and Ireland, some of the most affluent countries in Europe. But in all countries there is a wide spread of support for all three models of the family, and none receives majority support except in Denmark. Certainly, there are no sharp differences between northern and southern European societies, or by level of prosperity. Overall, a three-quarters majority of European men and women favour the idea of the working wife, but a clear majority also favour the wife retaining all or the major part of the home-maker role. Age has a strong influence on attitudes. These results reflect the development of core values over the lifecycle, as many women prefer greater role segregation after they have children and confront competing priorities for the first time (Hakim, 2003a: 106–9).

The European Commission's Eurobarometer surveys provide unique evidence on the diversity of sex-role preferences and ideologies[8] *within*

European countries, as well as across western Europe. They show that there is no single, dominant preference among women (or men), except among the youngest women, whose views are less stable (Hakim, 2003a: 65–6, 106–8). A minority of women choose to be primary earners throughout life and compete in the labour market on the same basis as men. Another minority of women, one in four in the European Union, prefer segregated family roles, which means that wives normally quit the labour market permanently after marriage, if they ever work at all. Finally, at least one-third of women enter the workforce as secondary earners: they expect (or hope) to be supported by a husband for most of their adult life, so that they only supplement his earnings rather than being equal co-earners. An appropriate label for this last arrangement would be the *modern sexual division of labour* in the family.

Equivalent data for the USA in the 1980s reveals a similar pattern of plans and preferences among women of working age who had married in the period 1965–84 (Whyte, 1990). Prior to marriage, 30 per cent had aimed to be full-time housewives; 44 per cent wanted to work for some of the time after marriage; and only 25 per cent desired a life-long employment career. In the USA, there was a massive decline in the popularity of the marriage career in the decades up to the 1980s. But it was replaced by the new ideal of the modern sexual division of labour, with the wife as secondary earner, rather than by a swing towards lifelong employment, which was chosen by a minority of wives (Whyte, 1990: 48–9).[9]

There are several Eurobarometer surveys every year, but after 1987 the Commission dropped the question on family models from the survey because it was not producing the results they wanted. Relevant results from national surveys, and the International Social Survey Programme, indicate that views on the family division of labour have fluctuated since the 1980s, but have not substantially changed. In particular, there is no clear trend in data on this topic (Hakim, 2000a: 89–94). This is consistent with the absence of any trend across age cohorts (Hakim, 2003a: 106–8). We carried out new surveys in Britain and Spain in 1999 which included the Eurobarometer question on family models.

## The British survey

Qualitative studies based on depth interviews can readily identify the diversity of lifestyle preferences, and the way they impact on women's choices and behaviour – as illustrated by Gerson's brilliant study of how women decide about motherhood and careers (Gerson, 1985: Table C22; Hakim, 2000a: 149–54). Our aim was to identify a small number of classificatory questions that might be included in any large interview survey, so that this variable could be created within all major survey datasets, including cross-national comparative studies (Hakim, 2003a: 33–48).

Our shortlisted questions were included in a British survey carried out as one of 27 projects selected for the ESRC Research Programme on the Future of Work running over six years (1998–2004) in Britain. The interview survey was carried out for the author by the Office of National Statistics (ONS) in January and February 1999.

The survey was based on a probability random sample of households in Britain, and face-to-face interviews with one person aged 16 and over chosen randomly within each household. The proportion of the households in which the selected informant was the head of household or spouse was 81 per cent in our sample. From a sample of 5388 eligible addresses, an overall response rate of 68 per cent was achieved, producing data for a nationally representative sample of 3651 persons aged 16 and over in Britain. Refusals accounted for 24 per cent of the initial sample, and non-contacts for another 8 per cent.

The final sample included 1691 men and 1960 women, with a substantial proportion (20%) aged 65 and over. Excluding the pensioners reduces the sample for the population of working age to 2900, including 2345 married and cohabiting couples.

The survey was used to examine sex differences in ideal models of the family division of labour, work orientations and lifestyle preferences, and to explore the impact of lifestyle preferences on behaviour, especially labour market participation and occupational choice. The full report is presented in Hakim (2003a), which also includes comparative analyses of an equivalent national survey in Spain carried out in late 1999, following standard procedures for cross-national comparative studies (Hakim, 2000b). A later analysis looks at the impact of lifestyle preferences on married women's fertility (Hakim, 2003c).

Apart from Table 4.1, all tables and evidence presented here are from the 1999 British survey and the equivalent Spanish survey.

## Family models, work centrality and lifestyle preferences

Three questions from the survey are the focus of our analysis here. Two questions were taken from the Eurobarometer series. The third, a question on work commitment, has been widely used, in slightly different versions, in research on work orientations in the USA and Britain (Hakim, 2003a: 72–7, 2004b: 101–6). The question on ideal family model addresses sex-role preferences in the family context. Two further questions cover work orientations from different angles and are combined into an index of work centrality. Table 4.2 shows the three questions, the index of work centrality produced by combining responses to questions 2 and 3, and the distribution of lifestyle preferences resulting from the combination of ideal family model and work centrality. All three questions produced results in line with those obtained in earlier Eurobarometer and other surveys. The survey also

*Table 4.1* The diversity of sex-role preferences in Europe

Percentage of adults supporting each of three models of the sexual division of labour:

| | Symmetrical roles | | Compromise | | Separate roles | | Total |
|---|---|---|---|---|---|---|---|
| | 1987 | 1983 | 1987 | 1983 | 1987 | 1983 | |
| Denmark | 58 | 50 | 29 | 33 | 13 | 17 | 100 |
| Spain | 50 | .. | 20 | .. | 30 | .. | 100 |
| United Kingdom | 49 | 39 | 32 | 37 | 19 | 24 | 100 |
| Portugal | 47 | .. | 26 | .. | 27 | .. | 100 |
| Netherlands | 46 | 41 | 30 | 27 | 24 | 32 | 100 |
| France | 46 | 42 | 30 | 27 | 24 | 31 | 100 |
| Greece | 46 | 53 | 30 | 23 | 24 | 25 | 100 |
| Italy | 43 | 42 | 32 | 28 | 26 | 30 | 100 |
| Belgium | 38 | 35 | 33 | 25 | 28 | 40 | 100 |
| Ireland | 37 | 32 | 22 | 26 | 42 | 42 | 100 |
| West Germany | 28 | 29 | 37 | 38 | 35 | 33 | 100 |
| Luxembourg | 22 | 27 | 34 | 23 | 44 | 50 | 100 |
| Men – all | 41 | 35 | 31 | 34 | 28 | 31 | 100 |
| 15–24 years | 59 | 49 | 28 | 33 | 13 | 18 | 100 |
| 25–39 | 50 | 40 | 31 | 38 | 19 | 22 | 100 |
| 40–54 | 36 | 28 | 34 | 36 | 30 | 36 | 100 |
| 55 and over | 27 | 26 | 30 | 28 | 43 | 46 | 100 |
| Women – all | 44 | 41 | 31 | 31 | 25 | 28 | 100 |
| 15–24 years | 62 | 60 | 26 | 25 | 12 | 15 | 100 |
| 25–39 | 52 | 45 | 29 | 32 | 19 | 23 | 100 |
| 40–54 | 39 | 36 | 33 | 34 | 28 | 30 | 100 |
| 55 and over | 28 | 31 | 34 | 29 | 38 | 40 | 100 |
| Total for EC of 12 | 43 | .. | 31 | .. | 26 | .. | 100 |
| Total for EC of 10 | 42 | 38 | 32 | 32 | 26 | 30 | 100 |

*Notes*: The question asked: People talk about the changing roles of husband and wife in the family. Here are three kinds of family. Which of them corresponds most with your ideas about the family?

A family where the two partners each have an equally absorbing job and where housework and the care of the children are shared equally between them.

A family where the wife has a less demanding job than her husband and where she does the larger share of housework and caring for the children.

A family where only the husband has a job and the wife runs the home.

None of these three cases.

Percentages have been adjusted to exclude the 3 per cent not responding to the question and the 2 per cent choosing the last response.

*Source*: Derived from European Commission, *Eurobarometer* No. 27, Brussels, June 1987. Data for people aged 15 and over, interviewed at home.

*Table 4.2* Ideal models of the family and work–life priorities

| | Women | Men | All |
|---|---|---|---|
| Q1. People talk about the changing roles of husband and wife in the family. Here are three kinds of family. Which of them corresponds best with *your* ideas about the family? | | | |
| – A family where the two partners each have an equally demanding job and where housework and the care of the children are shared equally between them. | 42 | 46 | 44 |
| – A family where the wife has a less demanding job than her husband and where she does the larger share of housework and caring for the children. | 42 | 35 | 39 |
| – A family where only the husband has a job and the wife runs the home. | 17 | 19 | 18 |
| – None of these three cases | | | |
| NB For half the sample the order of the 3 models was reversed. | | | |
| Q2. If *without* having to work you had what you would regard as a reasonable living income, would you still prefer to have a paid job, or wouldn't you bother? | | | |
| % who would still work | 58 | 62 | 60 |
| Q3. Who is the *main* income-earner in your household? | | | |
| Is it yourself? | 33 | 69 | 50 |
| Your partner/spouse? | 46 | 6 | 27 |
| Both of you jointly? | 10 | 12 | 11 |
| Or someone else? | 11 | 14 | 12 |
| Work centrality: | | | |
| % who are work-centred | 26 | 52 | 38 |
| % other reasons for work | 74 | 48 | 62 |
| Lifestyle preferences: | | | |
| home-centred | 17 | ? | |
| adaptive | 69 | < 48 | |
| work-centred | 14 | 52 | |
| Base = 100% | 1960 | 1691 | 3651 |

*Notes*: Tiny numbers of respondents saying Don't know or rejecting all three family models are excluded from all analyses of question 1. Tiny numbers of people giving a Don't know response to question 2 are grouped with those who would give up work.
*Source*: Hakim (2003a) *Models of the Family*.

allowed us to produce an index of patriarchal attitudes (Hakim, 2003a: 68–72) which, in contrast with lifestyle preferences, has little or no impact on behaviour (Hakim, 2003b, 2004a: 85–7).

The theoretical framework for the study was preference theory, as set out by Hakim (2000a). The methodology is person-centred analysis rather than variable-centred analysis (Magnusson and Bergman, 1988; Cairns, Bergman and Kagan, 1998; Magnusson, 1998). A key feature of this approach is that it reveals how variables may have a hugely different impact, depending on the context (social group or situation) where they occur. Person-centred analysis recognises the heterogeneity of respondents; denies that people are homogenous in their responses to social and economic influences and experiences; and takes account of extreme cases, which can amount to 20 per cent of cases at either end of a distribution. The alternative perspective of person-centred analysis differs qualitatively from variable-centred analysis.

The family models question identifies women we classify as *home-centred* or *family-centred*: women who prefer to focus their time and energy on home and family work, and thus seek a marriage with complete role segregation. Just under one-fifth (17%) of the sample fell into this category.

The two questions on work orientations identify people for whom market work is central to their identities and lifestyle. The question on work commitment identifies people who claim they would continue with paid work (not necessarily in the same job) in the absence of economic necessity. The introduction of a national lottery in Britain in the 1990s made this hypothetical situation more realistic than previously. The lottery proved enormously popular, and there is substantial publicity for the millionaires it regularly creates, many of whom give up their usual job soon afterwards. About two-thirds of men and women say they would continue in paid work.

Primary and secondary earners were identified by a Eurobarometer question asking about the main income-earner(s) in the household. People who classified themselves as sole, or joint, main earner(s) were classified as primary earners; all others were classified as secondary earners. The question was treated as an opinion question, and analyses of responses show clearly that it reflects a subjective personal identity more than income level or job status (Hakim, 2003a: 77–83). For example, married men adopt the identity of primary (co)earner irrespective of income level, and retain it even when they are not in employment. In contrast, women who regard themselves as primary earners when single switch immediately to the secondary earner identity after marriage, almost irrespective of their income level and whether they have a job or not. Work centrality is defined as a combination of adopting a primary earner identity and having non-financial commitment to one's paid work. For married women, this means in practice those who regard themselves as joint main earner as well as being committed to their employment activities. Less than one-fifth of married women passed this test, and overall only one-quarter of women compared to half of all men were classified as work-centred.[10] Work-centred women who also prefer the symmetrical roles model of the family were classified as *work-centred* in the final classification of lifestyle preferences in Table 4.2.

Women who were neither home-centred, nor work-centred, were classified in the residual, middle category of adaptives: roughly two-thirds of women. This group comprises those choosing the compromise model of the family, with women as secondary earners, plus those choosing the symmetrical roles model who do not pass the work-centrality test. Men's lifestyle preferences are less well defined because all three family models involve full-time permanent income-earning roles for men, so we are unable to identify home-centred men, who would anyway constitute a tiny minority. Because the question on family models does not differentiate between men, the work centrality index alone was used to separate work-centred men from the adaptive group (which must include a few home-centred men). The final composite variable, lifestyle preferences, works well for women, because of the way the survey questions were focused on women's choices, but works less well for men.

In sum, our nationally representative survey shows that at the start of the 21st century, after three decades of equal opportunities policies in Britain, there remain substantial differences between women and men in work orientations and sex-role ideology. The new survey also shows that these are core values, not superficial or ephemeral attitudes, which have substantive implications for labour market choices and behaviour.

## Women's desire for financial dependence

It is notable that there are no sex differences on the questions on preferred family model and work commitment. It is the question identifying primary and secondary earners that creates most of the sex difference in lifestyle preferences. It is remarkable that women today continue to look to a partner to provide a family income, even when they are capable of earning their own living, even when they have a job, even when they are highly qualified, and despite the fact that they claim to prefer symmetrical family roles! There is no objective reason for women's reluctance to adopt the primary earner role and identity, nor for men's continuing, almost universal, acceptance of this responsibility.

The majority of men, in both Britain and Spain, adopt the primary earner identity irrespective of income level. The sense of obligation to provide for themselves and their family does not depend on job grade or earnings level among men, so there is clearly no necessary, causal relationship between the two variables (Hakim, 2003a: 81–3, 99–105). The results for men invalidate the easy argument that women's work orientations are simply a response to their lower grade (part-time) jobs and lower earnings. Men are just as likely to be work-centred whether they have low or high earnings, low or high grade occupations. The weak association observed among women is due to self-selection into the workforce, and into careers offering higher rewards, by work-centred women. It is worth underlining that women in our study were classified as primary earners if they reported that they were jointly responsible for household income with their partner. This response option did not specify the relative contributions of each partner, which could have been very unequal, while accepting that both contributions were essential. However only one in ten women reported that they were jointly responsible for household income; men were slightly more likely to report this. Also, there is no evidence that women's work orientations were affected by responsibility for children in Spain, and the association was very weak in Britain (Hakim, 2003a: 139, 158). Today, there is a sharp contrast between women's stated commitment to paid employment, and their unwillingness to take responsibility for earning their own income.

Comparative studies of black and white women in Britain provide further, strong evidence that adoption of the primary earner identity is a matter of personal choice rather than education, income, and job grade. Siltanen's case study of men and women, primary and secondary earners, working for the Post Office demonstrates this clearly. Married men were almost invariably primary earners, working unsocial hours, and long overtime hours when necessary, in order to support a dependent wife and children. The few men in secondary earner jobs were generally young single men still living with their parents. White women were typically secondary earners if they were married, and primary earners if they were not supported by a husband. In contrast, black women behaved like primary earners throughout the lifecycle: always choosing jobs that ensured their financial independence, whether they were married or not, even when they had young children (Siltanen, 1994: 85–7). Black women demonstrate that there is nothing inevitable about white mothers becoming secondary earners, or financially dependent, as a result of childbirth; it is a choice that white women choose to make. Black women do not have privileged access to childcare services, or to better-paid jobs, that are not available to white women – quite the contrary. Black British women prove that adoption of the primary or secondary earner identity is essentially a personal, subjective choice of identity and life goals, rather than an inevitable consequence of a weaker position in the labour market.

Black and white British women are subject to the same social structural constraints, the same fiscal system and welfare state, and the same labour market with a substantial degree of occupational segregation (Hakim, 1998). Our survey shows there are only trivially small sex differences in the proportion of black people who are work-centred, while white people resemble people with origins in the Indian sub-continent (Table 4.3). Interestingly, patriarchal attitudes are quite separate from responses on the work-centrality index.

The work orientations of black women are closer to those of white men than white women. It is thus not surprising that employment rates among black British women are markedly higher than among white and Asian women. These differential workrates have been confirmed by successive censuses, special surveys of the ethnic minority population, and analyses of the Labour Force Survey (Owen, 1994: Table 6.2; Hakim, 2003a: 143–7). In particular, black women are far more likely to work full-time rather than part-time hours. The likelihood of choosing a part-time job in preference to a full-time job is twice as high among white women as among ethnic minority women in Britain, after controlling for lifecycle stage and level of qualifications (Dale and Holdsworth, 1998: 84). Work-centrality is a core value, with real consequences for behaviour.

There are thus continuing sex differences in acceptance of the income-earning role, at least within the white population in Britain. Role reversal couples (with the wife as main earner) are just as rare as couples who share responsibility for income-earning: 10–15 per cent of couples in each case in Britain. Surprisingly, there is no association between preferred family model and acceptance of the primary earner identity, in either Britain or Spain (Hakim, 2003a: 80). So the lifestyle preferences classification is a complex combination of the core values of work centrality and preferred family model, and is not a simple reflection of a woman's position in the labour market.

Similar results are reported for the USA. Winkler (1998) found that among dual-earner couples aged 25–64 years, only one-quarter of wives were primary earners, earning more than their husbands, and these couples

*Table 4.3* Sex-role ideology among ethnic minority groups

| | White | | Black | | Indian | | Others | |
|---|---|---|---|---|---|---|---|---|
| | M | F | M | F | M | F | M | F |
| Ideal family model: | | | | | | | | |
| symmetrical roles | 46 | 40 | 40 | 64 | 21 | 33 | 43 | 47 |
| compromise | 36 | 43 | 30 | 21 | 36 | 45 | 33 | 43 |
| role segregation | 18 | 17 | 30 | 15 | 43 | 22 | 24 | 10 |
| % work-centred | 51 | 26 | 63 | 51 | 58 | 21 | 62 | 26 |
| % accept patriarchy | 61 | 61 | 72 | 64 | 98 | 88 | 62 | 54 |
| Base = 100% | 1459 | 1718 | 21 | 32 | 48 | 31 | 11 | 32 |

*Notes*: People aged 16 and over who have completed their full-time education.
*Source*: Table 5.11 in Hakim (2003a) *Models of the Family*.

were generally in lower-grade, lower-paid jobs. At all income levels, wives' earnings made up a constant one-third of the couple's combined earnings, rising to 40 per cent among couples with both spouses in full-time employment. In effect, the majority of wives in the USA are secondary earners, irrespective of educational level or earnings (Winkler, 1998).

Qualitative researchers and theorists have struggled to make sense of modern women's insistence on financial dependence on a male partner, and their opposition to role reversal, even when they achieve occupations and incomes that unquestionably allow them to be the primary earner in a family. For example, a study of young educated women in the USA demonstrates that even the most educated modern career women still expect to have a husband with equal or higher earnings. None of the women were prepared to support a dependent husband, and only 9 per cent earned more than their husband. A two-thirds majority had ensured they married men with even higher earnings than themselves (Gerson, 1985: 113, 143). The pay gap between spouses thus cuts across all education and income groups (Winkler, 1998: chart 1).

Other qualitative studies of successful women reiterate their concern about the dangers of marrying down, and the need to find a partner who does not expect the successful woman to pick up all the bills (Hanauer, 2003). Despite the elimination of sex differences in educational qualifications, women in Europe and the USA continue to marry up if at all possible (Hakim, 2000a: 193–222). A study of marriage markets in France concluded that it is women (not men) who insist on their partner being taller, older, richer, and dominant – symbolically as well as substantively (Bozon and Heran, 1988, 1990a,b; Bozon, 1991). The same pattern is found in numerous studies (Feingold, 1992). Brannen (1991) found profound contradictions between women's stated ideals and day-to-day reality. Mothers who had returned to work full-time still regarded their husband as the main breadwinner for the family, and their own earnings as secondary or peripheral. While the majority of the mothers paid lip service to the idea of symmetrical family roles, reality was organised on different principles that were agreed between spouses. Most of the mothers took responsibility for childcare and domestic work, and the great majority were content with their partner's limited contribution. The husband's job was treated as more important, while children were the main concern of the mothers. Private realities can be quite separate from public discourse.

At present, preference theory (Hakim, 2000a) and evolutionary psychology (Buss, 1989, 1995) are the only theories that offer explanations for women's continued reluctance to be main providers.

## Lifestyle preferences and outcomes

The vast majority of men work full-time continuously throughout adult life after completing their full-time education. If couples are genuinely adopting symmetrical family roles, we should expect wives to adopt the same employment patterns as men, while husbands contribute an equal share of domestic work and family work. Our survey did not collect information on domestic and family work, but we can examine full-time workrates among spouses and partners.

Table 4.4 shows that the ideal family model and work centrality together raise full-time workrates from a low of 21 per cent among women who prefer differentiated family roles and for whom market work is not central, to 72 per cent among women who are work-centred and who prefer symmetrical family roles. Work-centrality and family role preferences each have a substantial impact on workrates, doubling them among women. There is no impact among men, because all three family models allocate a breadwinner role to them, and because the dependent husband in a role reversal marriage is as yet too rare for this to be a genuine choice for men. McRae (1986) shows that couples have social and psychological problems when the wife's occupation is higher-status than the husband's. Atkinson and Boles (1984) report similar problems in couples with a wife who earned substantially more than the husband.

Detailed analyses in the main report (Hakim, 2003a: 131–41, 149–58) show that lifestyle preferences predict workrates, but (full-time) employment does not predict women's lifestyle preferences and core values. Lifestyle preferences are not simply a rationalisation of employment decisions already made. The causal impact is essentially one-way. These results for Britain and Spain confirm those already obtained from the major longitudinal studies in the USA (Duncan and Dunifon, 1998; Hakim, 2002).

The main report also shows that lifestyle preferences cut across socio-economic groups, income levels and educational levels, among men and, with few exceptions, among women. Social, economic and cultural capital

*Table 4.4* Impact of ideal family model and work centrality on full-time workrates (%) among couples

| | Ideal family model | | |
|---|---|---|---|
| | Symmetrical roles | Differentiated roles | All |
| Wives aged 20–59 | 53 | 26 | 36 |
| work-centred | 72 | 60 | 67 |
| all others | 47 | 21 | 30 |
| Husbands aged 20–59 | 80 | 87 | 84 |
| work-centred | 79 | 89 | 84 |
| all others | 81 | 85 | 83 |

*Notes*: Married and cohabiting couples aged 20–59 who have completed their full-time education.
*Source*: Table 5.7 in Hakim (2003a) *Models of the Family*.

are not important as correlates or predictors of lifestyle preferences (Hakim, 2003a: 93–122).

The impact of lifestyle preferences on employment is separate from, and stronger than the impact of education. One of the most often-repeated conclusions in social research is that women with higher education qualifications have higher workrates (in Britain, higher full-time workrates) than women with only secondary school (high school) education. This pattern is repeated in our survey, with a 20 percentage point difference in full-time workrates between women with higher education and other women (Table 4.5). Because education has an impact on social and political attitudes (Davis, 1982), it is usually assumed that it must have a major impact also on gender ideology and lifestyle preferences. There is evidence in our surveys that educational level has a big impact on some aspects of gender ideology, in particular acceptance or rejection of patriarchal values. However educational level has very little impact on women's (and men's) lifestyle preferences (Tables 4.5 and 4.6). Highly educated women are just as likely as others to prefer a marriage with completely separate roles (14%). The only difference between the two educational groups is that there is a higher proportion of work-centred women in the small group of highly educated women, 22 per cent compared to 14 per cent, an 8 percentage point difference that is small enough to be the result of differential self-selection into higher education. This means that four-fifths of women who enter higher education are not 'investing' in a continuous employment career, as conventional human capital theory assumes, but in the equally profitable marriage market (Hakim, 2000a: 193–222).

*Table 4.5* The relative importance of lifestyle preferences and higher education

| | % working full-time | | Distribution | |
|---|---|---|---|---|
| | Highly qualified | Other women | Highly qualified | Other women |
| Lifestyle preferences: | | | | |
| work-centred | 82 | 56 | 22 | 14 |
| adaptive | 46 | 32 | 64 | 72 |
| home-centred | 54 | 37 | 14 | 14 |
| All women 20–59 | 56 | 36 | 100 | 100 |
| Base = 100% | 245 | 1008 | 245 | 1008 |

*Notes*: Women aged 20–59 who have completed their full-time education. In the absence of information on educational qualifications, the highly qualified are defined as those completing their full-time education at age 21 and over, because in Britain first degrees are normally completed by age 21. People completing full-time education at age 20 or earlier are assumed to have qualifications below tertiary education level.
*Source*: Table 5.5 in Hakim (2003a) *Models of the Family*.

Despite the fact that higher education has no important impact on lifestyle preferences, Table 4.5 shows that lifestyle preferences have a huge impact on full-time workrates, particularly among more highly educated women. A work-centred woman who does not have higher education qualifications is more likely to be in full-time work than a highly educated woman who is adaptive or home-centred. Among the highly educated, there is a 36 percentage point difference between the workrates of adaptive and work-centred women, a far larger gap than the 20 percentage point difference between the two education groups. Women with higher education tend to marry spouses with similar education, and high incomes. They are thus even better able to make choices uninhibited by financial constraints.

Sex-role ideology has no impact on men's full-time workrates. Parental responsibilities also have no effect, because men's role in most families is primarily as income-earner, not as carer. Our results confirm the lack of genuine choices in men's lives, as compared with women's lives in Britain in the 21st century.

Home-centred and work-centred women constitute two minority groups, but they have distinctively different lifestyles from the adaptive majority (Table 4.6). Two-thirds of work-centred women are in full-time employment. In contrast, two-thirds of adaptive women work part-time or not at all. Almost half of the home-centred women are not in employment, and a small minority have never had a job. A relatively high 40 per cent of home-centred women have full-time jobs. The reasons for this unexpected result are explored in the full report, and show that in certain circumstances, economic necessity overrides personal preferences (Hakim, 2003a: 141–3, 211–33).[11]

Home-centred and adaptive women are most likely to marry or cohabit, and to stay married. This is not surprising, as their preferred lifestyle is heavily dependent on having a breadwinner spouse who is in regular employment. Work-centred women are least likely to marry, and most likely to be separated or divorced. Women who regard themselves as financially independent anyway have less motive to marry and to stay married. Further, home-centred women have twice as many children as work-centred women, many of whom seem to be childless. The fertility measure here is demographers' 'own child' measure: the average number of children aged under 16 years living at home per woman aged 20–55 years. It does not include older children (who may no longer live at home anyway), so it understates total fertility. Nonetheless, it shows clearly that fertility levels vary dramatically between the three preference groups, along with marriage rates and employment patterns. Further analysis shows that fertility differences are sharper among highly educated wives than among non-graduate wives (Hakim, 2003c). Work-centred men have higher fertility than other men, but there is otherwise no difference between the two groups of men (Table 4.6).

*Table 4.6* Characteristics of women and men by lifestyle preference group

| | Women | | | Men | |
|---|---|---|---|---|---|
| | Home-centred | Adaptive | Work-centred | Work-centred | All others |
| % employed full-time | 40 | 35 | 63 | 82 | 80 |
| part-time | 16 | 37 | 15 | 3 | 4 |
| % not in employment | 44 | 28 | 22 | 15 | 16 |
| % married/cohabiting | 71 | 80 | 45 | 79 | 66 |
| average number of dependent children aged 0–15 at home | 1.28 | 1.02 | 0.61 | 0.91 | 0.60 |
| % left full-time education: | | | | | |
| by age 16 | 54 | 55 | 42 | 59 | 56 |
| 17–20 years | 28 | 28 | 32 | 21 | 24 |
| age 21+ | 18 | 17 | 26 | 20 | 20 |
| Base = 100% | 171 | 870 | 194 | 554 | 551 |
| National distribution of the three groups | 14% | 70% | 16% | 50% | 50% |

*Notes*: Women and men aged 20–59 who have completed their full-time education.
The fertility indicator is shown for women and men aged 20–54 years.
*Source*: Hakim (2003a) *Models of the Family*.

Further analyses in the main report show that women in the three lifestyle preference groups do not differ on other dimensions. Most notably, lifestyle preferences have no impact on occupational choice in Britain at the start of the 21st century. However lifestyle preferences do inform choice of job, with adaptive and home-centred women frequently choosing part-time jobs, and hence displaying the higher labour turnover that is typical of this section of the workforce (Hakim, 2003a: 165–89). The implication is that women in all three preference groups might be found working side by side in the same occupations. This means that occupational choice cannot of itself be used as an indicator of women's career orientations. This has major implications for employers' policies, and also for government employment policies.

Polachek's thesis, based on data for the USA, is that lifestyle preferences determine women's choice of occupation (Polachek, 1979, 1981, 1995). We find that lifestyle preferences have a powerful impact on women's employment decisions, and on the type of job chosen, but not, as Polachek predicted, on women's choice of occupation. Equal opportunities legislation has been effective: women are no longer excluded from certain occupations because they are (assumed to be) not as work-centred as men. But it does not mean that all women will behave exactly like men in the occupations they share. Case studies of desegregated occupations, such as pharmacy, in the USA, Britain and Canada (Reskin and Roos, 1990: 111–27; Bottero,

1992; Crompton and LeFeuvre, 1996; Hakim, 1998: 221–34; Hassell, Noyce and Jesson, 1998; Tanner *et al.*, 1999; Hakim, 2003a: 185–6) show that women gravitate towards employee jobs with limited responsibilities, part-time and short-term jobs, while men gravitate towards self-employment and their own business, or full-time jobs in large retail chains offering the prospect of promotion into management. If this is happening in occupations that require higher qualifications, it is even more likely to happen in less qualified occupations.

## Conclusion: the rising importance of lifestyle preferences

The Future of Work research programme was intended to provide pointers to likely future developments. Our study confirms preference theory, building on the pathbreaking, but little-known results of the early American longitudinal studies, which showed just how important life goals and aspirations could be in the long term (Hakim, 2002, 2003a: 125–9). Preference theory posits that these motivations only become powerful after the contraceptive revolution and the equal opportunities revolution gave women genuine choices as to the relative balance between market work and family work in their lives. Preference theory constitutes a major break from the teleological theories implicit in the expectation that male and female employment patterns will converge, and that sex differentials will disappear in the workforce.

While the theory is empirically based, our 1999 British survey is the first to attempt to operationalise and test it with freshly collected data. The survey showed that three questions can be sufficient to identify and differentiate home-centred, adaptive and work-centred women. The resulting taxonomy worked well, displaying sharp differences between the three groups in terms of employment patterns, marital and fertility histories.

There is still scope for the three questions to be developed and refined. For example, the question on ideal family models might be complemented by an extra question assessing the acceptability of role-reversal family models.[12] This would permit the lifestyle preferences of men to be identified more completely. Second, questions on work-centrality might need modification for other cultural settings, and different labour markets.

Preference theory can thus be operationalised with a limited number of tried-and-tested survey questions that are sufficiently simple and self-explanatory to be included in any large-scale survey exercise using structured interviews. Our three questions have all been used in numerous surveys, in different countries and time points. The excuse that attitudes and motivations are too difficult to measure is open to challenge. Some core values can be measured without large batteries of questions, even though social psychologists usually insist on them.

Preference theory does not deny the impact of social, economic and institutional factors. These will continue to ensure continuing differences in female employment patterns in modern societies. However women's motivations and core values are independent factors with causal powers that must now be investigated more thoroughly. Preference theory brings values back into the multidisciplinary investigation of future developments in female labour force participation, and the implications for work–life balance.

In sum, preference theory works well in predicting women's employment choices. One of the benefits of this approach is that it forces us to take a long hard look at the overall position of women in each society, instead of treating all western European and northern American countries as effectively equivalent, despite their differences. However the main theoretical and empirical development is the insistence that lifestyle preferences and lifegoals can no longer be ignored, or be assumed to be known, or to be homogenous.

## Policy implications

In the second half of the 20th century, sex discrimination was seen as the main barrier to women's achievement in the labour market, and the focus was on legislation to prohibit and neutralise discrimination. Today, the main barrier is presented as the problem of work–life balance, and the focus is on organisational change, family-friendly employer policies, and what the European Commission calls 'the reconciliation of work and family life', which in practice means public childcare services (Moss, 1996). Most academic discussions of work–life balance focus on the legal and institutional context, or else employer policies (Lewis and Lewis, 1996; Drew, Emerek and Mahon, 1998; Haas, Hwang and Russell, 2000; Parcel and Cornfield, 2000; OECD, 2001). Studies of couples' strategies are rare (Moen, 2003). Here, the focus has been on what women want, and we are therefore concerned with empirically discovered realities and evidence-based policies. Much research on work–life balance consists of arguments for social engineering to impose unisex family and employment roles on everyone.[13] Social scientists generally assume that women are a homogeneous group, with a single set of interests regarding work–life balance,[14] and there is astonishingly little research on men's and women's preferences.[15]

Preference theory offers a different perspective, and shows that differences between the three lifestyle preference groups are more important than sex differences in work orientations and job values. Policies that are of interest to work-centred people (men and women) will be of little interest to adaptive people (men and women). Work-centred people are most ambitious and give priority to their careers over family life throughout life. Parental leave schemes are of no interest to careerists. Sabbaticals are used for further training and career development rather than family life. In contrast, adaptive people seek a more even balance between the competitive world of paid work and the non-competitive context of family work. It is they alone who are interested in parental leaves, unpaid sabbaticals for family activities, reductions in working hours, and other family-friendly workplace schemes. Careerists may use subsidised childcare services, but they would make appropriate arrangements anyway. Childcare services are crucial for adaptive women because they are most responsive to social signals and economic pressures.

In sum, employers and national governments need to recognise the diversity of lifestyle preferences among women *and* men, and devise policies that are neutral between the three lifestyle preference groups. Where this is impossible, they need to ensure that their policies are even-handed: that a scheme favouring careerists is balanced by another scheme favouring the home-centred or adaptives.[16] One-size-fits-all policies may be administratively convenient, but they are bound to fail – as illustrated by low take-up rates for compulsory paternal leave schemes even in Sweden (Haas and Hwang, 2000; Hakim, 2000a: 242; OECD, 2001: 145–6), and even lower take-up rates in Britain.[17] Policy-makers should in future cater for the increasing diversity of the workforce, and the polarisation of lifestyles, rather than assuming convergence on a single, universally-attractive model of the family and the good life. Sex differences are indeed fading away, but they are being replaced with other, equally profound and enduring divisions within the workforce, between work-centred careerists and adaptive people who want an even balance between family work and paid work. Policy-makers should accept that there are several, equally valid and productive, models of the employment career in the 21st century.

## Notes

1. In a 1996 interview, Allan Larsson, Director General of DGV in the European Commission, complained that women's workrates were still much lower than men's employment rates. He insisted that the days of the male breadwinner taking responsibility for household financial well-being throughout working life while women assume the bulk of domestic responsibility had effectively gone, and dismissed the 'old social contract' with a division of responsibilities between spouses as 'no longer valid' (European Commission, 1997b: 4). In this interview, Larsson effectively outlawed what is often described as the 'traditional' sexual division of labour, but is in fact a modern arrangement, and he insisted that the Scandinavian model must be extended to all EU citizens, thus reducing women's choices to his own preference.
2. Beck (1986/1992: 123) argues that under current institutional conditions the single-person household is in fact the logical outcome of feminist ideology, which is ultimately antipathetic to the interdependence of married couples.
3. The distinction between dual-earner and dual-career couples is important, yet is not always made (Blossfeld and Drobnic, 2001).

4. The Eurobarometer series of surveys are run by the European Commission to inform European Union policy-making. They cover all EU member states, and focus on social and political attitudes.
5. The symmetrical roles family model attracts disproportionate support in Table 4.1 partly because it was the first response listed in the Eurobarometer surveys and partly because it is currently the politically acceptable response in western Europe, as indicated by the positive connotations attached to the words 'egalitarian' and 'equal'. Methodological work with this survey question (Hakim, 2003a: 65–6) shows that if the order of responses is reversed (with the role-segregated family listed first and the symmetrical roles family listed last), around 10 per cent of respondents transfer their allegiance from the symmetrical roles model to the role-segregated model (with much larger swings among young women in the 16–24 years age cohort). This produces a more even distribution of about one-third of respondents supporting each of the three models in 1987. This latter distribution is probably closer to reality.
6. European historians are documenting the rise and decline of the male breadwinner family, as a popular ideal which was often achieved for at least part of the lifecycle in working class families, and show that it became dominant in Holland, Britain and the USA, but not in France, for example (Pedersen, 1993; Pott-Buter, 1993: 285–7; Seccombe, 1993: 202–9; Janssens, 1998). They have also sought an explanation for it within contemporary historical developments and trade union demands for a family wage for men (Creighton, 1996, 1999). In countries such as Japan, where the transition from an agricultural economy to an industrial economy is recent enough for people to remember the heavy labour required of both spouses on family farms, the single breadwinner family is a relatively recent innovation, and is regarded as modern and progressive rather than traditional (Tanaka, 1998: 95).
7. There is evidence that young people are most susceptible to social pressure when reporting their attitudes and values (Hakim, 2003a: 54, 66). This means that responses for people aged under 25 years in Table 4.1 are the least stable.
8. The term ideology refers to a set of beliefs and theories people construct to make sense of the world and guide their actions in it.
9. An interesting study by Agassi (1979, 1982) studied sex-role ideology and work attitudes among women (and men) in the USA, West Germany and Israel in the late 1970s. She too found that women's role preferences polarised: one-third chose to prioritise the homemaker role (without necessarily regarding it as obligatory or traditionally appropriate for all women); one-fifth consistently rejected the homemaker role in favour of a focus on market work in their own lives; and the remaining half of her study sample held more complex or contradictory views, sometimes giving priority to the maternal role over market work (Agassi, 1982: 221). Unfortunately, Agassi does not show the distribution of personal choices separately for each of the three countries in her study, although she does say that the three groups all included younger women as well as older women.
10. The sex differential in work centrality stands in contrast to the absence of differences between men and women in some job values (Tolbert and Moen, 1998). However when the list of job values is increased from just 5 to 14, sex differentials reappear again (Kirkpatrick Johnson, 2001).
11. In contrast, an analysis of differences between ethnic minority groups shows that the impact of ideology and values sometimes over-rides social and economic constraints (Hakim, 2003a: 143–8).

12. A study by Björnberg (1996) suggests that such a question could be particularly difficult to specify. She found that men who claimed to be family-oriented were a diverse group, whose values did not correspond to those of family-centred women.
13. The European Commission, national governments, and social scientists ignore research findings on the diversity of women's preferences in order to pursue their own policy agendas (Hakim, 2000a: 85–94). One recent example is the Commission's insistence on public childcare services as essential for all women, even though its' own research contradicts this strategy. When a Eurobarometer survey asked about the choice between more childcare services or financial help for a mother to stay at home, opinion was evenly divided between the two options, across the EU as a whole. However in countries that already had the experience of good childcare services, such as Finland, Sweden, France and Denmark, majority opinion favoured a salary for full-time mothers instead; in Finland, 70 per cent preferred this option (European Commission, 1998: 44–5).
14. The proselytising (rather than evidence-based) character of discussions of social policy, even among social scientists, is illustrated by the tendency, in some countries, for writers to assume that the facts immutably show their own nation to be 'superior' on some indicator that demonstrates the superiority of their national policies. Just one example is the routine insistence, by French social scientists, that France has one of the highest female employment rates and highest birthrates in western Europe (similar to those in Scandinavian countries), due to successful policies supporting working mothers. One illustration of this widespread belief is Fagnani's claim that France has one of the highest activity rates for mothers in the EU, despite specific evidence to the contrary in other papers in the same book that show France, Germany and Britain all have similar, *average* female employment rates (Drew *et al.*, 1998: 58, 155, 163). Similarly, in a special section on female employment in the OFCE journal, Mendras insists that France is similar to Scandinavian countries, and unlike Britain, in having the highest female workrates and the highest birthrates. In fact, other contributors in the same volume demonstrate that France, Germany and Britain all have very similar, and average, female workrates, and birthrates in Britain and France are almost identical (Mendras *et al.*, 2001). French social policy is in reality bifurcated, supporting non-working mothers as well as working mothers, but this diversified policy portfolio is never admitted by French social scientists (Hakim, 2000a: 229–34), even though independent cross-national comparisons routinely show that France, Germany and Britain all have diverse employment profiles in families and among mothers (OECD, 2001: 134–5).
15. Two other studies in the ESRC Future of Work Research Programme also addressed women's preferences, as illustrated by the chapters by Houston and Sigala in this book.
16. Balanced policies, and neutral policies are discussed in Hakim (2000a: 222–53).
17. In July 2004, Inland Revenue estimated that only a fifth of working fathers had made any use of their right to paid paternity leave in Britain – far fewer than the 80 per cent predicted by the Department of Trade and Industry. Swedish studies of extensions to the paternity leave scheme in January 2002 in Sweden also admit that many fathers use it purely to extend their summer holiday and Christmas holiday (Ekberg, 2004).

## References

Agassi, J.B. (1979) *Women on the Job: The Attitudes of Women to Their Work*, Lexington MA: Lexington Books.

Agassi, J.B. (1982) *Comparing the Work Attitudes of Women and Men*, Lexington MA: Lexington Books.

Anker, R. (1998) *Gender and Jobs: Sex Segregation of Occupations in the World*, Geneva: ILO.

Atkinson, M. and Boles, J. (1984) 'Wives as senior partners', *Journal of Marriage and the Family*, 46: 861–70.

Beck, U. (1986/1992) *Risk Society: Towards a New Modernity*, London: Sage.

Bernard, J. (1981) 'The good-provider role: its rise and fall', *American Psychologist*, 36: 1–12.

Björnberg, U. (1996) 'Family orientation among men: a process of change in Sweden', pp. 200–7 in Drew, E. *et al.* (eds), *Women, Work and Family in Europe*, London and New York: Routledge.

Blossfeld, H-P. and Drobnic, S. (eds) (2001) *Careers of Couples in Contemporary Society: From Male Breadwinner to Dual-Earner Families*, Oxford: Oxford University Press.

Boh, K., Bak, M., Clason, C., Pankratova, M., Qvortrup, J., Sgritta, G.B. and Waerness, K. (eds) (1989) *Changing Patterns of European Family Life: A Comparative Analysis of 14 European Countries*, London: Routledge.

Bottero, W. (1992) 'The changing face of the professions? Gender and explanations of women's entry into pharmacy', *Work Employment and Society*, 6: 329–46.

Bozon, M. and Héran, F. (1988) 'La découverte du conjoint – Les scènes de rencontre dans l'espace social', *Population*, 43: 121–50.

Bozon, M. and Héran, F. (1990a) 'Les femmes et l'écart d'âge entre conjoints: une domination consentie – I – Types d'union et attentes en matiere d'écart d'âge', *Population*, 45: 327–60.

Bozon, M. and Héran, F. (1990b) 'Les femmes et l'écart d'âge entre conjoints: une domination consentie – II – Modes d'entrée dans la vie adulte et représentations du conjoint', *Population*, 45: 565–602.

Bozon, M. (1991) 'Les femmes plus âgées que leur conjoint sont-elles atypiques?', *Population*, 46: 152–59.

Brannen, J. (1991) 'Money, marriage and motherhood: dual earner households after maternity leave', pp. 54–70 in Arber, S. and Gilbert, N. (eds), *Women and Working Lives*, London: Macmillan.

Buss, D.M. (1989) 'Sex differences in human mate preferences: evolutionary hypotheses tested in 37 cultures', *Behavioural and Brain Sciences*, 12: 1–49.

Buss, D.M. (1995) 'Psychological sex differences: origins through sexual selection', *American Psychologist*, 50: 164–8.

Cairns, R.B., Bergman, L.R. and Kagan, J. (eds) (1998) *Methods and Models for Studying the Individual*, London and Thousand Oaks CA: Sage.

Creighton, C. (1996) 'The rise of the male breadwinner family: a reappraisal', *Comparative Studies in Society and History*, 38: 310–37.

Creighton, C. (1999) 'The rise and decline of the male breadwinner family in Britain', *Cambridge Journal of Economics*, 23: 519–41.

Crompton, R. and Le Feuvre, N. (1996) 'Paid employment and the changing system of gender relations: a cross-national comparison', *Sociology*, 30: 427–45.

Dale, A. and Holdsworth, C. (1998) 'Why don't ethnic minority women in Britain work part-time?', pp. 77–95 in O'Reilly, J. and Fagan, C. (eds), *Part-Time Prospects*, London: Routledge.

Davis, J.A. (1982) 'Achievement variables and class cultures: family, schooling, job and forty-nine dependent variables in the cumulative GSS', *American Sociological Review*, 47: 569–86.

Davis, K. (1984) 'Wives and work: the sex role revolution and its consequences', *Population and Development Review*, 10: 397–417.

Drew, E., Emerek, R. and Mahon, E. (eds) (1998) *Women, Work and Family in Europe*, London and New York: Routledge.

Duncan, G.J. and Dunifon, R. (1998) 'Soft skills and long run labor market success', *Research in Labor Economics*, 17: 123–49.

Ekberg, J. (2004) 'Sharing responsibility? Short and long-term effects of Sweden's daddy month reform', paper presented to Department of Trade and Industry seminar.

European Commission (1987) *Eurobarometer* No. 27, Brussels: European Commission.

European Commission (1991) *Lifestyles in the European Community: Family and Employment within the Twelve*, Special Report on Eurobarometer No. 34, Brussels: European Commission.

European Commission (1997a) *Equal Opportunities for Women and Men in the European Union 1996*, Employment and Social Affairs Report, Luxembourg: Office for Official Publications of the European Communities.

European Commission (1997b) 'Interview with Allan Larsson', *Equal Opportunity Magazine*, 1: 3–4.

European Commission. 1998. *Equal Opportunities for Women and Men in Europe? Eurobarometer No. 44.3*, Luxembourg: Office for Official Publications of the European Communities.

Feingold, A. (1992) 'Gender differences in mate selection preferences: a test of the parental investment model', *Psychological Bulletin*, 112: 125–39.

Gerson, K. (1985) *Hard Choices: How Women Decide about Work, Career and Motherhood*, Berkeley and Los Angeles: University of California Press.

Haas, L.L. and Hwang, P. (2000) 'Programs and policies promoting women's economic equality and men's sharing of child care in Sweden', pp. 133–61 in Haas, L.L., Hwang, P. and Russell, G. (eds), *Organizational Change and Gender Equity: International Perspectives on Fathers and Mothers at the Workplace*, London and Thousand Oaks, CA: Sage.

Haas, L.L., Hwang, P. and Russell, G. (eds) (2000) *Organizational Change and Gender Equity: International Perspectives on Fathers and Mothers at the Workplace*, London and Thousand Oaks, CA: Sage.

Hakim, C. (1996) *Key Issues in Women's Work: Female Heterogeneity and the Polarisation of Women's Employment*, London: Continuum Press.

Hakim, C. (1998) *Social Change and Innovation in the Labour Market*, Oxford: Oxford University Press.

Hakim, C. (2000a) *Work-Lifestyle Choices in the 21st Century: Preference Theory*, Oxford: Oxford University Press.

Hakim, C. (2000b) *Research Design: Successful Designs for Social and Economic Research*, London and New York: Routledge.

Hakim, C. (2002) 'Lifestyle preferences as determinants of women's differentiated labour market careers', *Work and Occupations*, 29: 428–59.

Hakim, C. (2003a) *Models of the Family in Modern Societies: Ideals and Realities*, Aldershot: Ashgate.

Hakim, C. (2003b) 'Public morality versus personal choice: the failure of social attitude surveys', *British Journal of Sociology*, 54: 339–45, September 2003.

Hakim, C. (2003c) 'A new approach to explaining fertility patterns: preference theory', *Population and Development Review*, 29: 349–74, September 2003.

Hakim, C. (2004a) 'Lifestyle preferences versus patriarchal values: causal and non-causal attitudes', pp. 69–91 in Giele, J.Z. and Holst, E. (eds), *Changing Life Patterns in Western Industrial Societies*, Amsterdam: Elsevier.

Hakim, C. (2004b) *Key Issues in Women's Work: Female Diversity and the Polarisation of Women's Employment*, London: Cavendish Press.

Hanauer, C. (ed.) (2003) *The Bitch in the House: 26 Women Tell the Truth about Sex, Solitude, Work, Motherhood and Marriage*, Viking.

Hassell, K., Noyce, P. and Jesson, J. (1998) 'White and ethnic minority self-employment in retail pharmacy in Britain: an historical and comparative analysis', *Work, Employment and Society*, 12: 245–71.

Janssens, A. (ed.) (1998) *The Rise and Decline of the Male Breadwinner Family?*, Cambridge: Cambridge University Press.

Kirkpatrick Johnson, M. (2001) 'Change in job values during the transition to adulthood', *Work and Occupations*, 28: 315–45.

Lewis, S. and Lewis, J (eds) (1996) *The Work-Family Challenge: Rethinking Employment*, London: Sage.

Magnusson, D. (1998) 'The Logic and Implications of a Person-Oriented Approach', pp. 33–64 in Cairns, R.B., Bergman, L.R., Kagan, J. (eds), *Methods and Models for Studying the Individual* , Thousand Oaks, CA: Sage.

Magnusson, D. and Bergman, L.R. (1988) 'Individual and variable-based approaches to longitudinal research on early risk factors', pp. 45–61 in Rutter, M. (ed.), *Studies of Psychosocial Risk: The Power of Longitudinal Data*, Cambridge and New York: Cambridge University Press.

Marín, G. and Marín, B.V. (1991) *Research With Hispanic Populations*, Newbury Park: Sage.

McRae, S. (1986) *Cross Class Families*, Oxford: Clarendon Press.

Mendras, H., Benoit-Guilbot, O., Clémencon, M., Hakim, C. and Wierink, M. (2001) 'Sociologie de l'emploi feminin', *Revue de l'OFCE: Observations et Diagnostiques Economiques*, 77: 251–324.

Moen, P. (ed.) (2003) *It's About Time: Couples and Careers*, Ithaca and London: ILR Press.

Moss, P. (1996) 'Reconciling employment and family responsibilities: a European perspective', pp. 20–33 in Lewis, S. and Lewis, J. (eds) *The Work-Family Challenge: Rethinking Employment*, London: Sage.

OECD (2001) 'Balancing work and family life: helping parents into paid employment', pp. 129–66 in *Employment Outlook*, Paris: OECD.

Owen, D. (1994) *Ethnic Minority Women and the Labour Market: Analysis of the 1991 Census*, Manchester: Equal Opportunities Commission.

Parcel, T.L. and Cornfield, D.B. (eds) (2000) *Work and Family: Research Informing Policy*, London and Thousand Oaks, CA: Sage.

Pedersen, S. (1993) *Family, Dependence, and the Origins of the Welfare State: Britain and France, 1914–1945*, Cambridge: Cambridge University Press.

Polachek, S.W. (1979) 'Occupational segregation among women: theory, evidence and a prognosis', pp. 137–70 in Lloyd, C.B., Andrews, E.S. and Gilroy, C.L. (eds) *Women in the Labor Market*, New York: Columbia University Press.

Polachek, S.W. (1981) 'Occupational self-selection: A human capital approach to sex differences in occupational structure', *Review of Economics and Statistics*, 63: 60–9.

Polachek, S.W. 1995. 'Human capital and the gender earnings gap: a response to feminist critiques', pp. 61–79 in Kuiper, E. and Sap, J. (eds), *Out of the Margin*, London and New York: Routledge.

Pott-Buter, H.A. (1993) *Facts and Fairy Tales about Female Labor, Family and Fertility: A Seven-Country Comparison, 1850–1990*, Amsterdam: Amsterdam University Press.

Reskin, B.F. and Roos, P.A. (1990) *Job Queues, Gender Queues: Explaining Women's Inroads into Male Occupations*, Philadelphia: Temple University Press.

Seccombe, W. (1993) *Weathering the Storm: Working Class Families from the Industrial Revolution to the Fertility Decline*, London: Verso.

Siltanen, J. (1994) *Locating Gender: Occupational Segregation, Wages and Domestic Responsibilities*, London: UCL.

Tanaka, S. (1998) 'Dynamics of occupational segregation and the sexual division of labor: a consequence of feminization of white-collar work', pp. 85–122 in Sato, Y. (ed.), *1995 Social Stratification and Social Mobility (SSM) Research Series 3: Social Mobility and Career Analysis*, research report to the Ministry of Education, Science, Sports and Culture, Tokyo: University of Tokyo, Seiyama's Office.

Tanner, J., Cockerill, R., Barnsley, J. and Williams, A.P. (1999) 'Gender and income in pharmacy: human capital and gender stratification theories revisited', *British Journal of Sociology*, 50: 97–117.

Tolbert, P.S. and Moen, P. (1998) 'Men's and women's definitions of good jobs: similarities and differences by age and across time', *Work and Occupations*, 25: 168–94.

Turner, C.F. and Martin, E. (eds) (1984) *Surveying Subjective Phenomena*, 2 vols, New York: Russell Sage.

Walby, S. (1990) *Theorising Patriarchy*, Oxford: Blackwell.

Whyte, M.K. (1990) *Dating, Mating and Marriage*, New York: Aldine de Gruyter.

Winkler, A.E. (1998) 'Earnings of husbands and wives in dual-earner families', *Monthly Labor Review*, 121/4: 42–8.

# 5

# Working, Caring and Sharing: Work–Life Dilemmas in Early Motherhood

*Diane M. Houston and Gillian Marks*

During the last two decades of the 20th century the work participation of women with preschool children almost doubled from 28 per cent in 1980 to 53 per cent in 1999 (McRae, 2003). This increase now appears to have stabilised, with Labour Force Survey (LFS) figures for 2004 showing that 53 per cent of women with preschool children are in employment (Clegg, 2004). McRae (2003) and Houston and Marks (2002; 2003) demonstrate that this increase in part represents a greater likelihood of returning to work after the first child and that longitudinal analysis of individual women's employment shows a marked decrease in work, particularly full-time work, during the first child's early childhood, especially when women have second and subsequent children. McRae's (2003) longitudinal analysis demonstrated that only 10 per cent of first-time mothers had maintained full-time employment by the time their first child was 11 years old. McRae argues that this suggests that 'a complete explanation of women's labour market choices after childbirth, and the outcomes of these choices, depends as much on understanding the constraints that differentially affect women as it does on understanding their preferences.' (2003: 334–5).

There has been considerable controversy around the conceptualisation of women's work orientations (e.g. Hakim, 1991; Fagan and Rubery, 1996; Ginn *et al.*, 1996; Crompton and Harris, 1998). Crompton and Harris (1998) have argued that the work patterns of women are a product of their particular circumstances, their opportunities and constraints, and the decisions that they make in response to these. They suggested that work and home orientations might fluctuate according to occupation, lifecycle and national context. By contrast, Preference Theory (Hakim, 2000; 2003a) states that women in affluent societies can make a real choice between family work and market work. Hakim argues that women can be classified as home-centred (20%), adaptive (60%), or, work-centred (20%). She states:

> A minority of women have no interest in employment, careers, or economic independence and do not plan to work long term unless things

> go seriously wrong for them. Their aim is to marry as well as they can and give up paid employment to become full-time homemakers and mothers. The group includes highly educated women as well as those who do not get any qualifications.... In contrast, other women actively reject the sexual division of labour in the home, expect to work full-time and continuously throughout life, and prefer symmetrical roles for the husband and wife rather than separate roles. The third group is numerically dominant: women who are determined to combine employment and family work, so become secondary earners. They may work full-time early in life, but later switch to part-time jobs on a semi-permanent basis, and/or to intermittent employment. (Hakim, 2000: 189)

Hakim argues that adaptive women do not want to make a choice between work and family – they want both and 'if they give priority to family or to paid work, it is a temporary emphasis rather than a lifetime commitment.' (Hakim, 2000) Only adaptive women are influenced by life-cycle changes, as a consequence they are less likely to make significant achievements in the world of work because they prefer a balanced life. By contrast, work and home-centred women remain committed to these domains across the lifespan. Hakim (2000) suggests that even childless women may be home-centred, prioritising the domestic sphere, and that women who are work-centred may choose to be childless or will have children 'in the same ways as among men, as an expression of normality and a weekend hobby'. Hakim's primary argument is that women can now make choices about the balance between work and home, and these choices underpin different behavioural outcomes.

McRae (2003) conducted analyses of longitudinal data relating to women's work histories and attitudes and concluded that her findings provided support for Hakim's argument that employment careers are centrally important for only a minority of women, but that there was little evidence to support the assertion that it is preferences that determine work behaviour. McRae (2003) further argues that women with similar preferences, but different capacities for overcoming constraints, may have very different work patterns.

In this chapter we report findings from a longitudinal study of over 400 women which examined the determinants of first-time mother's intentions about work and childcare and their experiences during the three years after the birth of their child. This work has also resulted in analysis of women's preferences and the extent to which they are able to work in accordance with the preferences they express before their first child is born (Houston and Marks, 2002, 2003, 2004). Houston and Marks (2003) found that the majority of women were able to return to work after the birth of their first child, in a manner consistent with their preferences. However 24 per cent of women who expressed an intention to work after their maternity leave either did not work or worked less than they had intended to. The study demonstrated that the amount of planning women had done prior to their maternity leave and the support provided by their workplace (but not their partner or family) were causal factors in determining whether women were able to carry out their intentions to return to work. While these findings can be interpreted as consistent with Preference Theory (Hakim, 2000; 2003a), they also support the argument that personal and structural constraints determine whether women are able to fulfill their ambitions for work, if they also choose to have children.

In the present chapter we examine women's attitudes and experiences at around the times of their child's first and third birthdays, consider the changes that occur across the sample, and illustrate conclusions from quantitative data with qualitative evidence. Our focus will be on women's identity – the extent to which they identify with the role of worker and mother (Hogg, Terry and White, 1995), on their evaluation of their lifestyle, and with the impact of their lifestyle on their own psychological health, their children's temperament and their relationship with their partner. We also examine their preferences for childcare and work, and compare this with their actual lifestyle. In line with our previous work (e.g. Houston and Marks, 2003), and in response to the debate about women's work orientation, we compare women who do no paid work with those who work part-time and those who work full-time.

## Methodology

The research was conducted in the UK between 1999 and 2003. First–time mothers were recruited through antenatal classes held by NHS hospitals and the National Childbirth Trust. A researcher attended clinics and asked women to complete a questionnaire as the first part of a longitudinal study and return it in a post-paid envelope. Respondents were asked to send the researchers a birth announcement card when their baby was born and then to complete follow-up questionnaires at a series of intervals up to their child's third birthday. A variety of telephone and postcard follow-ups were also made in order to maintain the addresses and details of the sample. Six hundred questionnaires were given out to pregnant women and a total of 412 valid responses were received from women who met the criteria of working full-time and expecting their first child (a response rate of 69 per cent). At the child's first birthday 349 questionnaires were returned, at the second birthday 325 were received, and at the third birthday 312. This represents a longitudinal response rate of 76 per cent. Incentives in the form of vouchers and samples for baby care products were used to enhance response rates. In addition to structured questionnaires, qualitative data were obtained by asking respondents to write about any aspect of their experience as a new mother on a page of A4 at the end of the questionnaire.

## The sample

Prior to the birth of their child the majority of women in the sample were in jobs which were classified, in 1999, according to the SOC (OPCS, 1990) as social class II with incomes between £12,000 and £30,000. About 20 per cent of the sample earned in excess of £30,000 and another 20 per cent less than £12,000. The sample was therefore predominantly middle class, but included representation from high and low earning women.

## Questionnaire measures

Women were asked about their intentions and actual outcomes in relation to work and childcare. They were asked to provide information about their family, lifestyle, work and income as well as responding to questions designed to measure attitudes and beliefs. The questions and scales discussed in the present chapter are listed below.

With the exception of the General Health Questionnaire (GHQ, Goldberg and Hillier, 1979) all questions were responded to on a seven-point scale, where one indicates the lowest level of agreement and seven the highest.

Role identity as a mother – Being a mother is an important part of who I am; being a mother is important for my personal development; it is important to me to be a competent mother (three item scale, Cronbach's Alpha = .80.)

Role identity as a worker – Being a worker is an important part of who I am, being a worker is important for my personal development, it is important to me to be a competent worker (three item scale, Cronbach's Alpha = .87)

Evaluation of lifestyle decision – Doing no paid work, working part-time or working full-time was termed 'lifestyle decision' for the sake of brevity. Women were asked to evaluate this on the dimensions of 'my lifestyle decision is the best thing for me' 'my lifestyle decision is the best thing for my child' 'my lifestyle decision is the right thing to do'.

Specific Outcomes of lifestyle decision – Evaluation of the outcome of their lifestyle decision in terms of the extent to which their lifestyle facilitated the following specific outcomes – spending time with my child, influencing my child's development, experiencing my child's development, feeling lonely, being independent, having a conflict of roles, having good social contact, facilitating my career, having a sense of balance in my life, feeling bored, having interests outside the home, maintaining skills and knowledge, having a positive sense of self identity, getting a break from childcare.

Psychological well-being – The General Health Questionnaire (GHQ, Goldberg and Hillier, 1979) is designed to detect psychological distress in community settings and has been widely used in survey research as a measure of psychological well-being. Responses are measured on a four-point scale where four is the highest; a mean score approaching four would represent a clinical level of psychological distress.

Mother's ratings of child's temperament – Mothers were asked to rate their child's temperament on a scale of eight items – happy, secure, content, settled, sad, confused, distressed and fretful. Factor analysis demonstrated that these eight mood states formed two clear scales and on this basis the four positive items and four negative items were combined to provide two scales of positive (Cronbach's alpha .96) and negative mood (Cronbach's alpha .91). Mothers were also to assess their own child in comparison to other children of the same age on dimensions of energetic, relaxed, sociable, shy, fretful and easygoing.

Relationship satisfaction – Following Bradbury and Fincham (1992) relationship satisfaction was measured by a general five-item scale (e.g. my relationship with my partner is strong, is stable, etc.) and a one-item measure designed to evaluate overall happiness derived from the relationship.

Childcare Preferences – In the first birthday questionnaire women were asked to rank in order all possible forms of non-maternal childcare in terms of their own preference. In the third birthday questionnaire they were asked to state their most preferred option.

Childcare Practices – Women were asked to state what forms of childcare they were actually using and why (e.g. work, sport, shopping).

Lifestyle preferences – In the third birthday questionnaire women were asked to choose their 'ideal world' option in terms of work and childcare from a list of all possible permutations of full and part-time work for each partner combined with options for childcare or parental care e.g. 'I would work part-time and my partner would work full-time and we would arrange childcare during my working hours.' 'I would work full-time and my partner would care for our child.'

Non-financial work commitment – In the third birthday questionnaire women who were working were asked to rate the item 'I would continue to work even if I had enough money to achieve the standard of life I want'.

## Findings

### Decisions about work and childcare

When they were pregnant, 20.4 per cent of women stated that they intended to do no paid work at the end of their maternity leave, 54 per cent stated that they intended to work part-time and 25.6 per cent to work full- time. At the child's first birthday[1] 27.9 per cent were doing no paid work, 51.4 per cent were working part-time and 20.7 per cent working full-time. The apparent similarity in the proportions of women who intended to pursue each work option and those who did so is caused by differential response rates and masks movement between categories. Of the 265 women who had intended to work, 76 per cent were working full or part-time consistent with their original intention. However 14 per cent of those who had intended to work were not actually doing so and 10 per cent who had intended to work full-time were actually working part-time.

### Reasons for not returning to work

A short questionnaire was sent to those women who had intended to return to work but had not done so. Content analysis of the explanations they provided revealed that reasons for their non-return could be divided into five clear categories. The first involved an actual failed return. These women stated that they had tried to return to work (part and full-time), but became stressed and/or exhausted and so resigned from their jobs. A second category involved having intended to work part-time, but once arrangements were confirmed the women discovered that their income was too little to cover childcare. A third category also involved part-time work, these were women who had wanted to work part-time but their employer would not let them return on a part-time basis. Fourth was a category of women who had experienced unforeseen events such as illness or disruption to their plans for childcare and once these were resolved they could not or did not return. Finally there was a group of women who reported a strong emotional change; they simply felt that they could not leave their baby to be cared for by someone else.

## The first birthday

The data collected around the child's first birthday were analysed according to whether women were doing no paid work, working part-time or working full-time. Analysis of variance was used to compare mean scores in each work category.

### Role identity

There were no differences in identity as a mother in relation to work status. There was a high level of identification with the role of mother with a mean score of 6.5 across the sample. Figure 5.1 shows that there were differences in worker identity, those who did no paid work had significantly lower levels of identification with the role of worker than those who worked ($F = 45.9$, $p<.001$). More notable was that those who worked full-time reported similar levels of identification to those who worked part-time.

### Evaluation of lifestyle decision

Figure 5.2 shows evaluations of lifestyle decision. There were no significant differences in evaluation of 'my lifestyle decision is the best thing for me' but there were significant differences on the other two items. Women who did no paid work had significantly higher ratings of 'my lifestyle decision is the best thing for my child' ($F = 86.9$ $p<.001$) and 'my lifestyle decision is

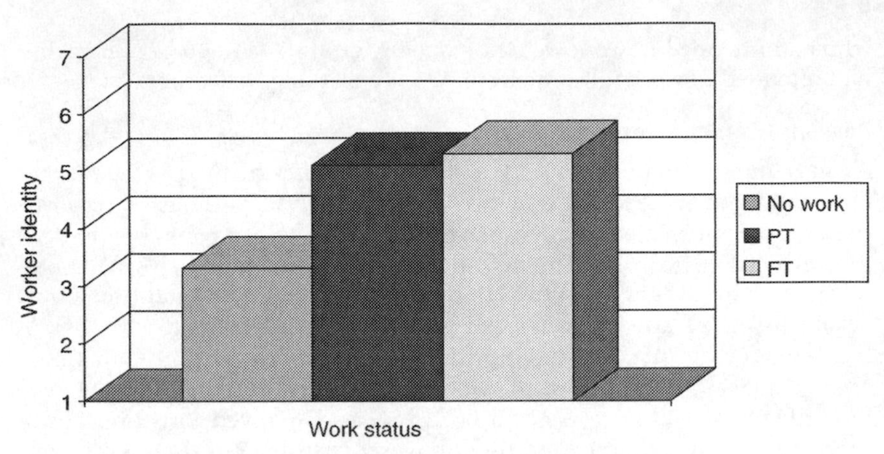


*Figure 5.1* Identification with role as worker at child's first birthday

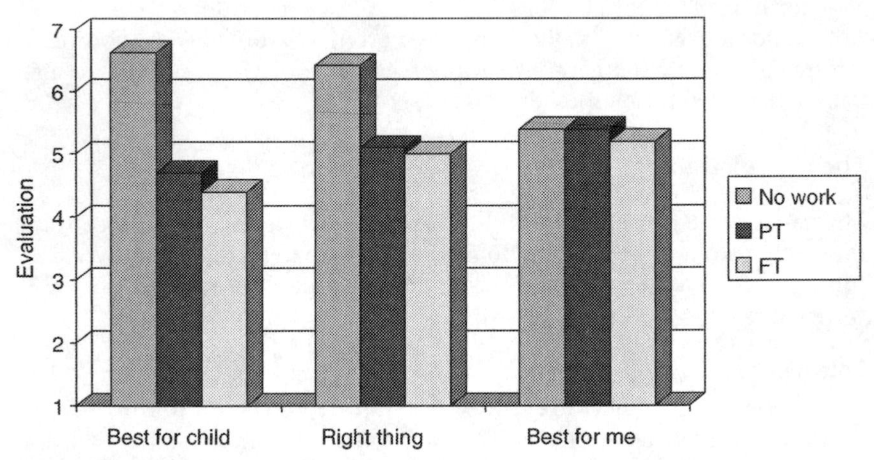


*Figure 5.2* Evaluation of lifestyle decision at child's first birthday

the right thing to do' ($F = 38.4$ $p<.001$). The ratings of 'best thing for my child' were low for workers. Amongst the full-time workers the mean for this item was 4.4, only just above the midpoint. None of the non-working mothers rated this item below four, whereas 16 per cent of the part-time workers and 25 per cent of the full-time workers rated the item below four.

## Specific outcomes of lifestyle decision

Figure 5.3 shows the mothers' evaluations of outcomes for their child. There were statistically significant differences between all three groups on all the outcomes listed, those who did no paid work agreed most strongly that their decision allowed them to spend as much time as they wanted with their child, influence and experience their child's development, and influence the kind of attention their child received (Multivariate $F = 33.55$, $p<.001$, all post hoc tests significant at $p<.001$).

On outcomes for the mother there were significant differences according to work status on all dimensions other than having social contact and a balanced life (Multivariate $F = 17.8$, $p<.001$, all post hoc tests significant at $p<.001$). Figure 5.4 shows those who did no paid work had significantly higher scores on the dimensions of bored and lonely, and less on independent, than those who worked. There were significant

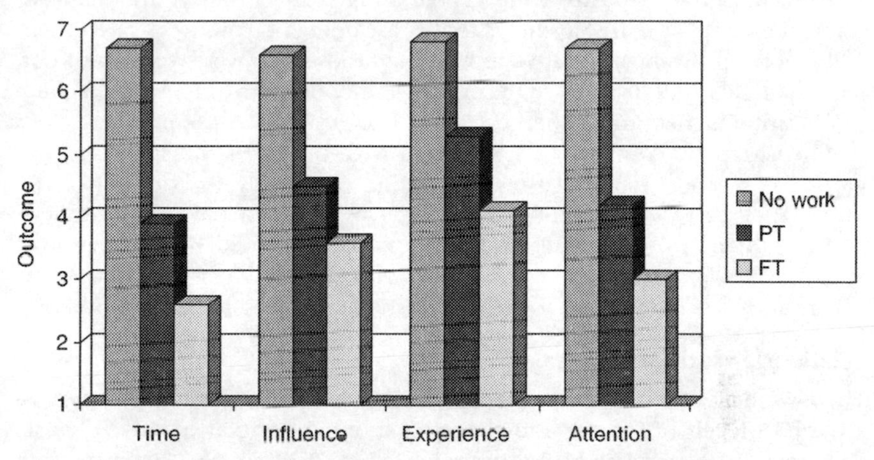


*Figure 5.3* Outcomes for child of lifestyle decision at first birthday

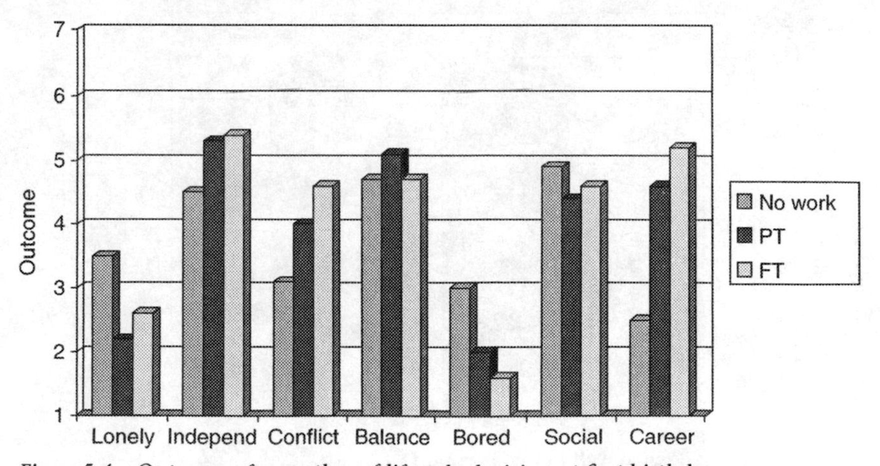


*Figure 5.4* Outcomes for mother of lifestyle decision at first birthday

differences between all groups on how much conflict they experienced, and how much their lifestyle had facilitated their career, this increasing from no work to part-time to full–time.

### Mothers' psychological well-being

The means shown in Figure 5.5 indicate that there were low levels of psychological distress across the sample, but those doing no paid work had significantly lower scores than those who were working, either full or part-time ($F = 3.6$, $p<.05$).

### Mother's ratings of child's temperament

The mean scores for positive moods were high, and negative moods low, across the sample. Figure 5.6 shows that those doing no paid work rated their child more positively on positive moods than those who were working full or part-time ($F = 9.9$ $p<.001$). On negative moods part-time workers had significantly higher ratings than the other two groups ($F = 4.6$, $p<.01$).

When asked to compare their children with others of the same age, all groups of mothers reported their own child favourably in comparison to others, but there were significant differences between part-time workers and the other two groups on the dimensions of relaxed ($F = 3.9$, $p<.01$) and fretful ($F = 4.8$, $p<.01$). Part-time workers felt their children were significantly less relaxed and more fretful when compared to other children.

### Relationship satisfaction

There were no differences between workers and non-workers in the (generally high) levels of satisfaction reported about their relationships. Those women who remained at home reported that their relationship had become more traditional.

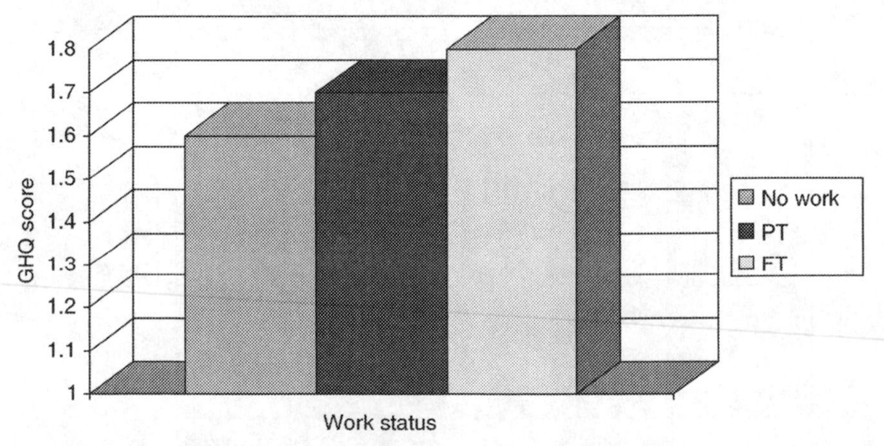


*Figure 5.5* Psychological well being at child's first birthday

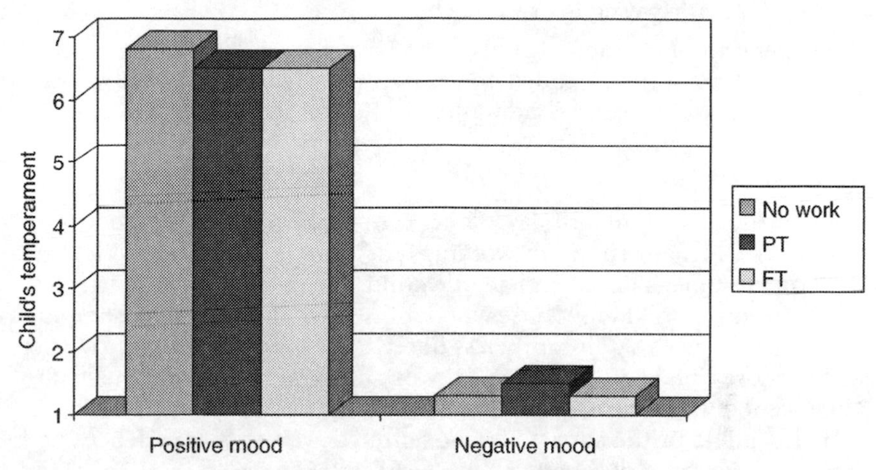


*Figure 5.6* Mother's evaluation of child's temperament at first birthday

Both workers and non-workers reported that work commitments prevented their partner spending time with their child (63 per cent of workers and 84 per cent of non-workers) and across the sample the majority of women reported that their partner was more stressed since the birth of their child.

## Childcare preferences

Seventy-five per cent of women rated the child's father as their first or second choice for non-maternal childcare, this was followed by grandparents – 59 per cent rated them as first or second choice. State-run nurseries were rated as first or second choice by only 5.6 per cent of women, private nurseries were more popular at 16.2 per cent, and employer provided day care at 17.1 per cent. Nannies or childminders were ranked first or second choice by 22.8 per cent.

## Childcare practises

Amongst women who were working, there was a high level of family and/or home-based childcare and many women used more than one form of childcare. Thirty-one per cent reported that their partner played some part in childcare whilst they worked and 21 per cent had help from grandparents. In most cases partners were responsible for childcare when women worked part-time or non-standard hours, or partner's care was mixed with some other form of childcare. In only a handful of cases were women reversing roles with their partner doing all the childcare. Twenty per cent were using a nursery, predominantly private provision rather than state or employer-owned. Thirty-six per cent paid for some form of home-based care, either a childminder (18%), a nanny (8%), or a friend (10%).

## What next? Anticipating the second child

Eighty per cent of the sample intended to have a second child and, of these women, 40 per cent intended to reduce their working hours or stop working once their second child was born.

## The third birthday

By the first child's third birthday, 35 per cent of the mothers were doing no paid work, 47 per cent were working part-time and 17 per cent were working full-time; 42 per cent had one child, 57 per cent two children and 1 per cent three children.[2] Those who had two children by the first child's third birthday were significantly less likely to be in work. Seventy-two per cent of those who were doing no paid work had two children, compared to 33 per cent of those working full-time.

At this point in the survey we re-examined women's experiences and views as a function of whether they were doing no paid work, working part-time or working full-time, whether they had one or more children, and examined any possible interactions between these two factors. In order to do this multivariate analysis of variance (MANOVA) was conducted to examine differences in mean scores as a function of work status and number of children.[3] While having more children was associated with less participation in work, MANOVA showed that it was work participation, not number of children or the interaction between the two, which resulted in differences in women's responses.

## Role identity

Consistent with the findings at the child's first birthday, identification with the role of mother did not differ according to work status or number of children with a mean score of 6.5 across the sample. Identification with the role of worker did differ according to working status, but not number of children. Both full and part-time workers showed the same level of identification with the role of workers, with a mean score of 5.4 and this was significantly different from those who did no paid work for which the mean score was 3.6 ($F = 47.7$, $p<.001$).

## Evaluation of lifestyle decision

Consistent with the ratings at the child's first birthday, those women doing no paid work reported a stronger conviction that their lifestyle was the right thing to do ($F = 33.0$, $p<.001$) and best for their child ($F = 47.1$, $p<.001$). A change from twelve months was that those doing no paid work scored significantly less strongly than those doing part-time work on the ratings of their lifestyle being the best thing for themselves ($F = 4.1$, $p<.05$) (see Figure 5.7).

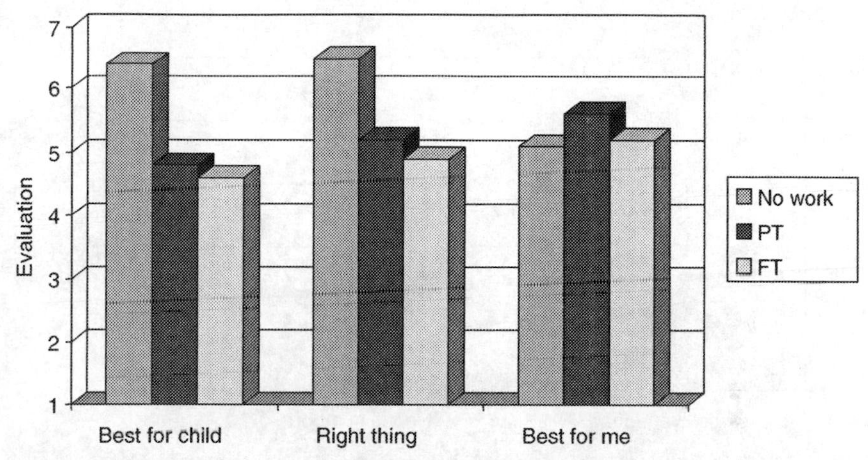


*Figure 5.7* Evaluation of lifestyle decision at child's third birthday

## Specific outcomes of lifestyle decision

The ratings of specific outcomes showed exactly the same pattern in relation to work behaviour as they did at the child's first birthday.

## Psychological well-being

Psychological well-being did not differ significantly between women with different work patterns. At the child's third birthday regression analyses revealed that psychological health could be predicted by marital happiness and whether the women felt that the distribution of childcare between themselves and their partner was fair.

## Mother's ratings of child's temperament

There was a significant effect of work behaviour on both positive ($F = 42.4$, $p<.001$) and negative ($F = 25.9$, $p<.001$) mood ratings (Figure 5.8). Post hoc tests showed that those doing no paid work rated their child significantly more positively and less negatively than either part or full-time workers.

When asked to compare their children with others of the same age all groups of mothers reported their own child favourably in comparison to others, but there were no longer any effects of work status at this stage in the survey.

## Relationship satisfaction

Figure 5.9 shows that, while the means across the sample were high, there was a significant effect of work on overall relationship satisfaction ($F = 4.0$, $p<.05$) and on the degree of happiness obtained from the relationship ($F = 3.2$, $p<.05$). Women working full-time reported significantly lower

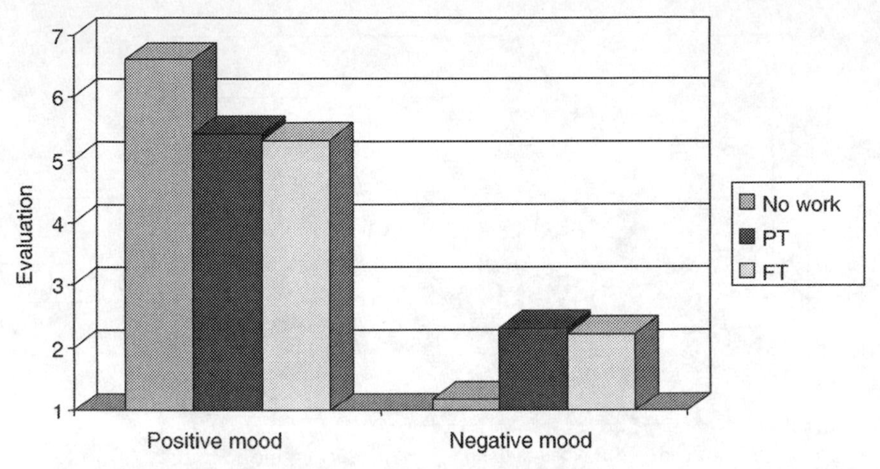


*Figure 5.8* Mother's evaluation of child's temperament at third birthday

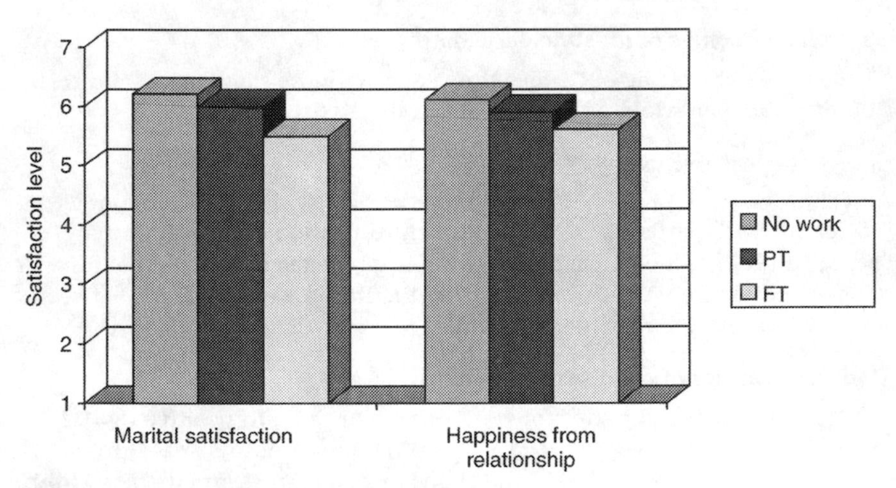


*Figure 5.9* Relationship satisfaction at child's third birthday

levels of satisfaction than those doing no paid work on both measures of relationship satisfaction, but there were no differences between those working part-time and those working full-time.

## Childcare preferences

At the child's third birthday women were asked only to indicate their preference for childcare, rather than rate all the possible options. By the time their first child was three years old, many women still indicated a preference for their partner (27%) to care for their child, however care by grandparents had declined in favour to 17 per cent. There was also an increase in preference for nursery care, 39 per cent indicated a preference for some kind of nursery provision, thought this was still heavily slanted toward private (27%) rather than state provision (6%). At this stage only 13 per cent indicated a preference for a nanny or childminder.

### Childcare practices

The primary source of childcare used by women in order to work at the child's third birthday this was: Nursery 42 per cent, childminder 22 per cent, nanny 7 per cent, grandparent 18 per cent, partner 6 per cent, friend or other family 5 per cent.

### Lifestyle preferences

From a list of all possible options for work and childcare only four were chosen by the women in the sample. As shown in Table 5.1, across the whole sample 30 per cent stated that they would prefer to stay at home and have their partner work full-time, 31 per cent chose to work part-time with childcare, whilst their partner worked full-time, 38 per cent chose the option of both parents working flexibly and sharing the care of their child. Just over 1 per cent chose for both parents to work full-time with childcare during working hours. None of the women chose to be the sole or main breadwinner by working more than their partner, despite the fact that a small number of women in the sample were doing so. When these preferences were examined in relation to actual working behaviour there was a stronger preference for the mother doing no paid work amongst those women who were not working, but a preference for equally shared work and care amongst both the full and part-time workers.

### Non-financial work commitment

The pattern of means for non-financial work commitment was opposite to work behaviour, part-timers (mean = 4.4) agreed slightly more strongly than full-timers (mean = 4.25) that they would continue to work if they had enough money for the lifestyle they wanted. The difference between the two groups was not statistically significant.

*Table 5.1* 'Ideal world' choices for work and childcare at child's third birthday

| | Whole sample | No paid work | Part-time | Full-time |
|---|---|---|---|---|
| Mother cares, father works full time | 30.0% | 52.9% | 21.1% | 9.4% |
| Mother PT, father FT, and childcare | 31.0% | 17.3% | 38.8% | 35.8% |
| Both parents PT and share care | 37.7% | 28.8% | 40.1% | 49.1% |
| Both parents FT and childcare | 1.3% | 1.0% | 0% | 5.7% |

## Discussion

### Work behaviour, choices and preferences

The evidence from this longitudinal study does demonstrate that women can be categorised according to their decisions about work and childcare in early parenthood. In the majority of cases women formed an intention in pregnancy and were able to carry out this intention when their first child was born (see Houston and Marks, 2003, 2004 for further discussion). However a substantial proportion of women found that their preferences were constrained by factors that resulted in their not working the way they had intended and there was increased likelihood of these constraints playing a larger role in work behaviour after the birth of second and subsequent children.

Interestingly, in this sample of new mothers, there were no differences in levels of identification with maternal roles in relation to work status; all groups of women reported a high level of identification with the role of mother. Part-time and full-time workers did not differ in their identification with the role of worker. In addition, both full and part-time workers showed the same levels of non-financial work commitment.

Houston and Marks (2002) reported that women who intended to do no paid work after their child was born, could be distinguished from those who intended to work, by their identity as both mothers and workers during pregnancy. During pregnancy, those who intended to give up work had developed a stronger identity as a mother and had lower identification with the role of worker. Thus role identity does seem to play a part in determining the intentions of what Hakim (2000) would describe as home-centred women. The present findings show that, once women actually have children, their work behaviour does not impact on their maternal identity and that working full or part-time does not appear to impact upon strength of identification as a worker. Thus while identity appears to play some role in shaping preferences for women who choose not to work, maternal identity does not distinguish between women once they are mothers, and work identity does not distinguish between women who combine work and motherhood whatever their hours of work.

Three years into parenthood the women in our study were asked about their preferences if all combinations of family patterns in relation to work and caring were available to them. Only 1.3 per cent of women chose the option of both partners working full-time. The most frequently chosen category was for both parents to work flexibly and to share the care of their children. The benefits of being able to share care and the frustrations of not being able to do so were a recurring theme in the qualitative data as illustrated in the following quotes:

> My partner would very much like to work part-time or have flexible hours to allow him to do more around the house and with our child.

> Ideally, we would both work part-time and split everything. Society prevents this and causes the strain and unhappiness. (*Part-time worker at child's first birthday*)

> Having a very supportive husband has made a huge difference. He negotiated a 4-day contract with his employers, and I too stay at home 1 day per week. This gives each of us a day alone with our son, and means he only goes to nursery 3 days per week. The fact that this is below 50 per cent of his waking time was important to both of us. (*Full-time worker at child's third birthday*)

Only a third of the sample indicated a preference for an option that involved paid childcare and none chose for the father to have the dominant role in caring for their children. More broadly it can be argued that the sample can be split 30:30:40 according to a preference for women as the sole carer, main carer or shared work and care. This is a rather more traditional pattern than reported by Hakim (2002, 2005), or than found in other comparable research (Houston and Waumsley, 2003), and may reflect the lifecycle stage of the respondents. However it is also important to note that only half of those who had given up work stated that doing this would be their preference if all options were available to them. For some women the key issue was not interest in work or willingness to be employed, but frustration in relation to difficulties in finding good quality part-time work that reflected previous experience and qualifications. Many women reported difficulty in finding part-time work which facilitated their career.

> At present, I am only working for 6 hours a week as that is all I have been able to find which suits my skills & experience. I am desperate to work, ideally two full days a week but there are no employment agencies in the Manchester area who are interested in part-time professionals. Also, the job papers only have menial positions advertised which are obviously no good. It's surprising that certain close people seem to think that, despite having a successful professional background, I would be happy to lower my ambition to zero and take any job. We do not need the money, but I feel that, without rewarding work of some kind, it is easy to feel isolated, worthless and as if you've dropped out of society. Also I have not suddenly lost all career ambition. I feel jealous of friends who have rewarding part-time work. Whether it is right or wrong, it's easy to feel as if you are 'old fashioned' and 'dependent' – for me this is very negative. ...My partner is supportive, although I resent the traditional role I find myself in. (*Part-time worker, at child's first birthday*)

Moreover there were professional women who decided not to work rather than take a menial part-time job. For these women not working at all allowed them to preserve their professional identity, rather than taking a job which was not at an appropriate level.

> When I planned to have a child, I thought that I would stay with him for about a year at home and then go to work, starting with a part-time job. Now I have started looking for a job, but was surprised to find out that it is very difficult to obtain a part-time job as an auditor or an accountant. I always hear that mothers were encouraged to find part-time jobs, so it was an unpleasant surprise to learn that it is next to impossible to find a part-time job in the field where I was making my career. I wanted to start with a part-time job because I didn't want to leave my child with a childminder full-time right from the start. (*No paid work at child's first birthday*).

These findings present some challenge to Preference Theory (Hakim, 2000). It is clear that we can distinguish a group of home-centred women on the basis of both their attitudes and work behaviour, but the attitudes and experiences of women who combine work with the care of preschool children seem remarkably similar, regardless of whether they work full or part-time. Moreover, in the present sample, there appeared to be remarkable reluctance to endorse a model of full-time work for mothers of small children. One possible explanation is that our sample of mothers does not include an adequate sample of work-centred women. Hakim (2000) argues that approximately 20 per cent of women are work-centred women and that these women are more likely to choose not to have children. Although 17 per cent of our sample were still working full-time at the time of their child's third birthday, two-thirds had only one child and the majority intended to have another child in the future. From the perspective of Preference Theory it could be argued that our full-time workers are actually adaptive women who will go on to reduce their work participation at some point in the future.

## Experiences in the first three years of motherhood

In our study, the women who gave up paid work in order to care for their child held a very strong belief that this is the best thing for their child and the 'right' thing to do and this view was also emphasised in the qualitative data.

> I have found that there is not so much support for women who want to stay at home with their children. And too much emphasis is put on going back to work. I feel that it is important to stay at home with your children and bring them up in the correct manner, after all that is the commitment you make when you decide to have children. I feel very strongly about this. (*No paid work at child's first birthday*)

A strong sense of making a decision based on morality, and sometimes sacrifice, emerged in the non-workers' comments.

> Neither my husband nor I have regretted our decision for me to stay at home full-time with the boys. Sometimes in the company of women who work (especially those who do not have children) I have lacked my usual self-assurance and confidence. I do feel as though the equality in my relationship with my husband has changed since I stopped work. He is able to go out when he wants to or needs to. For me, particularly since having our second child, finding time for myself has been impossible. I envy my husband the child-free times he has (watching or playing football or out drinking with friends). (*No paid work at child's third birthday*)

By the time their first child was three, non-working mothers were rather less certain that this was the best thing for them personally. This is further illuminated by their evaluation of the more specific outcomes where they indicated that they were able to have control over, and experience of, their child's development, but also found themselves feeling bored and lonely.

> Overall I am happy to have given up work to look after my child, but there are occasions when I feel a bit bored, cut off and out of touch with changing times. Life at home sometimes becomes a bit monotonous, but then so does work every day. (*No paid work at child's third birthday*)

> I believe I am making the right decision to stay at home with my daughter – for her benefit but not necessarily for mine as an individual! (*No paid work at child's third birthday, had initially returned to work part-time*)

By contrast, working mothers were not positive about the impact of their working on their child and this did not improve as the child reached the third birthday. A quarter of all full-time workers did not think that their lifestyle was the best thing for their child. In their written comments many women stated that working full-time was a financial or career necessity rather than a real choice.

> I would ideally like to be part-time if it could provide the financial support that we need (but it doesn't). I feel this would be perfect because having made the hard decision to go back to work, I have realised only now how important it is to me and to my self-esteem. However, I value my role as a mother above all else. I feel I would be able to provide him (my son) with the right stimulation when combined with the childminder's hours. My childminder however has him full-time and I have absolute trust in her and the stimulation she provides for my son. I do

> think however that only a mother can do it better. (*Full-time worker at child's first birthday*)

> I feel very proud to be able to work and bring up a child. I can feel good that I know I am working for a good reason and that is to be able to contribute to our household and financial commitments. I think if I had the choice financially, I would definitely work less hours, maybe a couple of days a week. I feel very, very sad that I am not with my lovely daughter as much as some mothers. I also feel annoyed when some people seem to act as if I'm being selfish working and leaving her with my mother-in-law. I work because I have to, and this means my daughter has a lovely warm safe home and everything she needs and wants. I can't wait until I can explain to her why Mummy is not with her all day, every day. I sometimes wonder what she thinks! (*Full-time worker at child's first birthday*)

At the child's first birthday working mothers had higher levels of psychological distress than those who were not working, but by the child's third birthday there were no differences between the three groups of women. The qualitative data do appear to reflect this in the number of references to stress, conflict and juggling at the child's first birthday. This is consistent with our previous findings which show that, the earlier women return to work, the more difficulties they experience (Houston and Marks, 2000). By the third birthday those mothers who had continued to work were more likely to be those who had found a way of making this work for their family, as illustrated in this quote:

> I have not regretted going back to work, especially when my hours were reduced. I found it stressful at first as I did not know what effect it would have on my son and I was very tired. Initially my husband just carried on as normal and didn't realise that, once I was back at work, I needed more help round the house. Otherwise it was like 3 jobs in one i.e. mum, wife and worker. Now, however he is much better and aware of my needs. (*Part-time worker, child's third birthday*)

The very positive lifestyle evaluations made by women who did no paid work were also reflected in their ratings of their child's temperament. At both the first and third birthdays these women rated their children as higher on positive moods and lower on negative moods. Interestingly this evaluation is not reflected in the comparative questions, where women are asked to evaluate their child's mood in comparison to other children. This reduces the probability that women who have given up paid work were simply motivated to present their experiences very positively in order to compensate for losing financial independence and career progression. It appears to be a real difference between the groups of women.

Part-time workers rated their child as experiencing more negative moods at the first birthday and this is also reflected in their evaluations of their child in comparison to other children. One possible explanation for this lies in the nature of part-time working patterns. Very few women in the sample worked the same number of hours everyday, there were all possible permutations of working hours, but many worked some full and some part days. Often their childcare patterns were also less straightforward than full-time workers, for example nursery for the whole days, grandparents for the half days – or vice versa. It may be that this is why they felt their children to be more fretful and less relaxed, as the children had less predictable routines than those whose mothers did not work or worked full-time.

> He screams when I leave him at the nursery, they tell me he is fine once I am gone, but I do wonder. With some of the week with me, a day with granny and nursery, he must be a bit confused as to what is happening to him. (*Part-time worker, child's first birthday*)

By the child's third birthday those doing full-time work reported significantly lower levels of relationship satisfaction than those doing no paid work. Given the differences in lifestyle satisfaction between these two groups, it is not surprising that this has impacted on their relationship.

> I enjoy my job tremendously which does compensate me for not being with my child. She is happy at nursery and again this reassures me. My partner and I have conflicting childcare views and for this and other reasons, we are splitting up. I expect to be living on my own with my child within a year. (*Full-time worker at child's first birthday*)

> I always thought I would be desperate to return to work after the birth of my son, but I was surprised as to how strongly the maternal instinct 'kicked in'. Due to financial constraints, I had to return to work even though I feel bitter and resentful about it. This has put considerable strain on my relationship with my husband and I have lost respect for him and view him with contempt a lot of the time. I know that he is trying his best to generate an income stream but I feel that I shoulder all the financial worries for the family but feel that I am unable to, as I would ideally want to leave work. I do the lottery every week! (*Full-time worker at child's third birthday*)

While working full-time may put a strain on relationships, full-time workers' comments contained frequent references to the importance of their partner's support in being able to work full-time. Both the qualitative and quantitative data appear to indicate that full-time work impacts most strongly on relationships and often leaves no time for couples to spend together.

> Having a very supportive husband has made a huge difference ... but my husband and I now have very limited social, leisure and sporting activities. (*Full-time worker at child's first birthday*)

### Childcare and work

Many mothers felt that nursery care was not beneficial to children before they had developed social awareness and a desire to play with other children. Another concern was the apparent disadvantages of having to adjust parenting values to fit in with an 'institution'. The detailed quote below summarises concerns expressed by a number of women:

> There are two main problems with combining work and motherhood – firstly most childcare situations involve a number of children together (nursery, childminder etc.) and subsequently the children pass on every bug going. My child has rarely been without a cold this winter and on top of that has had an ear infection, conjunctivitis twice, diarrhoea, and chicken pox. Needless to say, I have caught most of these colds and the conjunctivitis. This has worn us all down which makes keeping ourselves healthy (good food and exercise) much more difficult. What with trying to work at the same time (in a way that proves to my colleagues that just because I'm part-time now, I can still do the job), it becomes gruelling.
>
> The second issue is control over my child's upbringing and development. The nursery has a very strict food policy that doesn't allow the parents to send in food once they are 15 months old. As my child has always refused the nursery food, I foresee that when she gets close to 15 months, I will have to change childcare, either that or she will refuse to eat and hold out for food in the evening, setting up dreadful problems of waking hungry in the night etc. (We've already experienced this.) I had no idea this would be a problem when I started with the nursery. This is just an example of what must be common differences of opinion of how to treat a child's behaviour and development. It is also very difficult to know if these differences of treatment will have any long-term impact on my child – I have no idea and don't know how much to worry! (*Part-time worker at child's first birthday*)

While nurseries presented problems such as those described above, nannies and childminders were also considered problematic due to the difficulty in knowing what happened to children when they were alone with carers.

> I would not want a nanny, you read all the horror stories in the papers... (*No paid work at child's first birthday*)

By the child's third birthday, the increase in preference for nurseries reflected a view, that once children could talk, they would benefit from the company of other children, and would be able to relate their feelings and experiences about their childcare.

> Being at nursery has made (child's name) more sociable. She loves it and has lots of little friends, they do painting and modelling and all the messy stuff you put off doing at home. (*Part-time worker at child's third birthday*)

Although there was an increase in preference for nurseries at three, family care remained the most preferred option over the three years of the study. Overall the questionnaire data were consistent with findings from the qualitative data in which the women often expressed a very strong view that family care was preferable for preschool children.

> I feel it is largely down to the proximity of our immediate families (and our emotional closeness) that has enabled me to continue working. If anything, my mother urged me to work while I dithered! (*Part-time worker at child's first birthday*)

> The whole experience for myself and my son has been more positive than I expected. My son currently receives his childcare from my partner's parents, and he has developed an enjoyable and loving relationship with them. They also have far more time and patience when it comes to teaching him things, as his time during the day spent with me centres around the morning and early evening routines. (*Full-time worker at child's first birthday*)

> I am only able to work full time because my husband stays at home to care for our daughter. If he was not with her I doubt I could continue to enjoy my job. In fact if it meant childcare other than us (her parents) up to the age of 2 I doubt I would have continued with work. We have always felt that parental care was important for small children. I continued working as I earned significantly more than my husband who left his job to care for our child. (Also I enjoyed my employment more). (*Full-time worker at child's third birthday*)

## Conclusions

Women who have preschool children can be categorised into those who work, and those who do not, in terms of their work behaviour, attitudes and experiences. For a minority of women who have the financial support to do so, caring for their children themselves on a full-time basis is an important moral decision, in some cases, a moral sacrifice. With the exception of 1.3 per cent, none of the mothers in our sample favoured both parents working full-time as a model of family life with preschool children. Our findings do therefore support the basic premises of Preference Theory (Hakim, 2000) insofar as they show that a minority of women are home-centred and the majority of women seek some balance between work and family. However, our previous work, Houston and Marks (2003), has demonstrated that preferences alone do not determine work outcomes and that workplace support and planning – actions related to employers and work – can help in over-coming the constraints that women experience when trying to combine work and motherhood. In addition, our data do not provide evidence for a group of work-centred women.

We would suggest that home and work-centred women may be less prevalent than proposed by Hakim (2000).[4] In our study, half the women who had given up work to care for their child stated that this would not be their preference[5] if all possibilities were open to them, and some women appeared to have withdrawn from the labour market as a means of preserving their professional identity. Other studies have shown that while 20 per cent of women in the UK may remain childless, this does not appear strongly related to career orientation (McAllister and Clarke, 1998). Hakim (2003b) herself found that voluntary childlessness was much less prevalent than previously predicted, at around 7–8 per cent of women aged 42. In her analysis the majority of women without children were found to be in middle and lower grades occupations, rather than in professional and managerial work. Moreover, childless women did not have less traditional division of household labour than those with children.

Importantly, our findings challenge the notion that adaptive women are not committed to their working role or motivated by ambition. By contrast they show what extraordinary effort women have to make in overcoming both psychological and practical constraints in order to work. The majority of working mothers sought a more even balance of work and care between themselves and their partner. Over the course of the whole study there was an overwhelming number of comments relating to concern about the impact of working on children and the difficulty in achieving work–life balance. This may also reflect concerns about the importance of early childhood experiences in longer term educational and psychological outcomes (Francisconi and Ermish, 2000; Kurtz, 2004).

There is increasing evidence that men would also like to seek a better balance between paid work and family life (Houston and Waumsley, 2003; O'Brian and Shemilt, 2003). The present study shows that a third of fathers were involved in childcare in order to support their partner's work activities when the first child was twelve months old.

Women may not be a homogenous group, but the majority of women, and gradually increasing proportions of men, seek to combine both work and family life in an equal manner. Both employers and policy makers must address how the world of work can adapt to this desire for greater symmetry in gender roles and meaningful input into children's lives. This implies longer periods of leave for parents with very young children and greater availability of part-time and flexible work across all levels of employment. To achieve this will require a serious and challenging analysis of the relationship between working hours and productivity, and a more radical assessment of how work tasks and person hours can be divided.

## Acknowledgements

This research was funded by the Economic and Social Research Council Future of Work Programme, award number: L212252019. Thanks to Lizanne Allcock and Louise Hope who provided research and administrative assistance on this project.

## Notes

1. At the time this longitudinal survey began women were entitled to 18 weeks with statutory maternity pay and up to 29 weeks leave in total (if they had 12 months service with their employer. However the women in the sample had varied leave entitlements due to different employer practices and some of these extended to 52 weeks. Thus work behaviour when their child was 12 months old is used as the criterion for whether they have returned to work as intended.
2. Three families had three children, due to the birth of twins.
3. It would have been possible to examine change across the sample from pregnancy, to first birthday and third birthday as a function of work behaviour and number of children. However this form of analysis would have excluded the experiences of those who changed from one work category to another during the study. As actual experiences are likely to determine changes in behaviour this approach was not considered appropriate for the present chapter.
4. Hakim (2002, 2005) measures work centrality as having both non-financial work commitment and stating that you are the main or joint main earner. She argues that asking individuals to state whether they are the main or secondary earner is an opinion question because some men who earn less than their partners state that they are the main earner, and some women who earn more state that they are the secondary earner. However for the majority, occupational segregation (Miller *et al.*, 2004) and the gender pay gap (Anderson *et al.*, 2001), combined with the tendency for women to marry older men (Feingold, 1992), will ensure that men earn more than their partners. Thus this particular means of measuring work centrality may not be the most robust.
5. In our study preferences are measured in terms of personal choice, not general social attitudes. Hakim (2003) has argued that preferences measured at the level of general social attitudes can be unrelated to personal preferences and goals.

## References

Anderson, T., Forth, J., Metcalf, H. and Kirby, S. (2001) *The Gender Pay Gap*, Women and Equality Unit, London.

Bradbury, T.N. and Fincham, F.D. (1992) Attributions and behavior in marital interaction, *Journal of Personality and Social Psychology*, *65*, 613–28.

Crompton, R. and Harris, F. (1998) Explaining women's employment patterns: orientations to work revisited, *British Journal of Sociology*, *49*, 118–36.

Clegg, M. (2004) *Gender Briefings: Facts and Figures about Women in the Labour Market*, Women and Equality Unit Website.

Fagan, C. and Rubery, J. (1996) 'The salience of the part-time divide in the European Union', *European Sociological Review*, *12*, 227–50.

Feingold, A. (1992) Gender differences in mate selection preferences: a test of the parental investment model, *Psychological Bulletin*, *112*, 125–39.

Francisconi, M. and Ermish, J. (2000) *The effect of parental employment on children's educational attainment*, Working paper University of Essex; Centre for Economic Policy Research (CEPR).

Ginn, J., Arber, S., Brannen, J., Dale, A., Dex, S., Elias, P., Moss, P., Pahl, J., Roberts, C. and Rubery, C. (1996) 'Feminist fallacies: a reply to Hakim on women's employment', *British Journal of Sociology*, *47*, 167–74.

Goldberg, D. and Hillier, V.F. (1979) A scaled version of the General Health Questionnaire, *Psychological Medicine*, *9*, 139–45.

Hakim, C. (2000) *Work-Lifestyle Choices in the 21st Century: Preference Theory*, Oxford: Oxford University Press.

Hakim, C. (1991) 'Grateful slaves and self-made women: Fact and fantasy in women's work orientations', *European Sociological Review*, *7*, 101–21.

Hakim, C. (2002) 'Lifestyle preferences as determinants of women's differentiated labour market careers', *Work and Occupations*, *29*, 428–59.

Hakim, C. (2003a) 'Public morality versus personal choice: the failure of social attitude surveys', *British Journal of Sociology*, *54*, 339–45.

Hakim, C. (2003b) *Childlessness in Europe*. End of Award Report to ESRC.

Hakim, C. (2005) Sex differences in work-life balance goals, in Houston D.M. (ed.), *Work Life Balance in the Twenty First Century*, Palgrave.

Hogg, M.A., Terry, D.J. and White, K.M. (1995) A tale of two theories: A critical comparison of identity theory with social identity theory, *Social Psychology Quarterly*, *58*, 255–269.

Houston, D.M. and Marks, G. (2000) *Employment Choices for Mothers of Pre School Children: A Psychological Perspective*, End of Award Report to the Economic and Social Research Council.

Houston, D.M. and Marks, G. (2002) *Paid and unpaid work in early parenthood*, End of Award Report to the Economic and Social Research Council.

Houston, D.M. and Marks G. (2003) The role of planning and workplace support in returning to work after maternity leave, *British Journal of Industrial Relations*, *41*, 197–214.

Houston, D.M. and Marks, G. (2004) *Predicting the work intentions and behaviour of first-time mothers using the theory of planned behaviour*. Paper under editorial consideration.

Houston, D.M. and Waumsley, J.A. (2003) *Attitudes to flexible working and family life*, JRF, The Policy Press.

Kurtz, Z. (2004) *What works in promoting children's mental health: the evidence and the implications for sure start settings*, www.surestart.gov.uk

McAllister, F. and Clarke, L. (1998) Choosing Childlessness, Family Policy Studies Centre.

McRae, S. (2003) Constraints and choices in mothers' employment careers: a consideration of Hakim's Preference Theory, *British Journal of Sociology*, *54*, 317–38.

Miller, L. Neathey, F. Pollard, E. and Hill, D. (2004) *Occupational segregation, gender gaps and skill gaps*, Equal Opportunities Commission.
O'Brian, M. and Shemilt, I. (2003) *Working Fathers: Earning and Caring*. Manchester: Equal Opportunities Commission.
Office of Population Censuses and Surveys (1990) *Standard Occupational Classification (SOC), 3*, London: HMSO.

# 6

# Part-Time Employment among Women with Preschool Children: Organisational Cultures, Personal Careers and Sense of Entitlement

*Maria Sigala*

## Introduction

Part-time employment is popular among women with small children in the UK. Currently, one in every four employees works part-time and the vast majority (82%) of them are women (Summerfield and Babb, 2003). Between 1991 and 2001 the number of women in part-time employment increased by 13 per cent and in 2001 almost one in every three women with children under five years old were working part-time (Matheson and Babb, 2002; Twomey, 2002). Despite its popularity, part-time employment has been described as a 'trap which lowers women's lifetime employment prospects and earnings' (Tam, 1997: 243).

From their part, women with small children agree that working part-time employment enables them to manage work and family responsibilities successfully. They also, however, acknowledge the career trade-offs that such a decision often entails (Hill, Märtinson and Ferris, 2004). Cross-sectional research findings testify to the segregation of female part-time employees into low-skilled and low-paid jobs and analysis of longitudinal data reveals the downward occupational mobility that part-time employees experience (Rubery, Horrell and Burchell, 1994; Jacobs, 1999; Joshi, Paci and Waldfogel, 1999; Blackwell, 2001). Without exception, studies on female part-time employment as a family-friendly arrangement, paint a bleak picture of the present and future of these women in the labour market. Dex and Joshi (1999) summarise these findings when they describe the current state of female part-time employment as one whereby 'many women traded down, accepting a convenient job with reduced hours but lower status, as a way of combining family responsibilities and income-generating employment' (649).

Some authors maintain that women choose part-time employment because they are not committed to or interested in their working careers enough to choose full-time employment (see Hakim, 2000). Discussing differences within the group of female part-time employees, and similarities across female part-time and full-time employees, some authors challenge the assumption that time spent in the labour market indicates an individual's work orientations and preferences (Warren and Walters, 1998; Walsh, 1999). Instead it is argued that organisational cultures, particularly those promoting long working hours, 'encourage mothers to consider part-time work as the only viable form of employment' (Fagan, 2001: 244). The same cultures are held accountable for the way female part-time employees are singled out and discriminated against at the workplace (Lane, 2000; Whittock, Edwards, McLaren and Robinson, 2002). These cultures or ideologies are often conceived in the context of major discourses of time, productivity and commitment that dominate organisations and deny women in part-time jobs a sense of entitlement to better working conditions and career prospects (Lewis, 1997, 2001).

In an interview study with both male and female junior and senior managers in a UK high street bank, Liff and Ward (2001) found that women reported feeling unable to even ask for reduced hours of work on the grounds that 'in a culture in which long hours are valued as a major indicator of commitment, knowledge that one had been asking about reduced hours of work would count more than an assessment of the quality of one's work in determining one's future' (27). However, the same study reveals that organisational cultures can be diverse and at times conflicting: the target organisation's 'egalitarian' and 'family-friendly' agenda co-existed with a long working hours culture that discriminated against those seeking time outside work for caring responsibilities. The study also showed that organisational cultures are interpreted differently among organisational members: it was women more than men who feared the impact of a long working hours culture on their career since on account of their gender they, rather than their male colleagues, were expected to face discrimination following parenthood. Finally, Liff and Ward presented examples of organisational cultures 'in the making': both male and female interviewees avoided blaming women who did not work beyond their contractual hours, but by describing these women as being 'their own worst enemy', both male and female interviewees presented them as accountable for their own exclusion.

Halford and Leonard (2001) define organisational cultures as the products of social interactions and negotiations during which 'norms and behavioural arrangements are continually constructed and reconstructed' (67). If organisational cultures grow out of communicative practices, then it is important to look at popular narratives as stories that may be re-told to others – possibly others interested in part-time employment. Also, not only do stories give meaning to experiences but, more importantly, they 'fashion our sense of identity' and 'set certain limits over who we can be' (Gergen,

1999: 70). The sort of identities that can be fashioned by accounts of organisational cultures may convey what, according to Lewis (1997), is a 'sense of entitlement' for better working and career opportunities.

The term 'career' has become synonymous with upward mobility to the point that this rhetoric has become the 'reality' and it is taken for granted that pursuing a career means rising up in the organisational hierarchy (Mallon, 1998). However, the meaning of career is neither single nor fixed but rather 'it is used in meaningful ways, it is given meaning, and it creates meaning' (Young and Valach, 1996: 362; cited in Collin, 1998). Under the wider umbrella-term of social constructionism, the concept of career has been examined as it develops in the language that people use to make sense of their experiences in the labour market (Young and Collin, 2004; Cohen, Duberley and Mallon, 2004).

Coupland (2004), for example, focused on the concept of career both as a resource, drawn on and deployed by a group of graduate trainees, and the functions that this talk served. She found that participants would construct and deploy normative understandings of career, and they would then proceed into denying these constructions for themselves. According to Coupland (2004), her participants' denials that they followed a 'mainstream' career path, with the planning that such a path requires, enabled them to manage accountability 'in the event of not hitting the target'. In the case of female part-time employees, past research has shown that career talk may be a sensitive topic. Stephens (1996) found that female medical doctors in part-time jobs talked about the stigma of working fewer hours, and about 'career stagnation' and 'disadvantaged careers'. She noted, however, that 'during the interviews the suggestion that the male partner's career was advantaged exactly for the reason that the woman had taken time off for childrearing was met with some hostility' (49). This suggests that although women may talk about the career costs of their part-time employment, they refuse to accept the inferior position that this talk implies for themselves.

The present study will focus on mothers of preschool children, who are also part-time employees. It will deal with their accounts of organisational cultures and personal careers. One aim is to examine which narratives about organisational cultures women use when making sense of their status and of their power to command changes at the workplace. The other is to analyse how they use the concept of career in reference to themselves, and how they can exercise agency and fashion a positive self-identity.

The analysis centres on sixteen semi-structured personal interviews with women who were in part-time employment, had at least one child of preschool age, and lived in the wider area of Milton Keynes, an expanding new town with a low level of unemployment within commuting distance of London. This sample was recruited by advertisements in the local press, posters in local libraries, contacts with three major employers in the area, and through health visitors. It was part of a wider sample of mothers with preschool children. Interviews took place at the mother's home, her workplace or the interviewer's office. They lasted around 45 minutes, were tape recorded and fully transcribed. The average age of the interviewees was 33 years. The youngest participant was 19, the oldest 46. Participants differed in the number of children, marital status, and childcare arrangements. Seven interviewees worked in health care, generally in nursing, six were in secretarial, clerical and personal services jobs, two in managerial posts and one was a university lecturer.

## Organisational cultures and part-time employment

The narrative of the 'hegemonic' organisational culture was often used in the course of explaining how the interviewee took up her part-time hours.

> I feel very loyal to them especially since having children because there is not many companies that would (.) there's a lot of companies that I feel they would support you and give you your maternity leave but they've done more than that to me: they've made it a lot easier for me to have children and come back to work on my terms. They were very supportive and understanding and I think there's a lot of companies especially in industry that they wouldn't even contemplate coming back to your job part time. They would be: 'No, you have to go and do another job'. So, I feel very privileged the way I've been treated throughout the whole having children thing. (*Susan, personal assistant*)

> And he (immediate manager) then had to go back and put the case to the partnership, but he was, I think that the lawyers are very male-oriented and have got no concept of not working: 'why would you not want to work 90 hours a week?' I think he had to actually fight quite hard to get the part-time hours on my behalf. I didn't have to fight very hard at all because he just realised, she lives in (names place) it's an hour and a half commuting, can't do it, you know, it just doesn't work, so I think he was very keen to keep me. (*Louise, IT manager*)

> And it was me that went part-time rather than my partner because he is an engineer, he has now moved into software but IT, they are so male-dominated that the idea of part-time work, especially if you are you know, because you are father and you want to spend time with your kids is just unheard of. And it was very incredibly easy for me to arrange part-time work. (*Fran, university lecturer*)

> It's a brick wall, I couldn't afford (.) I asked, I took it up to the personnel, and the question was: 'well yes if they do it for you they will have to do it

> for them and we are not prepared to do that'. There is only so much you can do, when it comes to little things like going and getting yourself a part-time job, that is far easier than trying to fight the company that you are working for, where they definitely don't want part-time people. Sometimes everything you want doesn't work out. (*Rachel, cashier in supermarket*)

'Hegemonic' organisational cultures are constructed as the ideological positions of the organisational establishment. Descriptions of organisational cultures hostile to part-time employees become more persuasive with the use of certain rhetorical devices, such as extreme case formulations ('a lot of companies they wouldn't even contemplate', 'have got no concept of not working', 'so male-dominated that the idea of part-time work is just unheard of', 'they definitely don't want part-time people') and active voicing ('no you have to go and do another job', 'why would you not want to work 90 hours a week') (see Potter, 1996). The interviewees do not talk about hegemonic organisational cultures just to justify powerlessness, but also to argue that, despite the prevalence of a full-time working culture, their part-time employment is routine. Normality is achieved by contrasting the extremes of hostile organisational cultures with the present status of part-time employees as something 'easier' 'not very hard', 'incredibly easy' or 'far easier' to achieve. As the normality of part-time employment is built up in these accounts, women come to challenge the limited supply of part-time jobs at an organisational level. The problem with these stories is that they rely on the assumption that organisational cultures are stable and uniform and belong to an organisational oligarchy. So the part-time employee may challenge this culture but cannot claim to be part of it.

There were other narratives, however, of organisational cultures that emphasised change and part-time employees were presented as the driving force behind this change; these were stories about 'evolutionary' organisational cultures.

> Since I've got my part-time hours a couple of the lawyers have negotiated shorter hours, which is a big step forward for the firm, the female lawyers. We haven't at the moment got any female lawyers with kiddies but we have got a couple who have said they would like to work 4 days in the office and 1 day at home and I think the fact that I have shown that you can work at home and be productive has helped their case. (*Louise, IT manager*)

> (Mentor's name) next reaction was that: 'oh that's actually you know, if more people did that then that might shift the way'. You sort of work yourself to death and get lost in academia and it might shift a bit to improve it a bit if more women did it. And in fact I know a couple of sort of acquaintances, women academics who had done the same thing I

> have, a bit younger than me but done the same thing and gone back part-time. (*Fran, academic lecturer*)

> They have become a bit more flexible but I think it is because they have realised that there is a whole work force out there that have got children that will work for them if they give them the hours that they want.[ ] So you know they have kind of got their heads round thinking: 'let's ask the employee what they want to do and we will work our taskforce around them'. (*Carol, nurse*)

> Apparently only forty-five per cent of management women were coming back to the company after maternity leave at one point and they've realised, you know, that obviously some of those people had done ten years' service and they were taking their training and then they were going and working on the evening shift filling in the shelves at Homebase, you know, or Tesco's or whatever and realising that they were the capabilities don't go away just because you are unable to work a full week. (*Lucy, retail manager*)

Stories about 'evolutionary' organisational cultures construct these cultures as the attribute of a hierarchy. A gradual improvement is described here ('a big step forward', 'it might shift a bit to improve it', 'they have become a bit more flexible', 'they have realised') as the hierarchy develops to become more accommodating to the needs of the employees, particularly the female ones. These changes may be credited to one's personal efforts to secure a part-time job and to prove oneself in that position ('since I've got my part-time hours', 'I have shown you I can be productive'). Alternatively it is the departure of whole groups of employees in search of more accommodating employers that has been held accountable for these changes ('they (managers) were taking their training and then they were going and working on the evening shift filling in the selves'). Cultures are presented as organisms whose survival depends on the ability to adapt to changes. It was expected, for example, that employers need to change as more women come back to work after having children. The position of the part-time employee is still that of an outsider, so that employers have to 'work their taskforce around them' (see Carol's comments).

Bagilhole (2003) in her study with female Church of England priests, found that, despite being a minority within their profession, and despite reporting hostility and open opposition to their priesthood, these women insisted that their presence and practices will bring changes to organisational structures and cultures. However, drawing attention to the few changes undertaken in the Methodist Church in which women priests have worked for twenty years, the author's predictions are pessimistic for the future of these Church of England priests for whom 'an extremely hostile male culture remains' (375). On the future of part-timers in managerial jobs, Whitehead (2001) writes similarly: 'the emergent cohort of women managers may well be disruptive of gender stereotypes in terms of numerical visibility, but as regards organisational culture not much may change [...] while the discourse of performativity continues to pervade most public and private sector sites' (100).

A third distinctive way of talking about organisational cultures was in stories about 'inclusive' organisational cultures.

> I worry sometimes that...I have had that feeling where I worry that I should be there full time and I don't think that'll never stop 'cause I worry that the other (title of managers) are getting full support from their PAs whereas my (title of manager) has to put up with three days a week. Although I am quite flexible and they ring me at home if there is a real emergency. (*Susan, PA*)

> And I want to be able to go back to that ward and feel that I still really belong, that's quite important for me in a workplace to feel part of the team, and that is quite difficult when you only work, especially when I am only on nights. So what I have tried to do very hard is make sure that I do go in, we have a ward meeting once a month, so I have been to every single one since I have been back, and that is during the day time, which means it's quite a commitment on my part because I have to find someone to look after these two just for an hour. So I am sort of putting myself out but at the end of the day I think it's quite important that I get seen there and remembered that I am still part of the team and not just somebody who turns up for work 2 days a week. (*Rebecca, nurse*)

> It was also the fact that the job that I was doing, you had to do longer hours. You couldn't do it on the short hours just 5 mornings a week. I mean as it was I went to work, I dropped the children off at nursery I was there for 8.30, officially my shift should have ended at 4.30 every day but I was always there at 5.30. And then I had to literally put things down and go because I would be late for nursery otherwise. And I felt I wasn't doing the job properly as a result and I didn't think it was fair on the unit, for me to do shorter hours because the job needs somebody who could have been more flexible, do longer hours if needed and things. (*Bridget, bank nurse*)

Brooks and MacDonald (2000) adopted an ethnographic approach to study the night nursing sub-culture. They found that night shifts, instead of aiding career progression, created cultures that isolated women from the mainstream world of day nursing and made them feel 'second class' employees who were not 'part of the team'. This culture of 'presenteeism' was perpetuated by stories and myths among the day staff about 'unprofessional' and lazy night nurses. At present, some accounts report feelings and worries that reflect personal responsibility for the impact of one's part-time employment on the teamwork: 'I worry that I should be there full-time', 'I want to be able [...] to feel that I still belong [...] and that is quite difficult', 'I felt I wasn't doing the job properly [...] and I didn't think it was fair on the unit'. Stressing the impact of one's part-time employment on the team allows women to present themselves as important parts of the organisation. Stories of *inclusive* organisational cultures that construct camaraderie enable interviewees to talk about concerns and ways of coping with being part-time that confirm their involvement with, interest in and commitment to their team. So, even if a woman has to leave her part-time job for a more convenient post, it is not because of lack of commitment but rather because she cares for the impact of her part-time hours on the rest of her team (see Bridget's comments). In stories about *inclusive* organisational cultures women can construct for themselves the identity of someone who is committed to the productivity and performance of her working team. However in these stories women accept rather than challenge their exclusion from work teams on account of their part-time hours.

## Personal careers and part-time employment

Jenkins' (2004) study of different types of part-time employees in six different workplaces found that all groups of female part-time employees 'felt equally marginalised', and that for many part-time work 'symbolised the death knell of career development' (329). According to Jenkins, women's careers suffered because of the 'long hours' managerial culture that interpreted part-time employment as a lack of commitment.

In the present study, half of the interviewees in part-time jobs used the concept of 'career' when talking about their decision to work part-time after having children. Most of them had been in higher status jobs. One mother commented that only those in professional jobs had access to a career discourse: 'I am not career minded, I mean I am a secretary, I am quite happy doing it but I have never been like one of these people that wants to go off and be a Lawyer and have great things' (Maxine). All participants who talked about their careers predictably argued that pursuing a career is incompatible with holding a part-time job. Some women argued that as a result of working part-time their career 'had gone out of the window'. Others said that even if they aimed for promotion, 'nobody would appoint' someone in a part-time position.

The present analysis has identified four types of narratives used by interviewees, who, despite admitting the career costs of their part-time employment, could still construct a positive self-identity. A popular career narrative was that of the 'ex-career' self.

> I was working at (names employer) in London and I was working all the hours God sends to publish and you know, I was an academic when the

> RAE started and so that pressure to work and publish and produce, especially when it was quantity more than quality. I think I ended up feeling I was leading a very incredibly boring obsessive life really. [...] So I suppose that was the beginning of it, that I decided there were other more important things in life than just academic work. And then I met my partner there and I suppose you know you realise when we had a relationship that children seemed the thing we wanted to do. I suppose that logic of thinking that academic work is extremely important to me I would never consider giving it up, but it's no longer the be all and end all. (*Fran, academic lecturer*)

> I never sort of looked forward thinking about children. It was mainly my career that I looked forward about and getting married and everything. And I suppose children were on the horizon but it was certainly one thing that my husband and I never sort of, you know, as soon as we were married we had got to have children. And in fact I was actually quite anti children although I worked with them all the time, it wasn't something for me. But then suddenly my hormones got the better of me and that was that. (*Bridget, bank nurse, ex-ward manager*)

A personal career is put into some historical perspective to reveal that there was a time when the woman's career was the most important thing in her life until something happened to change that. Fran argued that working part-time had serious career penalties for an academic. The narrative of the 'ex-career' self allowed her to construct a version of her former academic career as a problematic state. Notice the extreme case formulations used: 'I was working all the hours God sends', 'I was leading a very incredibly boring obsessive life', 'the be all and end all'. Still, Fran attempts to repair the negative description of her career as an academic, particularly after mentioning her plans for children: 'academic work is extremely important to me I would never consider giving it up'. Bridget, on the other hand, was warier of losing her identity as a nurse and being mistaken for a housewife; she had admitted to this earlier in the interview. Bridget's 'ex-career' narrative serves to remind the interviewer of her professional identity and how it is against her nature to be a 'child-oriented' person. The use of a disclaimer ('I never sort of looked forward thinking about children') first acknowledges and then denies an interpretation of her part-time casual work as evidence of a child-oriented nature; in doing so she constructs a negative identity of a 'children-oriented' person (see Potter and Wetherell, 1987). Notice how her 'anti-children' self is constructed as exceptionally strong; even under circumstances when people would normally be children-oriented she still wasn't: 'I was actually quite anti-children, although I worked with them'.

Another interesting similarity between these accounts is the transition to motherhood. This is presented as a transition that occurred in a natural way, without women being forced into it, but also without detailed planning: 'you realise when we had a relationship that children seemed the thing we wanted to do', and 'suddenly my hormones got the better of me and that was that'. Here, the narrative of the 'ex-career' self enables women to talk about the time and effort that they have already invested in their working lives prior to motherhood.

Another career-related self-narrative was that of the 'strategic' self. Unlike the previous narrative, where the past is portrayed as a period of intense career building, the 'strategic' self-narrative refers to the past as an instant when career plans were first made.

> I have made the commitment and I have said I want to go back to work and I want to progress my career, they have seen that so that's my main commitment. I know a lot of nurses think: 'oh I am not going back to D grade having been a higher grade on the ward!', but you need to have that. If you want to choose something you have got to have a bit of a set back to start off with and then progress slowly. So I think that's my main commitment there, just getting there eventually. (*Hannah, nurse*)

> I always knew that the career would sort of like stay still, although I would continue nursing and at some stage I would be able to make another go of it as it were. But when would be anybody's guess and now is the time that it's actually fallen right as it were. (*Vicky, nurse*)

> I always knew I wanted children quite young, so that I could kind of have my children, get my family over and done with and have, you know, pick up my career later on. (*Carol, nurse*)

At times it may be argued that career progression is in the hands of one's manager (e.g. Liff and Ward, 2001), whilst at other times organisational systems may be held accountable for one's career (e.g. Coupland, 2004). In the 'strategic' self-narrative it is the individual employee who is presented as her own career manager. All previous accounts start with an assertion of a conscious decision about one's career, 'I have made the commitment', 'I always knew'. Interviewees then proceed to prove the claim that their part-time employment is part of a certain plan. Hannah had recently moved into a specialist area at the cost of her grade. Her account defends this decision as a career move despite the downgrade. She constructs corroboration ('they have seen that') to boost the veracity of her account (Potter, 1996). She also contrasts her ideas with those of her colleagues in order to challenge her membership of a certain category of nurses. This contrast enables Hannah to strongly claim that she made unique sacrifices to her career that her colleagues normally would not make (Dickerson, 2000). Finally, she explains her strategy: 'If you want to choose something you have got to have'. An 'if-then' structure is often used to constitute patterning in activity (Potter, 1996). Vicky argues that her strategy was to continue working as a nurse and to wait for the right moment to make a go of her career, whilst Carol's strategy all along was to build a family and then pick up her career. For Coupland's (2004) participants talking strategically about having a career implies the responsibility of potential failure to reach one's career target. For the part-time employees, constructing a 'strategic' self is nevertheless important if they are to claim that they are still interested in their future careers and working lives.

On the other hand, there were career stories in which women avoided strategic talk about motherhood. The 'adaptive' self-narrative described how motherhood could adapt in the light of career pursuits or biological factors. This narrative was often formed in response to the interviewer's question on preparations for motherhood.

> **Q: How much preparation had you put into being a mother?** Well I guess I was quite old when I started, 35 when I had her, I got married in 97 and had her in Nov 98, so we weren't married very long but basically it was a case of: 'well I'm getting to that age if I don't do it now, I'm not going to'. It's something I think (.) when I was younger I always thought (.) when I was much younger 21, 22 I thought I would get married, have kids and not have a career, even though I had been to university, I really was too lazy to be bothered with it and then through my 30s I got more into my career and thought: 'I'll never be able to give up the life style to have kids' and then decided, yes I did want to have kids and I was very sort of : 'if it doesn't happen I'm not bothered'. (*Louise, IT manager*)

> **Q: Before having children, have you ever thought about how you would like being a mother and how you would be like as a mother?** Hmm, yes I did actually, well I didn't think too much about it, no, I just knew it was something I wanted to be, yes. [...] **Q: Did you think that you would work?** Yes. **Q: Yes, you always thought that?** I was – how long was I qualified for, I am trying to think now – 1979 I started so I qualified in 1981. I then met my husband in 1985 and we both wanted children so that was we both thought: 'yes, we will have children'. I didn't have children for a long time. It just didn't happen. So I thought I am not destined to have children. I was doing my State Registered bit. So I did another year's training to become a Staff Nurse thinking I am never going to be a mother and then within 6 months of qualifying, I qualified in the June and in the October I fell pregnant. So therefore I thought as much as I have wanted to be a mother I am going to have the best of both worlds here and I am going to do 2 nights a week and come back. (*Hannah, nurse*)

The 'adaptive' self-narrative presents oneself as experiencing life transitions in which focus shifts between career, marriage and motherhood. Chronological and other details (such as active voicing) add authenticity to these accounts of transitions. This narrative appears to resonate with Hakim's (1996) label of a particular cohort of female part-time employees as 'drifters' having 'unplanned careers'; the instability and inconsistency implied by these labels boosts the author's arguments for the lower commitment of part-timers towards their careers. Here, however, denial of planning is expressed with reference to motherhood rather than to one's career. Accountability for the decision to become mothers is attributed to biological factors ('well, I am getting to that age') or to the way marriage works ('we both wanted children so that was we both thought: "yes, we will have children"). Also, both accounts make reference to a period when motherhood was considered impossible: 'I thought: "I'll never be able to give up the life style to have kids"' or 'thinking I am never going to be a mother'. On the other hand, career plans are detailed: 'I had been to the university', 'I did another year's training'. This narrative resembles that of the 'ex-career' self, as it draws from a discourse of career as a historical process. The interviewer is told again of the part-timer's investment in human capital.

Finally, the part-time employee used the narrative of the 'honest' self to defend her choice of part-time employment over a full-time job.

> I think that the media portray this modern woman I don't know that she really exists to be honest. **Q: Why?** Because politically correct you should be just as interested in your career once you had children as you should have been before, do you know what I mean? On the television and in the newspapers they seem to think that we all want it all and that we want to still be career women and that we want to (.) and most they are women like that but I don't think (.) I think you still feel this complete rush of love the moment you have a child and I don't really particularly want to have someone else enjoying the every day that is precious and I like to be I mean when we first got married we knew we wanted children but we always wanted to be in a position that I would only have to work the bare minimum amount of hours. I mean I obviously understand that there are people that theirs is different. (*Lucy, retail manager*)

> Well you know, have a child and then every day from 8.30 to 6.30 you don't see them, why not go part-time and it is literally she doesn't need to do those hours because she doesn't need the money. It's more of a power thing with this particular person. [ ] it's just a power thing because you are career minded, and I don't really see the point in having them. [ ] **Q: Do you think women shouldn't be career minded?** Oh no, I think everybody is to their own, it just wouldn't suit me, you

> know. All I ever wanted to do was get married and have children and have a little job, which is exactly what I have got so I am perfectly happy. But I am not one of these wives that runs around doing everything for everybody because I don't, I run around and do it for me. (*Sandra, bank clerk*)

These accounts draw from a discourse of 'career as power'. In this context, it may be problematic for a modern's woman identity as a modern woman to deny having a career and presenting oneself as a powerless woman. One way to deal with this is to undermine accounts which portray career-oriented mothers as modern women. Lucy blames the media and the press for creating the fictional character of a modern woman. She also questions the media's credibility as sources of unbiased information about women, motherhood and career by referring to the media's need to appear politically correct. Once the media's representations of career-oriented mothers as modern women have been undermined, their interpretation of the career interests of most modern mothers becomes questionable. By contrast, Lucy's expertise on the subject comes from her own experience of being a mother and feeling 'this complete rush of love the moment you have a child'. So, unlike the media who are biased sources of information about mothers' interests in their own careers, Lucy's experience of motherhood entitles her to furnish a realistic account of the subject (see Potter, 1996). Lucy's account of motherhood and career presents her as an honest person because, unlike the media, her account ignores issues of political correctness.

Another way of protecting one's identity as a modern woman and a part-time employee is to describe full-time employment as peculiar and abnormal (see Potter, 1996). Notice how Sandra talks about an acquaintance who works full-time: 'you have a child...you don't see them', 'she doesn't need to do those hours because she doesn't need the money'. Sandra can appear honest because she admits to her true and modest expectations ('all I ever wanted was'). By contrasting herself with other 'wives', who try to please everyone, she also portrays herself as someone true to herself.

## Organisational cultures, personal careers and sense of entitlement: A contribution to the 'work–life balance' debate

The 'work–life balance' rhetoric favours part-time employment. For female part-time employees with young children, however, their 'work–life balance' arrangement may come at a cost.

It has been argued that the success of a 'work–life balance' campaign within any organisation depends on the extent to which antagonistic cultures are challenged and changed (e.g. Lewis, 1996). The present study looked at whether and how such cultures can be challenged by mothers in various part-time jobs and organisations. Departing from theories of organisational cultures as products of social interactions (Halford and Leonard, 2001), this paper set out to explore the implications of popular narratives for part-timers' sense of entitlement.

The present analysis showed the multiple and often conflicting ways in which female part-timers talked about organisational cultures. At times these cultures were presented as dominant monolithic structures ('hegemonic cultures') that limited opportunities for part-timers. At others they were defined as flexible and adaptable to part-timers ('evolutionary cultures'). There were yet other instances when part-timers portrayed themselves as members of these cultures ('inclusive cultures'), albeit ones that could become liabilities to their teams. Each narrative enabled women to challenge their marginal position within organisations. For example, in the narrative of 'hegemonic' organisational cultures, the part-timer describes as abnormal those organisational cultures that are hostile to part-time employment. However, the present participants could not talk about themselves as 'typical' members of these organisational cultures. They were either outside of and in conflict with these cultures (see 'hegemonic' narrative), or in the process of proving themselves to the organisations (see 'evolutionary' narrative), or even at risk of letting their teams down (see 'inclusive' narrative). It is therefore difficult to see how these part-time employees can make demands for improved career opportunities, as long as women's part-time hours are deemed a great concession by the organisation.

It has been said that women experience career discontinuity due to their part-time employment (e.g. Jacobs, 1999). Some participants' narratives tried to bridge this gap by constructing a career past (investing time and effort into training, education and paid work) as a childless woman, and a career future with more time in paid work as children grow up. As women engaged in these narratives, another meaning of career came to life: career as a process rather than an achievement.

The findings of this study may help broaden the 'work–life balance' debate on part-time employment. For example, the idea that 'typical' members of an organisational culture even exist should be questioned; diversity needs to be acknowledged instead. Attention should be paid not only to the career costs of part-time employment, but to the continuity of part-time employees' careers: their work history and their plans for the future.

## References

Bagilhole, B. (2003) Prospects for change? Structural, cultural and action dimensions of the careers of pioneer women priests in the Church of England, *Gender, Work and Organisation, 10*, 361–77.

Blackwell, L. (2001) Occupational sex segregation and part-time work in modern Britain, *Gender, Work and Organisation, 8*, 146–63.

Brooks, I. and MacDonald, S. (2000) 'Doing life': Gender relations in a night nursing sub-culture, *Gender, Work and Organisation, 7*, 221–9.

Cohen, L., Duberley, J. and Mallon, M. (2004) Social constructionism in the study of career: Assessing the parts that other approaches cannot reach, *Journal of Vocational Behavior, 64*, 407–22.

Collin, A. (1998) New challenges in the study of career, *Personnel Review, 27*, 412.

Coupland, C. (2004) Career definition and denial: A discourse analysis of graduate trainees' accounts of career, *Journal of Vocational Behaviour, 64*, 515–32.

Dex, S. and Joshi, H. (1999) Careers and motherhood: policies for compatibility, *Cambridge Journal of Economics, 23*, 641–59.

Dickerson, P. (2000) 'But I'm different to them': Constructing contrasts between self and others in talk-in-interaction, *British Journal of Social Psychology, 39*, 381–98.

Fagan, C. (2001) Time, money and the gender order: Work orientations and working-time preferences in Britain, *Gender, Work and Organisation, 8*, 239–66.

Gergen, K.J. (1999) *An Invitation to Social Constructionism*, London: Sage.

Hakim, C. (1996) *Key issues in women's work: female heterogeneity and the polarisation of women's work*, London: The Athlone Press.

Hakim, C. (2000) *Work-Life Choices in the 21st Century: Preference Theory*, Oxford: Oxford University Press.

Halford, S. and Leonard, P. (2001) *Gender, Power and Organisations*, New York: Palgrave.

Hill, E.J., Märtinson, V. and Ferris, M. (2004) New-concept part-time employment as a work-family adaptive strategy for women professionals with small children, *Family Relations, 53*, 282–92.

Jacobs, S. (1999) Trends in women's career patterns and in gender occupational mobility in Britain, *Gender, Work and Organisation, 6(1)*: 32–46.

Jenkins, S. (2004) Restructuring flexibility: case studies of part-time female workers in six workplaces, *Gender, Work, and Organization, 11*, 307–33.

Joshi, H, Paci, P and Waldfogel, J. (1999) The Wages of Motherhood: better or worse? *Cambridge Journal of Economics, 23*, 543–64.

Lane, N. (2000) The low status of female part-time NHS nurses: A bed-pan ceiling? *Gender, Work and Organisation, 7*, 269–81.

Lewis, S. (1996) Rethinking Employment: An organizational culture change framework, in Lewis, S. and Lewis, J. (eds) (1996) *Work Family Challenge Rethinking Employment*, London: Sage, 1–19.

Lewis, S. (1997) 'Family-friendly' employment policies: A route to changing organisational culture or playing about at the margins? *Gender, Work and Organisation, 4*, 13–23.

Lewis, S. (2001) Restructuring workplace cultures: The ultimate work-family challenge? *Women in Management Review, 16*, 21–9.

Liff, S. and Ward, K. (2001) Distorted views through the glass ceiling: The construction of women's understandings of promotion and senior management positions, *Gender, Work and Organisation, 8*, 19–36.

Mallon, M. (1998) The portfolio career: pushed or pulled to it? *Personnel Review, 27*, 361–77.

Matheson, J. and Babb, P. (eds) (2002) *Social Trends, 32*, London: The Stationery Office.

Potter, J. and Wetherell, M. (1987) *Discourse and Social Psychology: Beyond Attitudes and Behaviour*, London: Sage Publications.

Potter, J. (1996) *Representing Reality: Discourse, Rhetoric and Social Construction*, London: Sage.

Rubery, J., Horrell, S. and Burchell, B. (1994) Part-time work and gender inequality in the labour market, in Scott, A.M. (ed.), *Gender Segregation and Social Change*, Oxford: Oxford University Press.

Stephens, J. (1996) From 'honorary chap' to mother: Combining work in the professions with motherhood, in Pilcher, J. and Coffey, A. (eds), *Gender and Qualitative Research*, England: Adelshort: Avenbury, 44–60.

Summerfield, C., and Babb, P. (eds) (2003) *Social Trends, 33*, London: The Stationery Office.

Tam, M. (1997) *Part-Time Employment: A Bridge or a Trap?* Aldershot: Ashgate.

Twomey, B. (2002) Women in the labour market: results from the spring 2001 LFS, *Labour Market Trends, March*: 109–24.

Walsh, J. (1999) Myths and counter-myths: An analysis of part-time female employees and their orientations to work and working hours, *Work, Employment and Society, 13*, 179–203.

Warren, T. and Walters, P. (1998) Appraising a dichotomy: A review of 'part-time/full-time' in the study of women's employment in Britain, *Gender, Work and Organisation, 5*, 102–18.

Whitehead, S. (2001) Woman as manager: A seductive ontology, *Gender, Work and Organisation, 8*, 84–107.

Whittock, M., Edwards, C., McLaren, S. and Robinson, O. (2002) 'The tender trap': Gender, part-time nursing and the effects of 'family-friendly' policies on career advancement, *Sociology of Health and Illness, 24*, 305–26.

Young, R.A. and Valach, L. (1996) Interpretation and action in career counselling, in Savickas, M.L. and Walsh, W.B. (eds), *Handbook of Career Counseling Theory and Practice*, CA: Davies Black, 361–75.

Young, R.A. and Collin, A. (2004) Introduction: Constructivism and social constructionism in the career field, *Journal of Vocational Behavior, 64*, 373–88.

# 7

# 'Daddy, I don't like these shifts you're working because I never see you': Coping Strategies for Home and Work

*Jeff Hyman, Dora Scholarios and Chris Baldry*

## Introduction

Recent evidence confirms that many working people, full-time as well as part-time, also carry significant caring and domestic responsibilities (Dex, 1999). With political and economic pressures exerted on people, including mothers, to enter into and remain in paid employment (Taylor, 2002), workers with caring responsibilities are faced with the need to develop strategies to organise their lives in order to negotiate between the demanding pressures of both home and work. This chapter examines the interplay between home and workplace pressures faced by employees and the sort of strategies that staff working in four call centres are adopting to cope with these compound pressures in order to maintain this precarious balancing act. Call centres were chosen for this study as representative of fast-growing 'new work' service sectors, increasingly typified by shift and seven-day working, integration with new communicative technologies and populated by high proportions of women operatives and team leaders, often working to tight performance targets (see e.g. Frenkel *et al.*, 1999; Taylor *et al.*, 2002). Drawing from our research observations we anticipate that domestic and work strategies can include some or all of: flexible patterns of formal working time; informal time accommodations between co-workers, such as swapping shifts; using paid leave to cover emergencies; opting to perform some part of the work at home, where this is feasible; and complex domestic arrangements between partners and families (extending perhaps to friends and neighbours) which balance maintaining the economic viability of the household with domestic responsibilities.

Following an examination of the literature on workplace and domestic pressures facing workers, this chapter goes on to describe the work routines in each of the call centres and then examines evidence for the incidence of employees with different caring responsibilities; working patterns of these employees; quantitative and qualitative work intrusions into people's non-work lives; attitudes toward domestic division of labour; the ways in which people cope; divisions of domestic labour and constraints posed by these divisions.

The study concludes that a high proportion of call centre employees with children were dependent upon grandparents as prime sources of childcare and/or relied upon partners to 'fill in the gaps'. It also found that tensions between work and domestic responsibilities for employees with caring responsibilities were rarely formally resolved through organisational policies. Rather, demands from employers for flexible patterns of work could present obstacles to greater employee control over their working time through the imposition of often unpredictable shift patterns extending into evenings and weekends. Unpaid working beyond contractual hours was evident, either through unpaid overtime or taking extra work home. The intensive and concentrated nature of call centre work was also expressed in reports of stress, exhaustion, health concerns and worries about family welfare.

## Workplace pressures

Contemporary working patterns are often complex as standard daytime working gives way increasingly to shift rotas, evening and weekend working, especially in the service sectors of the economy (Hogarth *et al.*, 2000). Moreover, there is a body of evidence that hours at work have increased (Green, 2001; Hyman *et al.*, 2003) and are continuing to grow, notwithstanding the *Working Time Directive* passed in 1998, heavily reported policy debates over the debilitating effects of the long hours culture and regular denunciation of endemic presenteeism in the UK economy (see e.g. Cooper *et al.*, 2001). Working time has expanded in a number of ways: through overtime, both paid and unpaid, and informally by significant numbers of people taking work home with them at the conclusion of the normal working day. Further, in today's flexible economy, additional working hours can be unpredictable and unexpected in their provision, especially in service sectors, where the rhetoric of customer service serves to shape both working hours and length of the working day (or night). But it is not just the number of hours spent at work which is a problem: there is growing evidence also for work intensification through greater use of information and communications technology, performance monitoring, appraisals and pressurised target setting (Green, 2001; White *et al.*, 2003; Burchell *et al.*, 1999). Long working hours coupled with intensive work can intrude into workers' domestic lives through feelings of exhaustion, stress and sickness and an inability to detach from thinking about work (Hyman *et al.*, 2003).

Both government and many employers at least now recognise the essence, if not the scale, of the problems facing employees. In recent changes to legislation (and in response to considerable criticism) the UK government has introduced two weeks' paid paternity leave and increased the periods available for paid maternity leave, following the relatively poor uptake of unpaid paternity and parental leave provided under earlier enabling legislation leave (see e.g. Bond *et al.*, 2002). Following these largely voluntary approaches which made little substantive impact on people's working lives, the Government has also now introduced legislation requiring employers to consider requests from parents with children under the age of six years for flexible patterns of work. Individual requests are, however, treated on their merits and can be turned down if employers can justify this action for operational reasons. Employers too are gradually shifting toward recognition that employees have domestic as well as workplace responsibilities and that tensions between the two domains may be unproductive for their businesses. In consequence, some commentators point out that there may be a sound business case for introducing family-friendly or work–life balance policies, typically by offering varying degrees of temporal flexibility through part-time working or more flexible working hours (Dex and Smith, 2002; Dex and Scheibl, 2002 ). There is, however, little evidence that employers are shifting to more profound approaches to balance work and life, such as through home-working, term-time working or the introduction of workplace nurseries (Hogarth *et al.*, 2000; Cully *et al.*, 1999: 75). So these policy and workplace developments have to be put into a context where overall working hours are high and still growing and where diverse work pressures can intrude into people's domestic lives.

Notwithstanding higher levels of governmental and employer support, it appears that balancing work and life remains a problem for many employees, their managers and of course the families of both. Legislation and employer policies have tended to be palliative rather than remedial and we have scanty knowledge of the ways in which people actually cope with the dynamic and multiple pressures they face. Exploring this issue is the main objective of this chapter.

## Domestic pressures

The focus on the household as the key social unit in analysing the work of production, reproduction and consumption owes a lot to the work of Pahl who argued that, historically, households must be seen as economic partnerships between men and women, and other household members, who develop household work strategies which make the best use of their combined resources for getting by under given social and economic conditions (Pahl, 1984: 20). The majority of households still tend to be made up of people related by marriage, partnership and kinship (McKie *et al.*, 1999) but the end of the 20th century saw a significant increase in diversity in the types of household. Households now include, in addition to married couples, one-person households, cohabitees, families with children and families without, single parents, gay and lesbian households and pensioners.

The widespread popular explanation is that these changes in household structure were due to the increase in labour force participation rates by women from just over half of all women in the 25–44 years age range in 1971, before the introduction of equal pay legislation in the UK, to over 75 per cent by the turn of the century (Hardill and Watson, 2004: 20). However, McRae points out that seen in historical perspective it is the period of the 'ideal family' of the 1950s and 1960s that seems unique and that high female participation and such characteristics as a higher age at marriage and birth of first-born, a drop in family size and increased childlessness were as true of the 1930s as of the 1990s (McRae, 1999: 2). The near continuous increase in the proportion of employed women since the 1960s seems to have been a contributory or necessary causal factor, but not a sufficient cause of changes to household profiles. Other less understood changes include a shift in values, particularly an increase in values of individual autonomy and rights to choose as applied to women, and structural changes such as the shift to services and accompanying deterioration in men's economic opportunities and shift in the gender composition of the workforce.

The greatest increase in women's employment occurred among married women (particularly educated women) in households where the male partner was already in work, resulting in a growing economic polarisation between two-earner and no-earner households (McRae, 1999: 6). Recent data for Europe show approximately half of all women in the EU between ages 16–64 are currently employed and two-thirds of this age group are married or living with a partner (European Foundation, 2000).

These trends have presented two areas of potential social adjustment: the care of children and other dependents, and the division of and responsibility for domestic labour in general. Within the EU the European Foundation's survey showed that in 2000, 70 per cent of working couples had children still living at home, 24 per cent of who were under six years old. Among working-age families in the UK with dependent children the proportion with two earners had risen to over 60 per cent by 1998 (McRae, 1999: 7). It seems however, from both EU and UK data, that the presence of children in the household has had very little influence on the combined levels of working hours of the employed couple, although it does seem to alter the distribution of both earnings and hours (European Foundation, 2000; Hardill and Watson, 2004). In practice there has usually been a prioritisation of the male partner's career and earnings potential; women are still expected to give a lower priority to their own career interests and 'invest more resource in the collective project called "family"' (Hardill and Watson, 2004: 21).

Since the work of Oakley in the 1970s (Oakley, 1974) a major focus on household study has been a gender-driven examination of domestic divisions of labour and ideologies of domesticity. Despite the ensuing debates and increase in feminist research, there still remains a gap between the expressed *preferences* of men regarding domestic labour and psychological responsibility for household and caring tasks, and actual practice (McKie *et al.*, 1999). As McKie and her colleagues point out, post-war social policies were premised on the idea of full male employment. Neither the reversal in the trend of economic opportunities for men and women in the labour market or the changes in household structures have been matched by equivalent changes in economic and social policies or in social values, so that women's lives continue to fragment around employed work, domestic labour and household-related caring to a far greater degree than for men (McKie *et al.*, 1999).

In Hardill's dual-career (professional) households, there was heavy reliance on non-household individuals, such as cleaners, childminders, nannies and au pairs, for help with non-market work (Hardill *et al.*, 1999). For households whose economic resources cannot stretch to the employment of externals, it seems likely that the wider family will be looked to for support. Findings from the ESRC Population and Household Change Programme (cited in McRae, 1999: 19) suggests that the increase in household diversity has not been accompanied by a decline in the importance which people still attach to the family; families still matter and most people maintain strong ties and regular contact with close relatives outside the immediate household.

The above review confirms the salience of both work and family under contemporary socio-economic conditions. Using case studies, this study aims to explore tensions between the competing claims of both domains and the strategies adopted by working people to reconcile the tensions presented by pressures of work and home responsibilities.

## Method

### Case studies

The data on which this study is based was drawn from four Scottish call centres collected between May 1999 and December 2001. The selection of case studies was intended to be representative of the profile of the sector in Scotland taking into account city/non-city location, establishment/workplace size and product/service. The sample focused on large workplaces (150 or more) representing four industries (see Table 7.1) – financial services (M), outsourced business services (T), telecomms/entertainment (E) and holidays and travel (H). Two workplaces were located in the city centre (M and T) and two in non-city locations (E and H).

*Table 7.1* Profile of call centre case studies

| Call centre | Location | Sector | Services provided | Year opened | Workforce size | Number of employee questionnaire respondents |
|---|---|---|---|---|---|---|
| M | City | Financial services | Sales, customer service | 1995 | 170 | 109 |
| T | City | Various/ outsourcer | Customer service, sales, IT/technical support, telemarketing | 1998 | 320–400 | 232 |
| E | Non-city | Telecomms/ entertainment | Customer service, sales, transfers | 1998 | 530 | 258 |
| H | Non-city | Holidays/ travel | Sales, enquiries, some customer service | 1997 | 340 | 256 |

## Data collection

Background data on company history, operating procedures, employment policies and staff characteristics was gathered as part of an intensive process of case study analysis and observation involving four researchers in each company for approximately four months. This was followed by the distribution of an employee attitude questionnaire and interviews. Distribution and collection of the questionnaire was conducted over several weeks to account for different shifts, sick/holiday leave, and variable work patterns. A total of 1476 questionnaires were distributed across the four call centres with an average response rate of 60 per cent resulting in 855 usable questionnaires from employees including team leaders and managers. Table 7.2 summarises the call centre employees' personal, job and home situations for the total sample and for men and women separately. The majority of the sample was female (70%) although there was sufficient numbers of men in the sample (231) to enable comparisons between the two groups. Around half of all employees were aged between 21 and 30 and over 90 per cent were on permanent contracts. The vast majority described themselves as customer service agents with no management responsibility; 13 per cent overall and a slightly greater proportion of men were team leaders or managers. Of these, 245 (29%) claimed that they had dependents or care responsibilities.

Exploratory interviews took the form of work observations and focused discussions with key groups of informants (management, inductees, trade union representatives) and provided initial discussion of the relationship between work and non-work life. Between 17 and 26 semi-structured interviews in each company also were conducted with a representative group of employees selected according to gender, age, job type and job/organisational level. These interviews explored three themes in greater depth: (a) previous work and educational history and how it led to their present job (b) experiences of working in the present company (content and control of work, commitment to company/peers/job, customer service, social relations) and (c) work–life linkages and the future (perceptions of job risk/uncertainty, relative importance of work, perceptions of society/class/status). A subset of these employees was contacted again for home-based interviews which explored work–life linkages in greater depth.

A total of 251 exploratory interviews or observation notes were conducted; with 77 semi-structured in-depth workplace interviews; 14 semi-structured in-depth home-based interviews; and three union interviews.

## Questionnaire measures

*Employee characteristics and home demands*: The questionnaire provided measures of gender; age (represented by an ordinal scale where 1 = '16–20', 2 = '21–30', 3 = '31–40', 4 = '41–50', 5 = 'over 50'); living arrangements (alone, with partner and/or children, parents or flatmates); dependents or

*Table 7.2* Employee characteristics and home demands

| | All employees | | Males | | Females | | | |
|---|---|---|---|---|---|---|---|---|
| | N | % | N | % | N | % | Chi² | Sig. |
| Gender | | | | | | | | |
| Male | 231 | 29.6 | — | — | — | — | | |
| Female | 550 | 70.4 | — | — | — | — | | |
| Age | | | | | | | | |
| 16–20 | 67 | 8.5 | 18 | 7.6 | 48 | 8.6 | | |
| 21–30 | 395 | 50.1 | 122 | 51.7 | 284 | 50.7 | | |
| 31–40 | 201 | 25.5 | 65 | 27.5 | 139 | 24.8 | | |
| Over 40 | 125 | 15.8 | 31 | 13.1 | 89 | 15.9 | 2.1 | .717 |
| Education | | | | | | | | |
| No qualifications | 30 | 3.7 | 11 | 4.6 | 19 | 3.4 | | |
| School/HNC/vocational/FE | 608 | 75.2 | 172 | 71.4 | 436 | 76.9 | | |
| Higher degree (ug/pg) | 170 | 21.0 | 58 | 24.1 | 112 | 19.8 | | |
| Contractual status | | | | | | | | |
| Permanent | 748 | 91.6 | 216 | 89.6 | 519 | 91.5 | | |
| Contractor/agency/temp. | 68 | 8.2 | 25 | 10.4 | 48 | 8.5 | .75 | .387 |
| Job status | | | | | | | | |
| Non-management | 698 | 86.8 | 199 | 82.6 | 505 | 89.1 | | |
| Team leader/project/sn. mgt | 106 | 13.2 | 42 | 17.4 | 62 | 10.9 | 6.4 | .012 |
| Living arrangements | | | | | | | | |
| on own | 89 | 10.8 | 31 | 12.9 | 55 | 9.8 | | |
| with partner and children | 206 | 24.9 | 43 | 17.9 | 152 | 27.1 | | |
| with partner only | 231 | 27.9 | 64 | 26.7 | 159 | 28.3 | | |
| with flatmates | 63 | 7.6 | 26 | 10.8 | 37 | 6.6 | | |
| with parents | 193 | 23.3 | 69 | 28.8 | 121 | 21.6 | | |
| with children only | 27 | 3.3 | 1 | .4 | 26 | 4.6 | | |
| other | 17 | 2.1 | 6 | 2.5 | 11 | 2.0 | 24.1 | .001 |

*Table 7.2* Employee characteristics and home demands – *continued*

| | All employees | | Males | | Females | | | |
|---|---|---|---|---|---|---|---|---|
| | N | % | N | % | N | % | $Chi^2$ | Sig. |
| Has dependents | 251 | 31.1 | 59 | 24.5 | 192 | 33.9 | 7.1 | .008 |
| Who provides care?[a] (N = 185) | | | | | | | | |
| Parents | 102 | 55.1 | 23 | 51.1 | 79 | 56.4 | | |
| Another relative (e.g. spouse) | 117 | 63.2 | 28 | 62.2 | 89 | 63.6 | | |
| Neighbour | 11 | 5.9 | 0 | 0 | 11 | 7.9 | | |
| Friend | 19 | 10.3 | 3 | 6.7 | 16 | 11.4 | | |
| Local authority provision | 34 | 18.4 | 6 | 13.3 | 28 | 20.0 | | |
| Private care provision | 38 | 20.5 | 9 | 20.0 | 29 | 20.7 | | |
| Domestic labour/primary resp. for: | | | | | | | | |
| Cooking | 401 | 46.9 | 78 | 32.4 | 308 | 54.3 | 32.7 | .001 |
| Shopping | 388 | 45.4 | 68 | 28.2 | 308 | 54.3 | 46.3 | .001 |
| Cleaning | 385 | 45.0 | 54 | 22.4 | 319 | 56.3 | 78.1 | .001 |
| Washing/ironing | 409 | 47.8 | 73 | 30.3 | 321 | 56.6 | 46.9 | .001 |
| Caring for small children | 101 | 11.8 | 7 | 2.9 | 90 | 15.9 | 26.9 | .001 |
| Caring for sick relative | 108 | 12.6 | 10 | 4.1 | 93 | 16.4 | 22.9 | .001 |
| Small repairs | 267 | 31.2 | 133 | 55.2 | 122 | 21.5 | 88.8 | .00 |
| Contribution to household income | | | | | | | | |
| None or almost none | 60 | 7.3 | 20 | 8.4 | 39 | 7.0 | | |
| Less than half | 280 | 34.0 | 63 | 26.6 | 208 | 37.5 | | |
| About half | 195 | 23.7 | 48 | 20.3 | 135 | 24.4 | | |
| More than half | 115 | 14.0 | 50 | 21.1 | 62 | 11.2 | | |
| All or almost all | 173 | 21.0 | 56 | 23.6 | 110 | 19.9 | 20.1 | .001 |

*Note*: [a] Multiple responses.

care responsibilities; primary responsibility for care (others, shared or self); care provision (parents, relatives, neighbours, friends, local authority or private provision); whether the employee was on a permanent or temporary contract; and whether the employee was a manager/team leader. Seven items relating to degree of responsibility for cooking; shopping; cleaning; washing/ironing; looking after small children/sick relative; and small household repairs also were included, scaled from 1 'always someone else's responsibility' to 5 'always my responsibility'. The sum of these responses was also used as an index of household responsibilities ranging from 1–35. Finally, employees were asked to indicate their contribution to household income based on five categories ranging from 'none or almost none' to 'all or almost all'.

*Work patterns:* Tangible indicators measured were whether employees frequently or always worked nights; whether employees frequently or always worked weekends; paid overtime per week (measured as an ordinal variable where 'zero hours' was coded 1, 2 'up to 10 hours', 3 '10–15 hours', 4 '16–29 hours', 5 '30 or more hours'); and unpaid overtime per week (measured as for paid overtime). Employees were also asked the extent to which they had to take work home with them. This was measured on a scale of 1 'never' to 4 'all of the time'.

*Work-home interaction*: Employee perceptions of how work affected non-work life were measured by six items. These statements were designed to represent the domains of time, behaviour and strain proposed by Greenhaus and Beutell (1985) to describe employee reactions to work–life interactions. One item which represented interference from home-life to work-life (the effect of household responsibilities) was also included. Responses to all items were on a four-point scale of frequency from 1 'never' to 4 'all of the time'.

*Attitudes towards division of labour:* Six items from the British Social Attitudes survey were used to measure attitudes towards gender roles. Employees were asked to rate each statement on a five-point scale of agreement.

## Company provision

The four call centres varied in the formal terms and provisions of working hours for their employees, though a common characteristic was the growing elasticity of working time and a management expectation that operatives should be flexible in order to staff required shifts. Hence at M, during the research period, staff core hours were expanded from 8am to 9pm to 7am to 11pm for new staff. Saturdays were included as regular shifts. Existing staff worked 140 hours over a four-week period, with maximum eight-hour shifts, though shifts could be adjusted either way by a maximum of two hours to 'meet business needs'. New staff had revised contracts with maximum ten-hour shifts and management had discretion to vary start and finish times by up to two hours with 48 hours' notice. For all staff, there was a requirement to work additional hours, again in accordance with 'business needs'.

Shifts at the outsourcing company T varied according to requirements of individual accounts, so that hours could fluctuate according to which account an employee was allocated. At E contracts stated that staff were required to work a flexible 24-hour shift pattern over a seven-day period and that shifts could be changed by management with 'reasonable notice'. Shift patterns at this company could be complex. Employees were hired at H on the basis of a 37.5-hour week over a five-day period which 'may contain a provision for Sunday working'. In addition, in some areas of the call centre, a continuous four days on – four days off 12-hour shift system was implemented.

In all four companies there was evidence of disruption and dissatisfaction among staff attributable to shifts. An operative at E, with aspirations toward becoming a social worker, complained that:

> Since I've moved up here [to E], I would like to go back to night school, but the shifts do have an impact on that, definitely, and it makes it very difficult ... I had thought about that but the shifts at work would make it almost impossible to do any sort of academic studies. (*E home interview, female, customer service advisor, age 41–50, married with children*)

In M, one operative complained that:

> I hate getting up in the morning to come to work, I really do, because I just think 'you are coming in and you are going to get hit with something else that's changed and you are expected to...'. They leave you messages on the phones saying 'next week on Monday we are doing 8–5 shift, we are getting our lunch at 11 o'clock in the morning. This is a new thing they are doing, sending you to lunch at 11. Canteen isn't even open at 11... They have sent a message can we stay and do overtime and take half an hour for our lunch. Just leave a bit of paper on your desk...They want you to take half an hour for your lunch and stay and do a couple of hours overtime. That would be a 12-hour day... They want us to be 100% flexible but they are not flexible in return. (*M workplace interview, female, customer advisor, age 31–40, divorced, no children*)

Shortness of notice was also a problem at H:

> We get our shifts out once a month and you usually get it like two days before they are about to start the next month which is pretty annoying ... because you don't know what shift you are working. That's the only

> downside of day shift. You can't sort of plan your life, you know. (*H workplace interview, male, sales consultant, under 20, single*)

More than one employee expressed family concerns. So, for example at E one team leader complained:

> I agreed to work constant backshift, why I've no idea, but I've been on secondment for two months to do this constant backshift ... and they pay me quite a lot more money to do it but the money's not enough, because my son was saying to me the other day, a couple of weeks ago, Daddy, I don't like these shifts you are working because I never see you... (*E workplace interview, male, team leader, age 31–40, married with children*)

Interference with family life was also expressed by another employee at M:

> [the shift pattern] gets in the way quite a lot. It's not very flexible at the moment. Just really because I've moved into the new team and find I'm doing an awful lot of late shifts like 1–9. Which really I don't find it very convenient because I get the bus now and I don't get home until after 10 at night ... I don't like my mum to be alone until that time herself ... I would just rather work 9–5 but you can't always have that and working the weekends is a bit inconvenient as well. (*M home interview, female, customer adviser, age 21–30, single*)

From the above narratives we can see that formally at least, the company work regimes which combine different shifts, evening and weekend working coupled with lack of notice of changes owing to holidays, staff absence and high labour turnover, can present practical and emotional problems for staff with caring responsibilities. As can be seen below, overtime, too, as well as less tangible spillovers from work, present further complexities for employees.

## Work patterns

Table 7.3 summarises the working hours of this sample of employees and compares these for men and women. Although only one-third of employees worked night shifts, over half worked weekends and of these a greater proportion of women than men ($\chi^2(1) = 11.7$, $p<.001$). More men claimed to work unpaid overtime than women. This is probably related to job status, as men were more likely to hold management responsibility and over 70 per cent of team leaders compared to 17 per cent of call centre operators claimed to work unpaid overtime ($\chi^2(1) = 145.94$, $p<.001$). The most common reason given for working unpaid overtime was not wanting to let down colleagues or customers.

*Table 7.3* Tangible extensions from work to home

| | All employees | | Males | | Females | | | |
|---|---|---|---|---|---|---|---|---|
| | N | % | N | % | N | % | $Chi^2$ | Sig. |
| Shifts | | | | | | | | |
| % freq/always work nights | 236 | 28.5 | 76 | 31.5 | 152 | 26.8 | 1.9 | .172 |
| % freq/always work Sat/Sun | 473 | 57.2 | 115 | 47.7 | 344 | 60.7 | 11.6 | .001 |
| Paid overtime[a] | | | | | | | | |
| No paid overtime | 669 | 82.5 | 197 | 82.1 | 472 | 83.2 | | |
| Up to 10 hours/week | 125 | 20.6 | 37 | 15.4 | 87 | 15.3 | | |
| More than 10 hours/week | 14 | 2.3 | 6 | 2.5 | 8 | 1.4 | .2 | .689 |
| Unpaid overtime[a] | | | | | | | | |
| No unpaid overtime | 611 | 73.9 | 165 | 69.0 | 446 | 78.7 | | |
| Up to 10 hours/week | 175 | 28.8 | 63 | 26.4 | 112 | 19.8 | | |
| More than 10 hours/week | 21 | 3.5 | 11 | 4.6 | 9 | 1.6 | 8.5 | .004 |
| Have to take work home[a] | | | | | | | | |
| Never | 547 | 68.3 | 150 | 63.3 | 393 | 70.3 | | |
| Occasionally | 220 | 27.5 | 76 | 32.1 | 145 | 25.9 | | |
| Quite often/all the time | 34 | 4.2 | 11 | 4.6 | 21 | 3.8 | 3.8 | .052 |

*Notes*: [a] Chi squared tests carried out on two categories due to small cell sizes.

Moreover, additional time at the workplace could easily accrue insidiously as demonstrated by experience from a team manager from H:

> At the moment I'm doing an 8–4.30 shift but I'll probably be in at about ten to eight and I am probably never out of here before quarter to five at night. ... when you add that up over a week or a month, you know, the hours total up. And the same with breaks as well. I always have my morning break and my lunch but very very rarely do I have my afternoon break. (*H workplace interview, female, team manager, age 21–30, cohabiting, no children*)

There was no difference in paid overtime between operators and management, or between men and women, and only 23 per cent overall claimed to work paid overtime. The primary reason given for this was the money. Nevertheless, around 30 per cent of the sample claimed to take work home at least occasionally. Again, when examined by job status, three-quarters of team leaders compared to one quarter of operators took work home ($\chi^2(1) = 105.7$, $p<.001$), with 16 per cent claiming that this happened quite often or all the time. In sum, an analysis of working hours gives indications of tangible interference of work into non-work life, with evidence for weekend shifts and unpaid overtime, particularly for females and team leaders.

## Work-to-home and home-to-work interference

Interference from work-to-home, assessed in terms of time, strain and behaviour-based effects, appeared to be focused mainly on feelings of exhaustion after work, effects on employees' health, and not being able to switch off after work. Table 7.4 summarises each item used in this study to represent interference from work on home life and shows these three issues to have received the highest rating for both men and women alike. In addition, women were more likely to claim work problems kept them awake at night, while men were more likely to say work prevented them from spending time with their friends. Very few of these employees showed home-to-work interference, although this was more likely amongst those with dependents ($\chi^2(3) = 35.4$). Further analysis by job status showed that team leaders/managers were more likely to report that work kept them awake at night ($\chi^2(3) = 21.1$) and to think about work when not there ($\chi^2(3) = 43.6$). These differences generally reflect behaviour-based effects. Some differences were also evident between those with and without dependents. Those with dependents were more likely to experience time-based interference claiming that work prevented them from spending as much time as they would like with their family or partner ($\chi^2(3) = 12.3$) and friends ($\chi^2(3) = 15.8$). All these differences were

*Table 7.4* Mean ratings of intangible extensions to work

| | All employees (N = 808) | | Males (N = 241) | | Females (N = 567) | | | |
|---|---|---|---|---|---|---|---|---|
| | Mean | S.D. | Mean | S.D. | Mean | S.D. | t | Sig. |
| My job has tended to adversely affect my health | 2.08 | .82 | 2.03 | .81 | 2.10 | .82 | 1.21 | .228 |
| After I've left work I continue to think about my job | 2.20 | .78 | 2.23 | .81 | 2.21 | .77 | .32 | .752 |
| I feel exhausted after work | 2.42 | .74 | 2.37 | .78 | 2.45 | .72 | 1.36 | .175 |
| Problems associated with work keep me awake at night | 1.70 | .77 | 1.62 | .75 | 1.75 | .78 | 2.28 | .023 |
| My job prevents me spending enough time with family/partner | 1.94 | .86 | 1.95 | .89 | 1.96 | .86 | .11 | .909 |
| My work keeps me from spending time I would like with my friends | 1.99 | .86 | 2.10 | .88 | 1.96 | .84 | 2.16 | .031 |
| Household responsibilities interfere with my ability to devote attention I would like to my job | 1.32 | .54 | 1.37 | .56 | 1.31 | .53 | 1.40 | .163 |

*Note*: Items were measured on a four-point rating scale: 1 'Never', 2 'Occasionally', 3 'Quite often', 4 'All of the time'.

significant ($p<.001$). A workplace interview with an operative at E pointed to the problems which can arise:

> It's very important for me, that, my main meal of the day, me and my family at the dinner table and have our dinner together and we don't get a chance to do that as often now and we'll sit and have a talk about our day and stuff ... and that's something that I miss, not having time with my family and not being able to socialise the same with my friends. (*E workplace interview, female customer service adviser, age 21–30, single*)

## Domestic circumstances of employees

Around half the sample of employees were living with a partner, some of these with children, and around 23 per cent still lived with parents (see Table 7.2). Only 10 per cent lived alone. Twenty nine per cent of all employees claimed to have dependents or care responsibilities, and significantly more women than men. Of those with care responsibilities, the majority seemed to rely on either or both parents or another relative, such as their spouse, although about one-third did mention friends or forms of state or private care.

In terms of domestic chores, around half of this sample claimed many household tasks were someone else's responsibility or they were shared, perhaps reflecting the relatively young age profile and the fact that almost a quarter still lived with parents. Nevertheless, domestic labour still seemed to fall more often on women in this sample than men; for all traditional female household chores, women were more likely to report having primary responsibility than men and all these differences were significant at the 99 per cent level. However, few were as abstemious as the partnered male employee from E, who when asked how his work affected the household division of labour, replied that:

> it affects it quite a lot in that I do nothing. It's as simple as that. (*E home interview, male, team leader, age 31–40, married with children*)

Only in the case of small repairs around the house were men more likely to report primary responsibility. Presented another way, the average household responsibility index for all employees was 20.13 which is above the midpoint of the 1–35 range for the sum of the responses for the seven chores. For men and women, respectively, the index was 18.7 and 20.7, a difference which was statistically significant ($t(525) = 4.9$, $p<.001$). Thus, women on the whole carried a greater burden of domestic labour. Finally, an examination of the contribution to household income showed that female call centre employees contributed, on average, less than male call centre employees.

## Coping strategies

Coping strategies can be divided between those that are predominantly work focused, such as swapping shifts, refusing to work extra time or rerouting work from office to home, to those that are essentially domestically instigated within households or extending to family and friends. Respondents were asked in work interviews, and to greater depth in home interviews, to describe any pressures they experienced and attempts made at their resolution.

### *(i) Workplace strategies*

There was evidence of informal shift swapping among operatives, though finding a 'partner' at weekends could be difficult, as indicated by an operative at E, where a formal process for nominating individual shifts was not recognised by the company:

> You would have to get somebody that was maybe off that Saturday and if you were working that Saturday they could swap with you. So you have to put out an email or put in a shift swap form and see if anybody is willing to do it for you, which is quite difficult because there is not a lot of work 9–1. (*E home interview, female, customer service adviser, age 21–30, single*)

The alternative would be: 'I'd have to apply for a holiday if I wanted it off ... we used to be able to get emergency holidays, like if it was a last minute's thing but even that's gone, you can request dependant's leave, but that is unpaid, that's a new thing'.

A more long-term workplace approach could be job sharing, though little evidence for this practice was found in any of the four call centres. Where it had been attempted, it has been either through the direct initiative of individual members of staff, or encouraged by management in order to cover awkward shifts, as explained by the same E operative:

> ...it's job sharing that suits them ... If you are prepared to work 1–9 they will give you job share. One of the girls who was in our team she applied, she's got two children and her husband's got two children from a previous marriage, so at the weekend she has four children and it was getting really difficult for her to arrange child-minding and everything, so she's asked to do the job sharing ... and she was told yes they would give her job sharing but she had to work a constant 1–9 shift.

Other, more individual, approaches to deal with work pressures include informal absence. One (male) team leader at E, required to work on regular Saturdays, which clashed with football, explained that:

> I just go. I presume that my manager knows that I just go to the football ... I'll maybe go in in the morning and just go to the football in the afternoon. (*E home interview, male, team leader, age 31–40, married with children*)

Another approach is simply to refuse to take on extra responsibilities, an approach which for obvious reasons is only rarely mentioned in interviews. After being told by his son that he never sees his father, the operator at E refused to continue with the better paid but disruptive backshift, despite the pleas of his manager that he should continue. There were no instances in any of the interviews of staff working at home instead of working in the office, a not unexpected finding for call centres. There was evidence, however, of team leaders and more senior managers taking extra work home after their regular work hours.

### *(ii) Domestic strategies*

Domestic strategies for coping with pressures embrace three main approaches; within the immediate household; in association with neighbours and extended family; and institutional, for example, childcare. We have already noted that one immediate pressure for women is that in addition to dealing with tangible and non-tangible spillover elements from work, they also undertake the bulk of the housework and domestic responsibilities. Surveys consistently show that men do considerably less routine housework than women, even in households where women work full-time. Nevertheless, the present study found instances of sharing which helped to relieve the immediate burden on women:

> Being truthful with you, I'm not a cook and whatever shift I'm on my husband's in in front of me and he makes the dinner ... so when I come in he has either fed my daughter, because she doesn't come in until 6 o'clock at night and if I'm late shift, obviously at eight o'clock they've had their dinner and my dinner is lying ... (*E, home interview, female, customer service adviser, over 50, married, no dependent children*)

And at M:

> There is an equal share. Basically my husband and I are both sort of taxi drivers for the kids now ... we both share whatever's to be done in the house. The mornings that I'm off will normally be my sort of housework mornings. G does all the ironing, I never ever iron. (*M, home interview, female, customer service adviser, no age reported*)

A more traditional response is perhaps offered by a male team leader at E with a partner working full-time who pointed out that:

> We're, well, I wouldn't say we were a modern couple, but I can cook, I love cooking. The other day, it was out of necessity, not out of pure passion, I did all the ironing, because it's killing Shelagh, standing up, given it some of that. Or if she is on a couple of days off, during the summer, I'll come home, the sweat blinding her, so she's out cutting the grass and that's a man's job, stop it, that's my job. [*E home interview, male, team leader, over 50, married with children*)

The data reported in Table 7.2 demonstrate that the most common and consistently applied coping strategy for respondents with care responsibilities was reliance upon family, with about half of these respondents pointing to family as a source of care provision. The interviews confirm the key role of the mother of the employee within the family network:

> Well, my Mum takes the kids for me. She knows when he (partner) is on standby ... so normally she will say bring them down the night before to save them getting up in the morning. (*E home interview, female, customer service adviser, age 21–30, cohabiting*)

The same employee also confirmed that 'Mum' takes the children if there is an in-service day at school or a similar event, but also confirmed her husband's role in taking the children to school in the morning, though 'that's one of the things that annoys me in winter because [her son] is really in school at about 8.25, so he is there quite a bit before the school goes in but...'

A call centre sales assistant at M made a similar point:

> My Mum gets the girls three days a week for me and watches them from 3 till 5 until my husband comes in from work. My mother in law gets them two days a week. So the two grans are widows, live on their own and it means that they enjoy... (*M home interview, female, customer adviser, dependent children, no age reported*)

Very little use was made by interviewees of institutional childcare which was often rejected on the grounds of expense, or less often, because childcare times did not conform with shift working times. When used, it tended to be adopted as a temporary solution to immediate childcaring problems.

### *(iii) Attitudes towards division of labour*

Whilst the study indicates that male partners do contribute to household strategies where women are working, men's attitudes toward women working and domestic labour roles are perhaps more resistant to change. Table 7.5 contrasts the responses of men and women to statements concerning gender roles at home and in the workplace. On the whole, the results confirm that women tended to be more positive towards women with families having full-time jobs, equal division of labour in the home (although the reality for these women, as shown above, was that they shouldered the greater burden of responsibility for domestic chores) and women's suitability for positions of responsibility. In each of these cases, the ratings given by women were significantly more positive towards women than those given by men. However, women also were significantly more likely to agree that it is a mother's responsibility to care for a sick child if both parents are working.

*Table 7.5* Mean ratings of attitudes to division of labour

| | All employees (N = 808) | | Males (N = 241) | | Females (N = 567) | | | |
|---|---|---|---|---|---|---|---|---|
| | Mean | S.D. | Mean | S.D. | Mean | S.D. | t | Sig. |
| On the whole women are not as ambitious as men in their jobs | 2.07 | .92 | 2.13 | .90 | 2.04 | .93 | 1.39 | .165 |
| If a child is ill and both parents are working it should usually be the mother who takes time off to look after the child | 2.56 | 1.11 | 2.42 | 1.02 | 2.62 | 1.14 | 2.39 | .017 |
| I'm not against women working but men should be main breadwinners for a family | 2.01 | .93 | 2.05 | .91 | 1.99 | .94 | .79 | .430 |
| There is no reason why family life should suffer when the women have a full time job | 3.77 | .99 | 3.65 | 1.03 | 3.82 | .97 | 2.13 | .034 |
| Nowadays men and women should share household tasks equally | 4.22 | .80 | 4.06 | .84 | 4.29 | .78 | 3.55 | .000 |
| Men are more suitable than women for positions of responsibility at work | 1.76 | .85 | 2.01 | .89 | 1.65 | .80 | 5.31 | .000 |

*Note*: Items were measured on a five-point rating scale: 1 'Strongly Disagree', 2 'Disagree', 3 'Neither Agree nor Disagree', 4 'Agree', 5 'Strongly Agree'.

The potential intensity of these compound pressures is illustrated by the response of an operator at M when asked whether work interferes with her private life.

> I can't get the housework done at all…It's quite tiring working all the time. Although I don't take work home, like tonight, by the time I get home tonight and I go and pick the kids up at my Mum's, go in there and have a talk for 15 minutes or something and then I go home, it will be about ten o'clock. Then they will have to rush into their beds because they've got school in the morning… It's difficult to do the homework thing and everything like that. Especially sometimes when I try to be involved and make sure they are doing their school work… (*M home interview, female, customer adviser, dependent children, no age reported*)

Table 7.6 looks at work values and finds that for both men and women their emotional attachment to work is not high, notwithstanding the pressures they face in terms of shifts and intense working conditions. More men than women claim that the main reason they work is to afford a good social life and that for them, leisure time matters more than work. As we see from the above quote, women may well perceive and treat their hours away from work more as domestic time rather than directed at leisure, reflected in the higher proportion of women who replied that their major satisfactions in life came from their family.

## Discussion and conclusions

This study of mainly women employees, many with caring responsibilities, and working in one of the new service sectors, has exposed a number of inter-related areas of potential tensions between their working and domestic lives and has also identified different ways in which these can be managed, albeit often partially and sometimes at personal cost. The tensions can be summarised as follows. First, the findings confirm earlier reported concerns that organisational flexibility in reality means imposing temporal flexibility onto workers to meet service demands rather than

*Table 7.6* Mean ratings of work values

| | All employees (N = 808) | | Males (N = 241) | | Females (N = 567) | | | |
|---|---|---|---|---|---|---|---|---|
| | Mean | S.D. | Mean | S.D. | Mean | S.D. | t | Sig. |
| I'm so involved in my work it is often hard to say where work ends & leisure begins | 2.03 | .99 | 2.08 | 1.06 | 2.02 | .98 | .75 | .456 |
| Most of my personal life goals are connected to work | 2.20 | 1.02 | 2.30 | 1.12 | 2.14 | 1.00 | 1.86 | .063 |
| If you have enough money there is no reason for having a job | 2.69 | 1.14 | 2.87 | 1.25 | 2.59 | 1.09 | 3.01 | .003 |
| The main reason I work is to afford a good social life | 2.87 | 1.13 | 3.04 | 1.16 | 2.82 | 1.13 | 2.41 | .016 |
| My leisure time matters to me more than work | 3.55 | 1.02 | 3.66 | .98 | 3.50 | 1.04 | 2.11 | .036 |
| The major satisfactions in my life come from my family | 4.09 | .93 | 3.88 | .95 | 4.14 | .93 | 3.60 | .000 |

*Note*: Items were measured on a five-point rating scale: 1 'Strongly Disagree', 2 'Disagree', 3 'Neither Agree nor Disagree', 4 'Agree', 5 'Strongly Agree'.

providing flexible but predictable working times suited to the needs of employees (see e.g. Purcell *et al.*, 1999). Shiftworking often extended late into the evenings and was especially prevalent at weekends. Balancing domestic responsibilities or simply maintaining a reasonably stable family and social life could be further compromised by management imposing unplanned extensions to shifts, often with short notice. Another source of uncertainty and irritation for planning domestic affairs was the lateness in publicising shift rotas, though this was probably attributable to unanticipated labour shortages. Informal unpaid overtime and taking work home by team leaders and other managers was also a common feature of the study. As interviews show, these tangible intrusions into domestic life, reported in depth elsewhere (Hyman *et al.*, 2003), did create emotional and practical difficulties for employees. These impositions, combined with the intense and occasionally fraught nature of much call centre work (see e.g. Taylor *et al.*, 2002; Taylor and Bain, 1999) led to reported problems with stress, sleeplessness, exhaustion and an inability to escape from thinking about work. In other words, the home lives of employees were also being affected by the nature of the work and work regimes. An operator at E described how she felt:

> I was off my work with stress, but never admitted to the work that it was stress, but it was stress and I actually got up off the seat one day and I threw a booklet and I was so happy I lifted a soft folder because the force I threw the booklet at the computer screen it would have went right through the screen and I actually got up and I had to go – I couldn't stay any longer and I took a really bad bout of the flu and I think it was just complete stress... (*E home interview, female, customer service adviser, age 21–30, single*)

A second substantive point derives from the finding that a substantial proportion of respondents and interviewees in the present study had childcare responsibilities for which the employers made little formal provision. Numerous studies have indicated that the major problem with institutional childcare is the cost (Labour Research, 2003). This was a point often referred to in interviews, coupled with the rigidity of formal childcare arrangements. For these reasons, nurseries and childminders were little used, and of course no workplace facilities were made available by the employers. Indeed, employers formally did little to help employees manage their working time: authorised shift swaps were rare, though an informal network of shift swapping clearly existed and was tolerated by at least some hard-pressed team leaders. Job share also was not actively promoted within the companies. With labour turnover high in all four establishments (between 25–37%), there might be a business case for employers to adopt a more liberal approach toward helping their employees to cope with home and work demands (see e.g. Dex and Scheibl, 1999).

There is little doubt that working parents with preschool children will continue to face difficulties combining work with childrearing as long as the cost of private nursery provision remains prohibitive and out of reach for many middle and low income earners. Most of the call centre respondents coped by relying on a combination of immediate partner and/or mother. Indeed, the extent to which the services of 'Grandma' were available and called upon was surprising, with at least some respondents taking a more strategic approach by moving house to be nearer to parents and hence to reliable childcare facilities. Reliance on extended close family ties also helped to resolve the problems of shift working and its lack of predictability. This 'service' may not, of course, be available throughout the country as proximity to extended family may be more prevalent in recently deindustrialised and Northern communities of the UK, where many call centres have been established. Perhaps because of the relative youth of the majority of call centre employees, there was little reference made to elder care, though with the reduction in public provision of elder-care facilities, one might anticipate additional problems here as well, if not now, then certainly in the near future (Graham, 1999).

Together, these factors clearly present obstacles to employees attempting to manage their work and domestic lives. Though attitudes toward household division of labour were still orientated toward the woman's role and this was reflected in the finding that domestic responsibilities were still largely carried out by women, there was evidence of male partners at least helping out by taking shift-bound partners to and from work, uplifting children from school and preparing meals. Partners could also offer emotional support to stressed-out employees though, of course, when such support is denied or not available, work–life tensions might become exacerbated. A trainee team leader expressed her feelings:

> My husband, every morning, God love him, but every morning he drops me off and he'll say, remember what I've said, keep your chin up and don't let them grind you down. Just go in and do what you've got to do and don't take it all on your shoulders ... People say things about you're always so bright and bubbly and I think how am I, because you don't know what is going on in my head. I go home and I'm like, oh, my face is tripping me. So I'll be quite honest, I don't think call centres are a perfect job for me, with the shifts and things like that I would prefer to be working a normal shift pattern where it didn't interfere with my home life. (*E workplace interview, female, trainee team leader, age 21–30, married, no children*)

The extent to which these often ad hoc domestic arrangements amounted to coherent and consistent strategies within a changing and uncertain world is open to question, though clearly some of the burden is borne by partners and close family, without whom many of our call centre respondents would have struggled to sustain employment let alone lead a reasonably balanced life. Notwithstanding the rhetoric and intensity of debate in recent years about work–life balance and flexible working, there was little evidence of employers implementing genuinely family-friendly policies.

## Acknowledgements

The work in this chapter derives from the project *Employment and Working Life Beyond the Year 2000: Two Emerging Employment Sectors*, ESRC Award No. L212252006. The full research team comprises Peter Bain, Chris Baldry, Dirk Bunzel, Nick Bozionelis, Kay Gilbert, Gregor Gall, Jeff Hyman, Cliff Lockyer, Abigail Marks, Gareth Mulvey, Dora Scholarios, Phil Taylor, Aileen Watson and the late Harvie Ramsay.

## References

Bond, S., Hyman, J., Summers, J. and Wise S. (2002) *Family-Friendly Working? Putting Policy into Practice*, York: York Publishing Services.

Burchell, B., Day, D., Hudson, M., Lapido, D., Mankelow, R., Nolan, J., Reed, H., Wichert, I. and Wilkinson, W. (1999) *Job Insecurity and Work Intensification: Flexibility and the Changing Boundaries of Work*, York: York Publishing Services.

Cooper, C., Dewe, P. and O'Driscoll, M. (2001) *Organizational Stress*, London: Sage.

Cully, M., Woodland, S., O'Reilly, A. and Dix, G. (1999) *Britain at Work*, London: Routledge.

Dex, S. (ed.) (1999) *Families and the Labour Market*, London: Family Policy Studies Centre.

Dex, S. and Scheibl, F. (1999) 'Business performance and family-friendly policies', *Journal of General Management, 24/4*, 22–37.

Dex. S and Scheibl, F. (2002) *SMEs and Flexible Working Arrangements*, York: York Publishing Services.

Dex, S. and Smith, C. (2002) *The Nature and Pattern of Family-Friendly Employment Policies in Britain*, Bristol: The Policy Press.

European Foundation for the Improvement of Living and Working Conditions (2000) EF/00/25/EN: *Combining Family and Work: the Working Arrangements of Women and Men*, Dublin: European Foundation.

Frenkel, S., Korczynski, M., Shire, K. and Tam, M. (1999) *On the Front Line: Organization of Work in the Information Society*, Ithaca, NY: Cornell University Press.

Graham, H. (1999) 'The informal sector of welfare: A crisis in caring?', in Allan, G. (ed.), *The Sociology of the Family*, Oxford: Blackwell.

Green, F. (2001) 'It's been a hard day's night: the concentration and intensification of work in late twentieth century Britain', *British Journal of Industrial Relations, 39*, 53–80.

Hardill, I., Dudleston, A., Green, A. and Owen, D. (1999) 'Decision making in dual-career households', in McKie, L., Bowlby, S. and Gregory, S. (eds) (1999), 192–206, Basingstoke: Macmillan.

Hardill, I. and Watson, R. (2004) 'Career priorities within dual-career households: an analysis of the impact of childrearing upon gender participation rates and earnings', *Industrial Relations Journal, 35 (1)*, 19–37.

Hogarth, T., Hasluck, C. and Pierre, G. (2000) Work-life Balance 2000: *Baseline Study of Work-Life Practices in Great Britain*, Summary Report, London: DfEE.

Hyman, J., Baldry, C., Scholarios, D. and Bunzel, D. (2003) 'Work-life imbalance in call centres and software development', *British Journal of Industrial Relations, 41*, 215–39.

*Labour Research* (2003), 'Childcare costs still prohibitive', June, 12–14.

McKie, L., Bowlby, S. and Gregory, S. (1999) 'Connecting gender, power and the household', in McKie, L., Bowlby, S. and Gregory, S. (eds) (1999), *Gender, Power and the Household*, Basingstoke: Macmillan, 3–21.

McRae, S. (1999) 'Introduction: family and household change in Britain', in McRae, S. (ed.) (1999), *Changing Britain: Families and Households in the 1990s*, Oxford: Oxford University Press, 1–33.

Oakley, A. (1974) *Housewife*, Harmondsworth: Penguin Books.

Pahl, R. (1984) *Divisions of Labour*, Oxford: Blackwell.

Purcell, K., Hogarth, T. and Simm, C. (1999) *Whose Flexibility?* York: York Publishing Services.

Taylor, P. and Bain, P. (1999), '"An assembly line in the head": Work and employee relations in the call centre', *Industrial Relations Journal, 30/2*, 101–17.

Taylor, P., Mulvey, G., Hyman, J. and Bain, P. (2002),'Work organization, control and the experience of work in call centres', *Work, Employment and Society, 16/1*, 151–69.

Taylor, R. (2002) *The Future of Work-Life Balance*, Swindon: ESRC UK Time Use Survey (2000), London: Office for National Statistics.

White, M., Hill, S., McGovern, P., Mills, C. and Smeaton, D. (2003) '"High performance" management practices, working hours and work-life balance', *British Journal of Industrial Relations, 41*, 175–96.

# 8

# Mens' Conditions of Employment and the Division of Childcare Between Parents

*Irene Bruegel and Anne Gray*

It has long been clear that the increase in women's paid employment has not evoked a compensating increase in the time men spend on childcare (Young and Willmott, 1973; Pilcher, 2000; Gershuny, 2000). Gershuny *et al.* (1994) suggested that adaptation was delayed in the 1980s by the childhood experience of that generation of parents, whose own parents generally have adopted a traditional sexual division of labour. Today, however, the majority of parents of young children grew up in the 1970s and 1980s, under a rather different domestic regime. Though attitudes have undoubtedly changed and there is good evidence that many men are spending more time with their children (Sullivan, 2000), the gender imbalance continues (O'Brien and Shemilt, 2003).

In this chapter we consider how changes in employment conditions and rights may have affected the division of childcare time between mothers and fathers, whilst recognising that a very wide range of factors will govern changing practices. This stance derives from research on the feminisation of employment in Britain and an interest in seeing how social context and social relations help explain behaviour beyond the preferences and characteristics of atomised individuals (Granovetter, 1985; Reskin, McBrier and Kmec, 1999; Blair-Loy and Wharton, 2002).

Our starting point is Carolyn Vogler's finding (1994: 59) that in the 1980s 'domestic sexism was directly related to segregation' in the British labour market in that 'men living in households with a more traditional division of labour were more likely to be working in segregated jobs' (1994: 61). Since that time a number of changes in conditions of employment can be argued to have affected the space for family life, some positive, others negative. There is little consensus on the scale of many of the changes, or their impact on different groups of employees (Bradley *et al.*, 2000), and there is still less about the potential effect on childcare practice.

This chapter is concerned with two related changes which could have raised the level of male involvement in childcare. The first is the numerical increase in the proportion of women employed in traditionally 'male' jobs. The underlying argument is that this form of quantitative feminisation has a qualitative effect. Insofar as more men are working alongside women, some loosening of the 'masculine ethic' and some convergence of working time regimes can be expected, which in turn could enable men to spend more time with their children. As Le Feuvre (1999) and Bruegel (2001) both point out, feminisation of the labour force – in the sense of an increased presence of women – takes many different forms. Here we are concerned specifically with increases in the numbers in mixed workplaces and consequent behavioural changes.

The second, related, change is the rising concern with the provision of 'family-friendly' working conditions and with the wider 'work–life balance', which could be expected to have loosened the constraints on fathers' involvement with their children's care, even if family-friendly employment is generally constructed as a means of reducing the stress on mothers in employment.

Against this is the evidence of rising working hours for fathers in the UK, up until 1999 (O'Brien and Shemilt, 2003), bucking the trend amongst many other groups of full-time workers. In 2000 over a quarter of fathers worked more than 48 hours per week, compared to less than one in five men without dependent children (ONS, 2001). As a result, convergence in working time between partners in a couple is limited to those without dependent children. Against this, too, are the arguments that considerable numbers of workers are experiencing pressure to work more unsocial hours, with less 'sovereignty' over the hours they work (Schor, 1991; Ferri and Smith, 1996; Perrons, 2003) and that even where men have access to parental leave many fail to take it up, even where it is paid (Brandth and Kvande, 2002), or where they are working outside 'traditional' workplaces, in parts of the so-called 'new economy' (Cooper, 2002; Perrons, 2003).

This chapter uses three large scale surveys to consider the relationship between fathers' employment and their involvement in childcare in Britain at the beginning of the 21st century. In the first section we document the way parenthood continues to differentiate fathers' and mothers' employment experience. In the life stage in which domestic labour is at a maximum, gender differences in paid labour are at their greatest. For this the Labour Force Survey provides the largest sample of people in employment available in the UK.

The second section draws on the Workplace Employment Relations Survey (WERS) of 1998 which has been used extensively to document the patterns of availability of family-friendly work practices (Cully *et al.*, 1999; Dex and Smith, 2001a). We examine how the gender composition of the immediate workgroup impacts on the perceived availability of family-friendly work provisions amongst parents and on their hours of work. This confirms the argument of Vogler (1994) about such effects; men working in the most male of workgroups, while often parents of dependent children, work longer hours and have a lower perception of the possibility of working more flexible hours. This may or may not reflect the actual availability of such an option.

The final section of the chapter draws on our ongoing analysis of the Time Use Survey 2000. We concentrate our analysis on the 739 couples with children under 16 where both partners completed detailed diary information, and in particular on the sub-set of 472 with children under 12 and fathers in employment. We look both at differences in the *share* of childcare taken by men as against women and at differences between men in how much time is devoted to childcare and paid employment. This is to see how far the gender environment of the workplace, work–life balance provision and hours regimes impact on resident father's recorded childcare practice.

## Parental divides in work time and work type

Though the feminisation of paid employment is associated with the demise of the sole male breadwinner, men remain the primary breadwinners in the majority of households and particularly in households with children (Table 8.1). Consequently, gender differences in patterns of employment, hours of work, types of employment and remuneration are now more centred on those who have, or who have had, dependent children. Mothers work shorter hours in more local jobs than other women and are therefore particularly concentrated in work traditionally regarded as 'women's work' (Hanson and Pratt, 1995). Men who have children are known to work longer hours than other men, even allowing for differences in age (Harrop and Moss, 1995; O'Brien and Shemilt, 2003). They now tend to work as unsocial hours as other men (Warin *et al.*, 1999), a change from the pattern of the late 1980s (Fagan, 2001). Table 8.1 shows differences in working time in 2002 and how it relates to the age of the youngest child in the family. Here hours of work are computed as the sum of all hours worked for pay, including in second jobs, and are averaged for each group, firstly, over all those in work including part-timers and, secondly, over all those under 60. The gender gap is expressed as the degree to which men's rates are higher, as a percentage of the average woman. The gender gap in hours of work is now relatively small for employed men and women who do not have children under the age of 16 – with men working around 25 per cent more hours than all women in this group; whereas differences of 40–101 per cent in working hours persist to this day between men and women with children. Fathers work on average twice as many hours as those mothers who are employed when their children are under five. Even

*Table 8.1* Gender differences between men and women by parenthood and age of youngest child in family

| | Hours of paid work (employees) | | | Hours of paid work (all under 60) | | | Hourly wage (those employed) | | |
|---|---|---|---|---|---|---|---|---|---|
| | Male | Female | % Gap | Male | Female | % Gap | Male | Female | % Gap |
| no child under 18 | 37.0 | 29.0 | 27.6 | 33.2 | 21.9 | 50.0 | £10.60 | £8.50 | 24.7 |
| married or cohabiting with: | | | | | | | | | |
| youngest child under 5 | 40.5 | 20.1 | 101.5 | 36.5 | 11.7 | 212.0 | £12.40 | £8.90 | 39.3 |
| youngest child 5–11 | 40.7 | 24.3 | 67.5 | 37.4 | 18.5 | 102.2 | £12.10 | £7.90 | 53.2 |
| youngest child 12–16 | 37.0 | 26.0 | 42.3 | 36.4 | 21.7 | 67.7 | £10.50 | £7.50 | 40.0 |
| n = | *20793* | *18533* | | *23832* | *25557* | | *5297* | *5477* | |

*Source*: Labour Force Survey, 2002 (Sept–Nov data set).

Putting together the information in column 2 Table 8.1 on hours of work with column 3 on hourly rates shows that men in households with children under five earned four times as much as their partners in 2002; those with children of primary school age earned three times as much and those with older children, almost two and a half times as much.

where the youngest child is at primary school, fathers' working hours are dramatically greater than mothers, though the difference declines as children enter secondary education. As one would expect, the differences are still greater when non-employed mothers are brought into the picture (column 2). Across all couples with dependent children, men do three times as much paid work as women, compared to just 50 per cent more where there are no dependent children.

Parenthood affects both men's and women's pay, but in diametrically different directions. As Sue Harkness (1996) has shown, in addition to working longer hours, fathers earn more per hour than other men, while mothers earn less per hour than other women, even when almost all the other factors known to affect pay are included in the analysis (Anderson *et al.*, 2001). The scale of the crude gender gaps in pay for parents and others are shown in the third section of Table 8.1. Some of the disparities between parents and others reflect the impact of pay on behaviour: low earning men may not become fathers; mothers with low earning potential may not seek employment. Even so, mothers earn 40 per cent less than their partners, compared to a 25 per cent gap for couples without children. While the lower hourly earnings of mothers can be explained from the tendency of mothers to work locally in part-time jobs and for these to be paid less per hour than other jobs, the positive association of hourly pay with fatherhood – other things being equal – still needs explanation.

In Table 8.2 the hourly pay of 25,000 male and female WERS 98 employees is analysed by occupational group and within that by the gender composition of the workgroup of respondents, for men and women separately in columns 1 and 2. Where they said their work colleagues (people doing the same kind of job as themselves at their workplace) were 'entirely' men or 'mainly' men, these were classed as 'male' jobs. 'Female' jobs were defined equivalently. In each occupation and for both men and women, those working in male environments invariably have higher pay. Thus the 114 male professionals who worked alongside women earned on average £9.80 an hour, compared to a rate of £11.60 for the 932 men who had professional jobs in more male environments. The second column of Table 8.2 shows a similar effect for women. The table also gives average pay for men and women in each occupation. This includes those in mixed jobs, for whom actual pay is not shown.

One possibility is that the positive 'fatherhood' pay premium reflects the tendency of fathers to work in more male-dominated types of work than other men. Table 8.3 shows how men with dependent children are more likely to be working in more male workgroups. For example, 36 per cent of those with children aged 12 to 16 said they worked exclusively with men, while only 28 per cent of men without children were working in such jobs. We created an index of the gender composition of workplaces to test how far this relationship simply reflected the increasingly likelihood that men work alongside other men as they get older. In practice age was an

*Table 8.2* Hourly pay by gender and gender profile of workplace 1998

| | | Men | | Women | |
|---|---|---|---|---|---|
| | | base | £ hourly | base | £ hourly |
| **Managers** | | | | | |
| 'male' job | | 856 | £11.40 | 92 | £11.10 |
| 'female' job | | 67 | £10.60 | 301 | £8.90 |
| | all | 1520 | £11.40 | 719 | £10.00 |
| **Professionals** | | | | | |
| 'male' job | | *932* | £11.60 | *104* | £10.80 |
| 'female' job | | *114* | £9.80 | *727* | £10.10 |
| | all | *1853* | £12.00 | *1488* | £10.30 |
| **Ass. Professionals** | | | | | |
| 'male' job | | *692* | £9.00 | *74* | £9.20 |
| 'female' job | | *79* | £7.20 | *845* | £7.80 |
| | all | *1089* | £8.90 | *1259* | £8.00 |
| **Clerical** | | | | | |
| 'male' job | | *186* | £6.97 | *72* | £5.97 |
| 'female' job | | *148* | £6.79 | *2411* | £5.99 |
| | all | *777* | £6.90 | *3380* | £6.10 |
| **Personal/Protective** | | | | | |
| 'male' job | | *561* | £9.10 | *52* | £8.90 |
| 'female' job | | *58* | £5.07 | *845* | £4.98 |
| | all | *955* | £8.10 | *1161* | £5.10 |
| **Sales** | | | | | |
| 'male' job | | *283* | £6.45 | *38* | £5.21 |
| 'female' job | | *96* | £4.30 | *1162* | £4.30 |
| | all | *704* | £5.70 | *1800* | £4.60 |
| **Operative** | | | | | |
| 'male' job | | *2009* | £6.20 | *83* | £6.70 |
| 'female' job | | *21* | £4.50 | *416* | £4.30 |
| | all | *2507* | £6.10 | *822* | £4.70 |
| **All** | | | | | |
| 'male' job | | *8618* | £7.87 | *596* | £8.29 |
| 'female' job | | *654* | £6.97 | *8276* | £5.90 |
| | all | *13226* | £7.90 | *12741* | £6.30 |

*Source*: WERS 1998 employee dataset.

important determinant of the gender composition of workgroups, but having a child, and the number of children under the age of 12 were independently and significantly associated ($p<.001$) with working in a more male environment.

## Hours regimes and the gender composition of workplaces

Though men and women working alongside one another can often work rather different hours, for example, as men take up opportunities for over-

*Table 8.3* Male employees: gender composition of work group by parenthood status

| | Gender composition of workgroup | | | | | |
|---|---|---|---|---|---|---|
| | Men alone % | Mainly men % | Mixed % | Mainly women | Total % | Base |
| Attribute | | | | | | |
| no child | 28.4 | 33.6 | 32.1 | 5.7 | 99.8 | *7973* |
| child 0–4 | 31.3 | 37.8 | 27.3 | 3.5 | 99.9 | *2218* |
| child 5–11 | 32.1 | 37.0 | 26.7 | 3.9 | 99.7 | *2782* |
| child 12–16 | 35.7 | 34.3 | 26.3 | 3.5 | 99.8 | *2750* |

*Source*: WERS 1998 employee dataset (weighted).

time, it is still evident that working hours are set at the workplace level, both formally as set out in conditions of employment and informally as cultures of 'fair' working hours develop. Case studies of workplaces have illustrated the strong pull of such cultures, even in the face of provision of more family-friendly working environments (Fried, 1999).

The WERS 1998 study shows that the gender composition of the workgroup has important effects on the average hours worked, even if occupations are separately considered. This is illustrated in Table 8.4, which is of a similar form to Table 8.2, contrasting in separate columns for men and women the effect of working mainly with men or mainly with women. Thus male professionals working in largely male environments tended to work a 42.5 hour week in 1998, compared to a 38.5 hour week for professionals who worked in more female environments. Similarly women who worked alongside men worked hours that were closer to the male level than women who worked in more female milieux. This is not surprising given the association of women's work with part-time work. What it suggests, however, is that those looking for higher paid areas of employment within their occupational groups may find themselves having to accept longer hours than they might desire by the nature of the 'hours regime' in such workplaces

A similar pattern emerges when the wider 'hours regime' is considered. In line with the longer hours they work, fathers are more likely to do overtime – 64 per cent of all fathers in the WERS sample were working some overtime hours, compared to 58 per cent of other men. Table 8.5 shows that this was partly to do with their tendency to work in more male environments in which overtime was more often compulsory. The first part of the Table shows that the proportion of men who worked overtime which they classed as compulsory varied by occupation, with professionals more likely to be working such hours than those in clerical or sales jobs. Within clerical and sales work the gender environment of the individual workplace again

*Table 8.4* Average total working hours by gender and job type

| | Men | Women |
|---|---|---|
| **Managers** | | |
| *base* | *1534* | *727* |
| 'male' jobs | 47.2 | 46.5 |
| 'female' jobs | 43.8 | 39.5 |
| **Professionals** | | |
| *base* | *1867* | *1499* |
| 'male' jobs | 42.5 | 40.2 |
| 'female' jobs | 38.5 | 34.2 |
| **Associate Professionals** | | |
| *base* | *1100* | *1269* |
| 'male' jobs | 41.6 | 37.3 |
| 'female' jobs | 35.6 | 30.7 |
| **Clerical** | | |
| *base* | *785* | *3436* |
| 'male' jobs | 38.5 | 37.7 |
| 'female' jobs | 36.1 | 31.5 |
| **Personal/Protective** | | |
| *base* | *956* | *1179* |
| 'male' jobs | 40.7 | 37.3 |
| 'female' jobs | 29.0 | 23.3 |
| **Sales** | | |
| *base* | *708* | *1812* |
| 'male' jobs | 39.9 | 36.0 |
| 'female' jobs | 21.7 | 21.6 |
| **Operatives** | | |
| *base* | *2533* | *838* |
| 'male' jobs | 44.7 | 39.0 |
| 'female' jobs | 36.1 | 35.6 |
| **All Jobs** | 41.2 | 30.1 |
| 'male' jobs | 43.0 | 39.0 |
| 'female' jobs | 33.0 | 28.0 |

*Source*: WERS 1998 employee dataset.

matters. The minority of men working in female dominated environments in shops and offices did much less compulsory overtime than those working in 'male' jobs. Only amongst professionals was there no significant difference in the degree of compulsory overtime working.

Table 8.5 also shows that there is no difference between fathers of young children and other men in the degree to which they do any compulsory overtime; the gender composition of their immediate job is far more critical. In line with the breadwinner model of fatherhood, fathers are more

*Table 8.5* Overtime amongst male employees

| | | All | 'Male' jobs | 'Female' jobs |
|---|---|---|---|---|
| **a. Proportion of group undertaking overtime and 'required to' by occupation** | | | | |
| Professionals | % on compulsory overtime | 24.4 | 22.6 | 21.7 |
| | *base* | *1904* | *962* | *115* |
| Clerical | % on compulsory overtime | 10.7 | 23.0 | 5.0 |
| | *base* | *784* | *189* | *152* |
| Sales | % on compulsory overtime | 17.4 | 24.0 | 6.0 |
| | *base* | *755* | *294* | *106* |
| **b. Proportion of group undertaking overtime and 'required to' by parenthood** | | | | |
| no child under 12 | % on compulsory overtime | 19.0 | 19.0 | 11.0 |
| | *base* | *9619* | *6129* | *517* |
| has child under 12 | % on compulsory overtime | 19.4 | 20.0 | 11.0 |
| | *base* | *4132* | *2873* | *154* |
| **c. Proportion of group undertaking overtime and 'needing the money' by parenthood** | | | | |
| no child under 12 | % on financially driven overtime | 19.5 | 22.8 | 15.1 |
| | *base* | *9619* | *6129* | *517* |
| has child under 12 | % on financially driven overtime | 24.3 | 28.9 | 7.1 |
| | *base* | *4132* | *2873* | *154* |

*Source*: WERS 1998 employee dataset.

likely to be under financial pressure to do overtime. Nearly a quarter of all fathers were doing overtime for financial reasons, compared to under a fifth of other men. Being in a 'male' job, organised traditionally to provide overtime working made an important difference to the degree to which men were actually working overtime mainly for financial gain. So only 15 per cent of non-fathers working in 'female' jobs did overtime predominantly for financial reasons, compared to 23 per cent in 'male' jobs. Numbers are small, but it looks as if fathers working in 'female' jobs are particularly unlikely to engage in overtime for financial reasons, despite the apparent financial pressures on them.

The composition of the workgroup also affects access to family-friendly work provisions, though not uniformly. In WERS all employees were asked whether, if they needed them, any of the family-friendly provisions listed in Table 8.6 would be available to them. They were also asked how understanding their managers were about family responsibilities. T-tests showed that in general the small minority of fathers who work in more 'female' types of jobs found management significantly ($p<.001$) more likely to offer better facilities and to be understanding of family pressures than those in more 'male' environments. In general, despite their tendency to work in more 'male' milieux, fathers appear slightly better off than men in general in access to family-friendly provision.

This could, however, be an artefact of the way the question was framed. Fathers, and especially those that work in more 'female' environments, are likely to be more aware of available facilities and more able to identify themselves as potentially having need for them. There is no way of testing this with respect to the difference between fathers and others, but in a

*Table 8.6* Family friendliness for men; fathers by job type

| % saying/having | Fathers | | | All men |
|---|---|---|---|---|
| | 'Male job' | 'Female job' | All including mixed | |
| Management understands family responsibilities | 46.4 | 59.0 | 49.4 | 50.1 |
| Flexible working | 22.0 | 38.0 | 25.0 | 27.0 |
| Job sharing | 4.6 | 32.1 | 9.9 | 9.9 |
| Parental leave | 24.3 | 45.4 | 38.1 | 24.1 |
| Can work from home | 10.4 | 12.8 | 12.7 | 10.9 |
| Nursery | 2.6 | 4.1 | 3.8 | 3.1 |
| *Base numbers* | *4162* | *218* | *5958* | *13550* |

*Source*: WERS 1998 employee dataset.

separate questionnaire managers in more 'female' workplaces reported better access to such facilities, alongside wider policies focused on equal opportunities (Bruegel, 2004). This suggests that the gender composition of the workplace makes a difference to the facilities available both to fathers and mothers, as O'Brien and Shemilt (2003) found in their analysis of the Work–Life Balance 2000 Survey.

## The impact of family-friendly policies on the gender division of childcare labour

The WERS study, however, tells us very little about the actual take-up of family-friendly policies in different types of work environments. Indeed given the fact that such policies are not generally available as of right, the gender environment of different workplaces is likely to affect take-up rates. As the American literature (Fried, 1999; Sandberg, 1999) makes very clear, both men and women in highly pressurised positions can be wary about being seen to take advantage of any parental leave arrangements. However, in more 'female' environments precedents and practices may emerge that help break any such taboo. On the other hand, family-friendly arrangements are often conceived as privileges which the firm may only find affordable while they apply to a few employees. In such circumstances, a more 'female' environment could militate against men's use of such provisions, nurseries being perhaps the prime example.

The Time Use Survey 2000 enables us to see how access to family-friendly provision impinges on fathers' involvement in childcare. The Time Use Survey uses the harmonised question about 'special working arrangements' also found in the Labour Force Survey. This refers to the individual's own working arrangements, rather than the more hypothetical access to flexible working found in WERS. Here we consider only whether or not men say their working arrangements include 'flexitime', since the number of fathers with access to other types of special working arrangements are too small for analysis.

Similarly, it is possible to identify men who sometimes work at home from the Time Use Survey, but this measure of ability to work at home is again rather different to that found in WERS. It will include all men, including the self-employed, who do *any* of the work relating to their main job either 'at' or 'from home' in their main job. This could be work outside normal working hours. The Time Use Survey contains a lot of information on childcare provided in nursery care, by childminders and other family members, but has no information comparable to WERS on employer support of nursery care.

The advantage of using a Time Use Survey as a measure of the domestic division of labour has been explained in detail by Gershuny (2000). The data in the UK Time Use Survey are derived from diaries filled in over two

24-hour periods. In principle measurement error should be less with diary records than where households are asked to estimate time and/or the share of responsibility (Bond and Sales, 2001). The Time Use Survey distinguishes between physical care, feeding, playing, teaching and talking to the child, but in this paper we only analyse the total number of minutes devoted to childcare on the days the diary was completed. Survey respondents are asked to record their primary activity in each ten-minute time-slot, and may also record a 'secondary' activity which they did simultaneously. No index of the gender composition of different workplaces equivalent to that of WERS 1998 is available from the Time Use Survey. Instead we classified fathers in the Time Use Survey by the gender composition of the detailed occupational unit of their employment, combining data from the Labour Force Surveys 2001 and 2002 to derive a reliable index for many of the units of the Classification of Occupations 2000.

Overall on about half the diary days both fathers and mothers of children under 16 contributed to childcare. In another 30 per cent men contributed no time at all and in a sixth, neither parent recorded any time spent in childcare. In a very small number, less than 5 per cent, fathers alone provided the childcare.

Table 8.7a shows the differences between these diary days, separating out those families in which no childcare was done that day (last column) and those in which the resident father did none (first column) and splitting those households that shared the childcare time between them into three groups: those where the man's contribution was around or below average (1–30%), above average (31–50%) more than 50 per cent of the recorded time. In Table 8.7a, *t*-tests show the significant differences in the profiles – father's age, hours of work etc – between households where men did no childcare and those in which he contributed some time.

*Table 8.7a* Characteristics of households by father's share of childcare on diary day

| | Father's share of childcare | | | | no childcare |
|---|---|---|---|---|---|
| | 0 | 1–30% | 31–50% | over 50% | |
| *Base* | *407* | *291* | *179* | *264* | *228* |
| Age of respondent*** | 38.6 | 35.8 | 35.9 | 37.8 | 42.0 |
| Mins. in main job*** | 431.0 | 300.0 | 178.0 | 136 | 378.0 |
| Gender comp. index* | 23.4 | 29.2 | 27.7 | 26.7 | 21.4 |
| External paid care* | 0.78 | 1.4 | 0 | 0.01 | 2.9 |
| Other family help*** | 1.0 | 0.5 | 0.5 | 1.2 | 4.5 |
| Number of children under 3*** | 0.19 | 0.47 | 0.44 | 0.34 | 0.03 |
| number of children 3–8* | 0.64 | 0.85 | 0.88 | 0.73 | 0.16 |

*Source*: Computed from ONS Time Use Survey 2000.
*Notes*: ***p<.001, **p<.01, *p<.05.

The age of the father, the number of minutes he worked on the day in question and the number of children under three all affect the share of the childcare undertaken by fathers, in generally predictable ways. Whether a father helps at all seems to depend on the presence of a young child, but families in which men do half or more of the childcare tend to have fewer, rather than more, young children. Again, whether he helps at all seems to reflect his age, but amongst those that undertake childcare, involvement appears greater amongst older fathers. Those that do no childcare are not only older, but are also more likely to work in more male occupations; on average amongst those that did no childcare, 21–23.5 per cent of the workforce in their detailed occupation was female, compared to 27–29 per cent amongst those that did a share. There was a clear, statistically significant ($p<.05$), difference in the work environment between men who provided no childcare in the week and those providing some, with those that made no contribution working in far more male occupations. However fathers who made a large contribution to childcare on a particular weekday generally worked less than three hours on that day and may therefore be less influenced in their childcare by their experiences at work.

Those households that appeared to not spend any time in childcare on the diary day had few young children, but also used much more external paid care (2.9 minutes, compared to less than a minute for other groups) and family help (4.5 minutes) than the average in the diary week. They do genuinely appear to be households in which childcare needs on the diary days were low, or met by other people.

In those cases where the father provided no childcare on the day in question he worked on average of just over seven hours (431 minutes in main job). Table 8.7b expresses this relationship another way: those fathers who worked over eight hours on the day in question contributed about 17 per cent of the childcare time of the couple, significantly below the average, though this may be made up by some fathers at the weekend (Yeung *et al.*, 2001). The division of childcare time between parents clearly reflects the division of paid labour between them, with the small number of non-employed fathers contributing nearly two-fifths of the childcare, but job-type appears to have no effect, with the self employed, managers, professionals and manual workers appearing to undertake similar shares of childcare. The Time Use Survey 2000 provides some evidence that men who are able to work from home and who have access to flexitime undertake a greater share of the total 'primary activity' childcare of a household (Table 8.7b). It suggests however, that where families use formal childcare, fathers provide significantly more of the total childcare than average ($p<.005$), an issue we explore further in the regression analyses below.

The Time Use Survey shows that father's childcare time peaks when the youngest child is two. This suggests that they are not just opting to play or watch TV with older children, though we can never know from a Time Use

*Table 8.7b* Father's share of childcare: Differences from mean contribution according to household characteristics

| Variable | All fathers of children under 16 | |
|---|---|---|
| | *base* | mean % |
| All | *1170* | 28.4 |
| Weekday | *605* | 25.6*** |
| Mother not employed | *329* | 23.7*** |
| Father not employed | *89* | 37.0*** |
| Father self employed | *190* | 24.6 |
| Father can work at home | *127* | 33.5** |
| Father has flexitime | *108* | 33.8** |
| Father works over 8 hours | *355* | 17.0*** |
| Father manager/professional | *532* | 28.8 |
| Father manual | *334* | 23.6 |
| Use formal childcare | *351* | 30.5** |
| Use other family care | *38* | 21.2 |
| Rural area | *84* | 21.8*** |

*Source*: computed from ONS Time Use Survey 2000. *t-test* of significant differences of means.
*Notes*: ***p<.001, **p<.01, *p<.05: T-tests of the difference between mean according to household characteristics and overall mean.

Survey how much care or attention they (or mothers for that matter) are putting into the time they spend with children. They may be like one father amongst Perrons' respondents who did his childcare while at work, arguing 'that children do not need a high input all the time' and that 'the notion of a special period of childhood is a particularly western concept' (Perrons, 2003: 85). Nor, for the moment, do we know whether fathers are solely responsible for children in the time they record as childcare.

If we confine the analysis to fathers of younger children and include the time fathers spend in childcare as an adjunct of another activity, like eating or cooking while tending the child, the proportions of fathers who record no childcare drops quite sharply. Looking first at single days, amongst fathers of under 12s, 26 per cent record no 'primary' childcare either in their weekday or weekend diaries, compared to 46 per cent of all those with children under 16, recorded in Table 8.7a. For fathers of under 5s, the proportion doing no 'primary' childcare on either diary day is only 12 per cent. When we construct an estimate of father's childcare per week from the two diaries combined (adding five times the weekday amount to twice the weekend amount), the proportion doing none declines. After adding 'secondary' childcare it falls further still, to 18 per cent for all fathers of under 12s and 7 per cent for resident fathers of under 5s.

Both mothers' and fathers' childcare time falls off with the age of the youngest child, but mother's falls more steeply. There is indeed a positive correlation between mothers' and fathers' childcare time, reflecting the different needs of children of different ages, different family sizes and different cultural patterns (0.269 between primary childcare of fathers and that of mothers; 0.131 between the total childcare time of each parent, including 'secondary' activity (both significant at $p<.001$).

Though the total time spent in childcare may reflect 'cultural' factors, we found no significant differences in the *share* of childcare taken by men across a range of cultural variables (Table 8.7b). Neither region, nor age, ethnicity, education, occupation, income, car ownership, or housing type, seemed to affect the distribution of recorded *primary* childcare between partners. There was some evidence that men who lived in 'rural areas' according to the 'Mosaic' classification of neighbourhood made a smaller contribution, possibly reflecting longer commuting times. There are too few ethnic minority families in the Time Use Survey to be sure that there is no ethnic effect.

Education and occupational status would seem to affect the recording of childcare. Men with more education and in managerial or professional jobs recorded rather more time undertaking childcare alongside other activities than other men. (Managers and professionals recorded five per cent more secondary childcare than the average, but only two per cent more aggregate primary and secondary care). As a result education and occupation appear to influence shares of aggregate childcare, though no difference is identifiable for primary care alone. Fathers of under 12s who left education before the age of 19 undertook a quarter of aggregate parental childcare compared to 35 per cent for those who stayed longer ($p<.001$). In line with this managerial/professional men recorded undertaking 29 per cent of combined primary and secondary childcare, compared to only 15 per cent for small employers and own account workers ($p<.001$).

The contribution of fathers would then seem to depend on two factors. Firstly the distribution of paid working hours between partners, and secondly – in complex ways – on the use of external care for the children. Later, we show that use of external care has a significant effect on fathers' childcare time where both partners have full-time jobs. Table 8.7b suggests that family-friendly provisions for fathers are too limited to have much effect on the division of childcare labour between parents: where men can work from home and where they use flexitime, they are responsible for a slightly higher than average share of childcare and do twice as much childcare as those fathers working over 8 hours. We do not know whether this is because men who are willing to take a larger share of childcare make more use of what facilities are available or whether the availability of flexitime and work from home stimulates fathers to provide more care. Later we see that the effect of flexitime in any case disappears when we control for fathers' working hours, as does any effect of the gender environment of the workplace.

## Regression analysis on the influence of father's hours of work on their childcare time

In analysing the interactions between the various factors that might determine the amount of childcare a father undertakes we concentrate in our regression analyses on the instances where fathers are most likely to provide some care. That is on the average weekly primary and secondary care of children below the age of 12. We do, however, ignore the small number of 'role-swap' families and exclude non-employed fathers.

Table 8.8 examines the determinants of father's weekly childcare in minutes, aggregating primary and secondary care, and including time in escorting children to school and elsewhere as time devoted to childcare. In Model 1 of the Table, we show that the age of the youngest child and the 'trade-off' between childcare, paid work and other activities accounts for some 43 per cent of variance in father's childcare. The effects of an extra hour of employment on childcare are of a similar order – a reduction of around 35 minutes – to that of an extra hour of any other activity. They are greater for fathers of under 5s but otherwise fathers of under 5s behave broadly like others, and separate regressions are not shown for them. The high proportion of the variance in aggregate childcare time explained in Model 1 emerges from the fact that all time in 'primary' activities must total to 24 hours, and primary activities account for 60 per cent of aggregate childcare time. Model 1 'explains' father's childcare time more in a statistical than a behavioural sense since other activities may be either causes or effects of variations in childcare time. It suggests, however, that for any given hours of work, men increase childcare time most at the expense of sports and related activities, rather than, say, domestic chores. Although work time will usually be determined by the employer and hence time for childcare might be assumed to be an outcome of such an external constraint, it is possible that for some men at least, a close relationship between hours of work and hours in childcare reflects a different dynamic; that men may *choose* to work longer hours in preference to childcare (Hochschild, 1997).

In Models 2 and 3 of the Table we show the influence on father's childcare time of his working hours (including commuting) and his socio-economic characteristics, including his partner's employment status. Once child's age, father's full-time education and occupation and mother's employment are held constant, the influence of hours of work on time spent in childcare drops considerably, but remains significant. For any given hours of work and job type, every extra year of full-time education increases the time a father spends on childcare, except where his partner is in full-time work (Model 3), or part-time work (Model 8), when his education has no significant effect. This may be because the differences in educational levels amongst husbands of mothers who work full-time or who work part-time are quite restricted.

Model 2 which includes a dummy for whether or not the mother works part-time, shows that father's childcare is greatest when his partner is in part-time employment and drops after that, with increases in hours of work amongst full-time women workers having no significant effect on hours of childcare provided by a man (Model 3). Model 6 suggests that this is associated with the use of external childcare amongst full-time worker-mothers. Where external childcare is used for at least one child, fathers spend an average of four hours a week less in childcare, conditional on hours of work, those of their partners and the age of the child. Model 5 suggests for the very small number of families using nursery care (less than 10 per cent of cases where the woman worked full-time), men's childcare time drops in line with hours of childcare. Otherwise no specific effects of external childcare time are identifiable, possibly because the variable available from the Time Use Survey is a broad brush measure, relating to total time in each type of childcare for all children in the household.

Amongst women in part-time employment in contrast, Model 7, shows no relationship between the use of external childcare and father's childcare time. Indeed, where the mother works part-time, use of external childcare is associated with a *larger* time input from the father (average 640 minutes per week) than if no external care is used (average 461 minutes per week; $p = 0.051$). Although this relationship is not statistically significant at the conventional cut off, it would seem that father's childcare time complements external care where the mother works part-time but tends to be substituted by external care to some degree when she works full-time. The observed complementarity may arise from the problems of scheduling part-time work and part-time care (La Valle *et al.*, 2002).

Taken together, including women not in employment, fathers can be seen (Model 9) to spend slightly less time in childcare when external care is used, once allowance is made for their working hours and the mother's working hours.

Whilst working at home sometimes does seem to increase father's childcare time on weekdays, even when working time is allowed for, less than 15 per cent of fathers have these privileges so that the numbers are too small to obtain reliable estimates of the difference. Flexitime and the gender composition of the father's occupation, do not seem to have any impact on childcare, once hours of work are kept constant.

In regression 8, we add the mother's childcare time to the list of variables. After controlling for age of youngest child, mother's work hours and father's socio-economic characteristics it has a small independent, positive effect on father's childcare time. There seems to be a disposition for some couples to spend more time in childcare than others independently of children's age or parents' work patterns, whether because of cultural factors, or particular children's needs, or because of differences in what they define as childcare.

*Table 8.8* Regression analyses with father's primary and secondary childcare (measured in minutes per week) as dependent variable

| | Model 1 | Model 2 | Model 3 | Model 4 | Model 5 | Model 6 | Model 7 | Model 8 | Model 9 |
|---|---|---|---|---|---|---|---|---|---|
| Population ('all' = families with under 12s ) | All | All | Mother f.t. employed | All | Mother f.t. employed | Mother f.t. employed | Mother p.t. employed | All | All |
| N | 472 | 430 | 100 | 426 | 97 | 106 | 197 | 432 | 398 |
| Adjusted R2 | 0.428 | 0.299 | 0.259 | 0.266 | 0.376 | 0.361 | 0.300 | 0.297 | 0.305 |
| F | 44.605 | 37.712 | 18.149 | 39.406 | 15.341 | 15.705 | 28.824 | 37.393 | 35.767 |
| Constant | 6300.18 | 462.756 | 1301.055 | 1130.593 | 718.518 | 1011.494 | 1401.066 | 411.630 | 0.178 |
| Beta coefficients which are significant (p<.05) | | | | | | | | | |
| Age of Youngest Child | –36.01 | –62.11 | –62.61 | –57.86 | –84.30 | –77.18 | –61.32 | –53.14 | –0.01 |
| Father's work time plus commuting (diary est.) | –0.61 | –0.18 | –0.18 | –0.17 | –0.16 | –0.18 | –0.21 | –0.18 | 0.00 |
| Father's domestic work | –0.45 | ~ | ~ | ~ | ~ | ~ | ~ | ~ | ~ |
| Father's other leisure | –0.60 | ~ | ~ | ~ | ~ | ~ | ~ | ~ | ~ |
| Father's personal care and sleep | –0.61 | ~ | ~ | ~ | ~ | ~ | ~ | ~ | ~ |
| Father's socialising | –0.56 | ~ | ~ | ~ | ~ | ~ | ~ | ~ | ~ |
| Father's sport etc | –0.67 | ~ | ~ | ~ | ~ | ~ | ~ | ~ | ~ |
| Father's voluntary activities | –0.45 | ~ | ~ | ~ | ~ | ~ | ~ | ~ | ~ |
| Age father finished full–time education | ~ | 41.57 | ns | ~ | ~ | ns | ns | 39.56 | 0.02 |
| Father = manager or professional | ~ | ns | ns | ~ | ~ | ns | 199.44 | ns | ns |
| Mother employed part time (dummy; 1 = yes, 0 = no) | ~ | 114.65 | – | 122.80 | – | – | – | ~ | ~ |

*Table 8.8* Regression analyses with father's primary and secondary childcare (measured in minutes per week) as dependent variable – *continued*

| | Model 1 | Model 2 | Model 3 | Model 4 | Model 5 | Model 6 | Model 7 | Model 8 | Model 9 |
|---|---|---|---|---|---|---|---|---|---|
| Population ('all' = families with under 12s ) | All | All | Mother f.t. employed | All | Mother f.t. employed | Mother f.t. employed | Mother p.t. employed | All | All |
| Mother's usual weekly work time in minutes | ~ | ~ | ~ | 0.05 | 0.29 | 0.24 | ns | ~ | ~ |
| Mother's weekly work and commuting time (diary est.) | ~ | –0.07 | ns | ~ | ~ | ~ | ns | 0.10 | 0.00 |
| Mother's weekly childcare time (primary & secondary) | ~ | ~ | ~ | ~ | ~ | ~ | ~ | 0.05 | ~ |
| All nursery care hours used by family in week | ~ | ~ | ~ | ns | -8.65 | ~ | ~ | ~ | ~ |
| All grandparent care hours used by family in week | ~ | ~ | ~ | ns | ns | ~ | ~ | ~ | ns |
| All childminder care hours used by family in week | ~ | ~ | ~ | ns | ns | ~ | ~ | ~ | ~ |
| Dummy for use of any external childcare (1 = yes, 2 = no) | ~ | ~ | ~ | ~ | –252.88 | ns | ~ | –0.07 | |

*Note*: ns = not significant, – not included in the model.

## Trends in father's childcare

Despite the possible over-estimation father's share of childcare, our estimates for 2000 at 28 per cent for all fathers and 30 per cent for fathers of those under five, is slightly smaller than the figure of 33 per cent for 1999 quoted by O'Brien and Shemilt (2003). This may reflect different methodologies for measuring the share of total parental childcare time.

Measures of total childcare time equally raise crucial questions of definition. Against our estimate of a total of 226.2 minutes per day ('primary' childcare only), by the average couple with a child under five years old in 2000, Fisher and Gershuny (1999) estimated a total of some 375 minutes for 1999. This makes for a rather different view of change since the early 1980s. Their estimate implies that there was an exponential rise in the total amount of time spent of childcare by parents – and hence by fathers – between 1984 and 1999, while our estimates suggest a continuing linear increase from 1974 in the time parents record as being spent in childcare as a primary activity.

The increase occurred in the context of rising working hours for fathers. On our estimates average total usual working hours for fathers computed from the Labour Force Survey rose by about half an hour, from 46.7 hours to 47.23 between 1984 and 2002. Thus the cross-sectional evidence of a negative relationship between working time and time spent with their children does not necessarily translate into cause and effect over time, on the evidence of the UK over the last 20–25 years. Clearly cultural changes, including increasing reliance on mother's earning power, have raised men's involvement with their children, above what it would have been just on trends in hours of work.

This point can be reinforced by looking at the different trends for professional, managerial and technical men from those for manual and clerical males. Over the period 1975–1997 Oriel Sullivan (2000) estimated that higher class men increased the time they spent with their children each day from an average of 7 to 18 minutes, while the rise for manual/clerical men was smaller, from 7 to 14 minutes. Using unpublished Labour Force Survey data for the same period we calculate that total usual working hours (including usual overtime) for fathers working in professional, managerial and technical jobs *rose* from an average of 45 hours and 20 minutes to just over 48 hours, while those for manual and clerical worker fathers *fell* from 49 hours 25 minutes to 47 hours 50 minutes. The change in time spent on childcare by the two groups identified by Sullivan thus bore little relation to the relative change in their working hours. It could have reflected changes in the number of young children between the two groups or differences in the patterns of change in the employment of their respective partners. Either way it reinforces the conclusion that some fathers have found it possible to increase the time they spend in childcare, despite rising working hours, though whether they were pushed or pulled and by whom, is another question.

## Conclusion

Whatever the evidence for families in general (Gershuny, 2000), the notion of a 'Time Famine' for parents of young children seems justified, especially for professional and managerial workers. It appears to relate to the traditional pattern of sex segregation in the labour market in which pay reflects, among other things, the gender composition of the particular labour market niche. Fathers continue, paradoxically perhaps, to be found in more sex-segregated workplaces with less child-friendly time regimes, exacerbating the sense of 'time-famine' for those with young children.

Our cross-sectional analysis tends to suggest that men's continued role as 'walking pay packages' may still constrain their involvement in childcare. Hence, as O'Brien and Shemilt (2003) point out, policies to increase mother's earnings, income support for working families, as well as policies to reduce the working day, could be important in enabling fathers to take a greater share in childcare within the household.

However, the picture is far from unequivocal and the constraints are not wholly economic. A decline in the degree of sex-segregated working as well as increases in the earning power of mothers since the 1980s would seem to have increased the choices open to men to engage more frequently in childcare. As the total amount of childcare undertaken has risen, so too, has the time men spend, and yet we are still far from gender convergence, expected on Gershuny *et al.*'s model of 'lagged adaptation' (1994).

The variation between families in the total childcare provided per child and in the share between parents suggests that the internal dynamics of family relations and differing concepts of children's needs interact with perceptions of economic pressures to produce a very complex picture of the division of childcare between parents. At base is the developing contradiction between the still dominant breadwinning conception of fatherhood and concepts of fatherhood as self-fulfilment and caring fatherliness. Even if they are working longer hours the evidence from our research is that some men can, and do, forgo other activities to spend more time with their children. In the British context fathers' support is especially important for mothers in part-time employment, sometimes because of difficulties organising external care to meet flexible and atypical part-time work hours, but sometimes as a preferred option, within wider constraints. On the other hand we have found, in line with Arlie Hochschild's (1997) more sceptical view of mens' commitment to childcare, that paid childcare and family childcare support is called upon to allow (some) fathers to continue to work long hours, when their partners are also employed for much of the working day.

These conclusions are based on a relatively limited analysis of the deployment of time in childcare across different couples. Unfortunately the Time Use Survey, while rich in detail, is not of a scale that would allow us to explore differences between families by class and education background any further. In this paper we also did not distinguish between 'child-minding' activities within the household, that is time spent looking after children to enable a partner to do something else and family engagement, the care of children as a joint activity of a couple and other children. Further analysis of the Time Use Survey which looked more deeply at what is involved in the time men record as being spent on childcare and at how they trade off different activities to gain time for childcare could provide a fuller understanding of the developing relationship between the sphere of paid work for men and the sphere of family in Britain today.

## Acknowledgements

This research was undertaken with the support of the ESRC Research Programme on the Future of Work L212252021 and the ESRC Family and Social Capital Research Group.

The authors would like to thank Mr. Eva Natamba for his assistance with computing tasks.

## References

Anderson, T., Forth, J., Metcalf, H. and Kirkby, S. (2001) *The Gender Pay Gap*, London: Cabinet Office; Women and Equality Unit.

Blair-Loy, M. and Wharton, A.S. (2002) 'Employees' Use of Work–Family Policies and the Workplace Social Context', *Social Forces* 80(3): 813–46.

Bond, S. and Sales, J. (2001) 'Household Work in the UK: An analysis of the British Household Panel Survey 1994', *Work Employment and Society* 15(2): 233–50.

Bradley, H., Erickson, M., Stephenson, C. and Williams, S. (2000) *Myths at Work*, Cambridge: Polity Press.

Brandth, B. and Kvande, E. (2002) 'Reflexive Fathers: Negotiating Parental Leave and Working Life', *Gender, Work and Organisation* 15(2): 186–203.

Bruegel, I. (2001) 'The Full Monty: The Feminisation of Employment and the unemployment of men' in Noon, M. and Ogbonna, E., *Work and Inequality*, Basingstoke: Palgrave.

Bruegel, I. (2004) 'Seeking the Critical Mass: Quantitative and Qualitative Aspects of Feminisation and Management in Britain in the 1990s', in Stewart, P. (ed.) *Employment, Trade Union Revival and the Future of Work*, Basingstoke: Palgrave.

Cooper, M. (2002) 'Fatherhood, Masculinity and Work in Silicon Valley' in Gerstel, N. (ed.), *Families at Work: Expanding the Bounds*, Nashville: Vanderbilt University Press.

Cully, M., Woodland, S. and O'Reilly, A. (1999) *Britain at Work as depicted by the 1998 Workplace Employee Relations Survey*, London: Routledge.

Dex, S. and Smith, C. (2001a) *Which British employees have access to family-friendly policies? An analysis of the 1998 Workplace Employee Relations Survey*, Judge Institute Research Paper No. WP/01, University of Cambridge.

Fagan, C. (2001) 'The Temporal Re-organisation of Employment and Household Rhythm of Work Schedules', *American Journal of Behavioural Science* 44(7): 1199–212.

Ferri, E. and Smith, K. (1996) *Parenting in the 1990s*, London: Family Policy Studies Centre.

Fisher, K. and Gershuny, J. (1999) 'Leisure in the UK across the Twentieth Century'. Working Paper 1999. 03 Institute for Social and Economic Research, Colchester: University of Essex.

Fried, M. (1999) *Taking Time: Parental Leave Policy and Corporate Culture*, Philadelphia: Temple University Press.

Gershuny, J., Godwin, M. and Jones, S. (1994) 'Domestic Revolution a Process of Lagged Adaptation' in Anderson, M., Bechhofer, F. and Gershuny, J. (eds), *The Social and Political Economy of the Household*, Oxford: Oxford University Press.

Gershuny, J. (2000) *Changing Times*, Oxford: Oxford University Press.

Granovetter, M. (1985) 'Economic Action and Social Structure: The Problem of Embeddedness', *American Journal of Sociology* 91: 481–510.

Hanson, S. and Pratt, G. (1995) *Gender, Work and Space*, London: Routledge.

Harkness, S. (1996) 'The Gender Earnings gap: Evidence from the UK', *Fiscal Studies* 7(2): 1–36.

Harrop, A. and Moss, P. (1995) 'Trends in Parental Employment', *Work, Employment and Society* 9(4): 421–44.

Hochschild, A. (1997) *The Time Bind: When Work Becomes Home and Home Becomes Work*, New York: Metropolitan Books.

La Valle, I., Arthur, S., Millward, C. and Scott, J. (2002) *Happy families? Atypical work and its influence on family life*', Bristol: Policy Press.

Le Feuvre, N. (1999) 'Gender, Occupational Feminization and Reflexivity: a Cross National Perspective' in Crompton, R. (ed.), *Restructuring Gender Relations and Employment*, Oxford: Oxford University Press.

O'Brien, M. and Shemilt, I. (2003) *Working Fathers: Earning and Caring*, Manchester: EOC Discussion Series.

Office of National Statistics (2001) *Social Focus on Men*, London: HMSO.

Perrons, D. (2003) 'The New Economy and the Work-life Balance: Conceptual explorations and a case study of the New Media', *Gender, Work and Organisation* 10(1): 65–93.

Pilcher, J. (2000) 'The Domestic Division of Labour in the Twentieth Century: Change Slow-a-coming', *Work, Employment and Society* 14: 4.

Reskin, B.F., McBrier, D.B. and Kmec, J.A. (1999) 'The Determinants and Consequences of Workplace Sex and Race Composition', *Annual Review of Sociology* 25: 335–61.

Sandberg, J. (1999) 'The Effects of Family Obligation and Workplace Resources on Men and Women's Use of Family Leave' in Hudson, R. and Parcel, T.L. (eds), *Research into the Sociology of Work* 7: 261–81.

Schor, J. (1991) *The Overworked American: The Unexpected Decline of Leisure*, New York: Basic Books.

Sullivan, O. (2000) 'The Division of Domestic Labour: Twenty Years of Change', *Sociology* 34(3): 437–56.

Vogler, C. (1994) 'Segregation Sexism and Labour Supply' in MacEwen Scott, A. (ed.), *Gender Segregation and Social Change*, Oxford: Oxford University Press.

Warin, J., Solomon, Y., Lewis, C. and Langford, W. (1999) *Fathers, Work and Family Life*, York: Joseph Rowntree Foundation.

Yeung, W.J., Sandberg, J.F., Davies-Keen, P.E., and Hollerth, S.L. (2001) 'Children's time with fathers in intact families', *Journal of Marriage and the Family* 63(1): 136–54.

Young, M. and Willmott, P. (1973) *The Symmetrical Family*, London: Routledge.

# 9
# Gender, Job Insecurity and the Work–Life Balance

*Nickie Charles and Emma James*

Policy discussions of the work–life balance normally focus on the need to reconcile the demands of paid employment with family life and, particularly, childcare. The work–life balance so defined is often seen as a women's issue which can be resolved by providing women with flexible hours of work. It is increasingly evident, however, that the work–life balance is something that concerns men as well as women and that there are men who value flexibility in paid work and want to spend more time with their children (Hatten *et al.*, 2002; EOC, 2003; Guardian, 2/1/03). Indeed this is recognised in the legislation introduced in Britain in April 2003 which improves fathers' as well as mothers' rights to request flexibility at work. What the legislation does not do, however, is move away from the assumption that the work–life balance is about balancing paid work and unpaid care work.

This assumption also characterises much research on the topic (see e.g. Forth *et al.*, 1997; Dex and McCulloch, 1995). Indeed it has been suggested that there is a gendering of the work–life balance such that, for men, it involves being able to fulfil their provider responsibilities through engaging in paid work while, for women, it involves facilitating the reconciliation of paid work with domestic and caring commitments (Drew and Emerek, 1998: 94). This gendering is reflected in the predominance of women in 'atypical', flexible or non-standard forms of employment, such as part-time working, and men's predominance in full-time, standard forms (Dex and McCulloch, 1995). There are, however, costs to engaging in flexible forms of employment and/or taking advantage of family-friendly policies. Thus flexible or non-standard working arrangements are often associated with low pay and/or insecure employment while taking advantage of family-friendly policies by going part-time after the birth of a child, for instance, is likely to jeopardise career prospects (Forth *et al.*, 1997; Dex and McCulloch, 1995; Wajcman, 1998; Veenis, 1998; Neathey and Hurstfield, 1996; Bell and LaValle, 2003). Indeed long hours of work are often seen as essential for furthering careers. It is, however, difficult to combine long working hours with childcare responsibilities and it is fathers who are more likely than anyone else to work long hours (Burghes *et al.*, 1997; EOC, 2003; O'Brien and Shemilt, 2003; Brannen *et al.*, 1998). The importance of more than full-time working for career progression makes it less likely that those with career aspirations will take advantage of family-friendly policies (Hojgaard, 1998; Crompton *et al.*, 2003). This, together with many men's feeling that they need to provide, goes some way towards explaining why it is that men are less likely than women to take advantage of opportunities for flexible working (Stevens *et al.*, 2004). Indeed there is considerable evidence that fatherhood is still associated with the provider role and that, where men have a choice, most choose to have a job rather than be primary carer for their children (EOC, 2003; Morris, 1990; Lupton and Barclay, 1997; Veenis, 1998; Giovannini, 1998: 196).

Increasing levels of job insecurity can, however, undermine men's ability to fulfil the provider role and may be leading to changes in the gendering of the work–life balance. Hitherto there has been little research exploring the impact of job insecurity on the work–life balance (although see La Valle, 2002; Bell and La Valle, 2003), neither has there been much attention paid to the balance between paid work and other dimensions of life such as social life, voluntary work and political activity. In this chapter we begin to explore these issues. We focus on how women and men balance home and work and the way this balancing is influenced by the presence or absence of family-friendly policies at work. We also investigate the importance attached to paid work in relation to non-market activities and the way life events can lead to a reassessment of the work–life balance. Throughout we are concerned to explore the wider meanings attached to balancing work and life and how the balance is affected by experiences of job insecurity.

## Methodology

Our study explored the gender dimensions of job insecurity in three different workplaces in a particular travel to work area in South Wales. It was a qualitative study exploring people's experiences of job insecurity through in-depth interviews with employees in a manufacturing organisation (Make-a-Lot), a public sector organisation (BureauGen) and a retail organisation (BigShop). Once access had been negotiated we wrote a letter to all the employees in each organisation asking them whether they would be prepared to be interviewed as part of a study exploring their experiences of paid work. The Human Resources and Personnel Departments distributed the letter and helped us select, from those that replied, a range of interviewees including those working on different contracts, in different parts of the organisation, with different hours of work and at different levels in the hierarchy. Our sample was not designed to be representative in any respect save that we wanted roughly to reflect the distribution of employees in each organisation's hierarchy (this can be seen in Tables 9.3 and 9.4). Furthermore the sample was, to a certain extent self selected. Our aim was to develop an in-depth analysis of the different perceptions and experiences of job insecurity amongst interviewees in different positions in the organisations' hierarchies and with different types of employment contract. To this end we interviewed 55 women and 56 men of different ages in a range of jobs and with different hours of work and contracts of employment in each organisation. The distribution of the sample can be seen in Tables 9.1 and 9.2.

The interviews were semi-structured and lasted between one and two hours; they were tape recorded and transcribed. With one exception they took place at work during working hours and were carried out between 1999 and 2000. The interviews explored experiences of paid work and interviewees' experiences of and subjective feelings about job insecurity. We also discussed the relation between domestic circumstances and paid

*Table 9.1* Distribution of sample by gender and age

| | BureauGen | | BigShop | | Make-a-Lot | | All |
|---|---|---|---|---|---|---|---|
| Age | Male | Female | Male | Female | Male | Female | |
| 16–19 | 0 | 1 | 3 | 0 | 0 | 0 | 4 |
| 20–29 | 3 | 4 | 6 | 2 | 1 | 1 | 17 |
| 30–39 | 5 | 5 | 6 | 4 | 8 | 5 | 33 |
| 40–49 | 5 | 4 | 1 | 7 | 7 | 9 | 33 |
| 50–59 | 5 | 5 | 1 | 4 | 4 | 2 | 21 |
| 60–69 | 1 | 1 | 0 | 1 | 0 | 0 | 3 |
| **Subtotal** | **19** | **20** | **17** | **18** | **20** | **17** | – |
| **Total** | **39** | | **35** | | **37** | | **111** |

*Source*: Gender Dimensions Sample (2000).

*Table 9.2* Distribution of sample by hours of work and type of contract

| | Female | | | | Male | | | | Total |
|---|---|---|---|---|---|---|---|---|---|
| | Full-time | | Part-time | | Full-time | | Part-time | | |
| | Perm | Temp | Perm | Temp | Perm | Temp | Perm | Temp | |
| **BureauGen** | 13 | 3 | 4 | 0 | 12 | 4 | 3 | 0 | **39** |
| **BigShop** | 8 | 0 | 10 | 0 | 9 | 0 | 8 | 0 | **35** |
| **Make-a-lot** | 17 | 0 | 0 | 0 | 18 | 2 | 0 | 0 | **37** |
| Total | *38* | *3* | *14* | *0* | *39* | *6* | *11* | *0* | **111** |

*Source*: Gender Dimensions Sample (2000).

*Table 9.3* Gender and seniority breakdown of the workforces of the three organisations (%)

| | BureauGen | | | BigShop | | | Make-a-Lot | | |
|---|---|---|---|---|---|---|---|---|---|
| Seniority | Men | Women | Total | Men | Women | Total | Men | Women | Total |
| 1. Most senior | 65 | 35 | 100 | 100 | 0 | 100 | 92 | 8 | 100 |
| 2. | 47 | 53 | 100 | | | | 85 | 15 | 100 |
| 3. | 33 | 67 | 100 | 65 | 35 | 100 | 100 | 0 | 100 |
| 4. | 21 | 79 | 100 | 50 | 50 | 100 | 100 | 0 | 100 |
| 5. Least senior | 28 | 72 | 100 | 24 | 76 | 100 | 89 | 11 | 100 |
| **Total** | 31.5 | 68.5 | 100 | 26 | 74 | 100 | 89 | 11 | 100 |

*Table 9.4* Gender and seniority breakdown of interviewees in the three organisations (numbers)

| | BureauGen | | | BigShop | | | Make-a-Lot | | |
|---|---|---|---|---|---|---|---|---|---|
| Seniority | Men | Women | Total | Men | Women | Total | Men | Women | Total |
| 1. Most senior | 1 | 1 | 2 | 0 | 0 | 0 | 1 | 1 | 2 |
| 2. | 1 | 1 | 2 | | | | 0 | 5 | 5 |
| 3. | 2 | 2 | 4 | 1 | 1 | 2 | 2 | 0 | 2 |
| 4. | 4 | 6 | 10 | 2 | 3 | 5 | 3 | 0 | 3 |
| 5. Least senior | 11 | 10 | 21 | 14 | 14 | 28 | 14 | 11 | 25 |
| **Total** | 19 | 20 | 39 | 17 | 18 | 35 | 20 | 17 | 37 |

*Notes for Tables 9.3 and 9.4*

For BureauGen levels 1 and 2 are managerial with level 1 being the most senior. Level 3 is the highest supervisory level. Figures in Table 9.3 for BureauGen are for July 1999.

In BigShop there were only 4 levels to the organisational hierarchy within the stores, two of them were managerial and are represented as levels 1 and 3 (there being no level 2). The figures for BigShop are for the three outlets together and are for May 2000.

For Make-a-Lot levels 3, 4 and 5 are production workers. Figures are for January 2001. Although women constituted 12% of the workforce at the time of interviewing, seniority data were not available for the whole workforce.

employment and how they influenced each other. There was a specific question which addressed the work–life balance by asking how work and life outside work fitted together and it is this material that we concentrate on in this chapter. In what follows we describe the different structure and culture of the organisations, commenting particularly on the availability of family-friendly policies. We then explore the different dimensions of the work–life balance as our interviewees talked about it in the context of job insecurity. Finally we suggest that the work–life balance can be influenced significantly by job insecurity and that it needs to be defined more broadly than has been the case hitherto.

## The organisations

The organisations were chosen because they contrasted in terms of the availability of standard and non-standard forms of employment. In the manufacturing organisation, henceforth Make-a-Lot, standard, full-time employment was the norm and the majority of the workforce was male. In the public sector organisation, BureauGen, and the retail organisation, BigShop, part-time as well as full-time working was available and the workforces were predominantly female. Contracts of employment also varied in the different workplaces. In Make-a-Lot and BureauGen temporary and casual contracts were in use as well as permanent contracts while in BigShop all contracts were permanent. Thus there was a marked distinction between Make-a-Lot and the other two organisations both in the gender composition of the workforce and in the absence of part-time working; two factors which are not unrelated.

### BureauGen

BureauGen is a large, public sector organisation where women outnumber men. At the lowest level women constitute 72 per cent of employees and at the highest level 35 per cent (see Table 9.3). Most employees work full-time with only 17 per cent working part-time. It is a classic bureaucracy with a clearly set out career structure. As well as providing good career opportunities, the organisation has a reputation locally for offering secure and stable employment, despite the use of temporary contracts. These positives outweigh the pay levels which are considered adequate but not generous. BureauGen prides itself on its family-friendly policies which enable employees to combine paid employment with caring responsibilities. It provides a workplace creche, runs holiday play schemes and offers a range of different working patterns including job sharing, part-time working, part-month working and different shift patterns so that some fit in with school hours. Career breaks of up to two years are available as is leave during the school holidays and there is generous maternity and paternity leave provision. In addition a system of flexitime operates and some of our more senior interviewees reported that they were able to work from home to accommodate childcare responsibilities. These policies were developed principally because the majority of BureauGen's workforce is female and were initially aimed at enabling mothers to pursue full-time employment and a career. In practice it is mainly women who take advantage of these family-friendly policies.

The gender culture at BureauGen is feminised and some of our male interviewees felt that women were favoured over men in terms of promotion. Others, however, welcomed the cooperative and supportive working environment which they attributed to a female-dominated workplace and contrasted this with their experiences of more macho working environments in male-dominated workplaces.

## BigShop

BigShop is a large store in the retail sector and our interviews took place at three outlets. Its workforce shows a similar gender distribution to BureauGen with 74 per cent of employees being women (see Table 9.3). Women are not so well represented in senior management positions, however, despite a 'flatter' management structure. There were no women store managers, women constituted 35 per cent of the lower tier of management compared with 76 per cent at the lowest level of the workforce. Part-time working was much more prevalent with 75 per cent of the workforce working part-time and part-time workers being heavily concentrated at the lowest level. Indeed this was the only organisation where we interviewed a significant number of part-timers.

BigShop was reported as offering secure and highly flexible employment; indeed flexibility was the main way in which employees were able to reconcile their out-of-work commitments with paid employment. Thus many of our interviewees were women who had young children to care for and who found BigShop provided the sort of flexibility that they needed. Others were students, whose main priority was studying and whose paid work had to fit in around this prior commitment, and older workers, who had left more demanding jobs and were working part-time in order to supplement a pension and to keep active and involved. This flexibility on the part of the employer engendered high levels of loyalty amongst those for whom part-time working enabled them to combine paid work with other commitments. For full-timers, however, hours were long and often unpredictable, thereby creating problems for out-of-work activities.

There was a clear gender division of labour operating in BigShop with the checkouts being 'very female orientated' while work 'outside on the trolleys' was the preserve of men (*033B,M,22yrs*). In other areas in the stores there was more of a gender mix and overall, unlike the other two workplaces, there did not seem to be a clearly defined gender culture.

## Make-a-Lot

Make-a-Lot is a factory and most of our interviewees worked on the shop floor operating machines or tending to them. In contrast to BureauGen and BigShop it is a male-dominated workforce with a culture which stresses the masculine nature of factory work. Women are in a small minority in this predominantly male workforce and there is only one woman in the senior management team (see Table 9.3). Much of the work on the shop floor is heavy, although in the view of one of our male interviewees, technology was making it less so which explained the influx of women in recent years.

This 'influx' was resented by some of the men who felt that this type of work was unsuitable for women. Some of the women agreed.

> I never thought I would end up on a factory floor. I think my father would turn in his grave if he knew I'd ended up on a factory floor... this is not what I wanted for myself. *(024C,F,50yrs)*

The work is seen as men's work which attracts a man's rate of pay, indeed Make-a-Lot was the only organisation which could be said to pay a breadwinner's wage. This made up for the relatively high levels of job insecurity and the possibility of further rounds of redundancies (Charles and James, 2003a).

There is a relatively flat structure on the shop floor and employees work in small groups which facilitates the establishment of close working relationships. Make-a-Lot operates a variety of different shift systems, all of which are full-time and attract significant shift premiums; overtime is also available. All employment is full-time and there are no formal provisions to enable employees to reconcile paid employment with family commitments. There are however informal arrangements which were agreed between interviewees and their immediate superiors and could involve flexible working and time off for family crises.

## Reconciling work and family life

There were several ways in which our interviewees reconciled paid work with caring responsibilities, particularly responsibilities for young children, and these differed in the three organisations. In BigShop part-time working enabled mothers to combine caring for children with paid employment while the norm for men with dependent children was to work full-time. Part-time hours were seen as ideal for those needing to combine paid work with unpaid care work as long as theirs was not the only wage coming into the household. In BureauGen the workplace nursery together with flexitime and other family-friendly policies enabled women as well as men to combine full-time paid employment with family responsibilities. In Make-a-Lot, where women and men worked full-time, family members were relied on for childcare and, for those in more senior positions, individual solutions such as engaging a nanny or informally agreed flexible hours were adopted. With few exceptions the responsibility of combining unpaid care work with paid employment rested with women. Almost all the men with family responsibilities worked full-time and, if they had young children, their wives generally worked part-time or were full-time housewives. This pattern could, however, be disrupted by men's experiences of job insecurity which, in some cases, had led to role reversal and a differently gendered work–life balance (cf. Crompton *et al.*, 2003).

These different patterns of reconciling the balance between paid employment and unpaid care work had different implications for gender divisions of labour at home and at work. Thus the part-time hours prevalent in BigShop, while facilitating the combination of caring responsibilities and paid work, were associated with women remaining responsible for unpaid care work within the home and men retaining the provider role. They were also seen as incompatible with higher levels of responsibility and career development at work. In BigShop, many of the women working part-time were happy with the status quo and did not want promotion. In BureauGen, however, there was some resentment at the incompatibility of part-time hours with more senior positions and far fewer employees were working part-time. Indeed the availability of a workplace nursery meant that women were able to combine paid work and childcare responsibilities by taking maternity leave and returning to work full-time even when their children were small. This pattern had been followed by several of our interviewees. One woman had returned to full-time working after having her children precisely so as not to jeopardise her career progression.

> Now had I said I wanted part time or job sharing I'd probably still be in the waiting list now for a post. This is where it is not very family friendly because although on the face of it it might well be, they don't really want the part-timer [senior manager]. I wouldn't have got my promotion if I'd wanted to restrict my hours. *(027A,F,40yrs)*

In BureauGen and BigShop there was, therefore, a recognition that taking advantage of family friendly policies, particularly by going part-time, could jeopardise career prospects. Conversely, many interviewees, men as well as women, did not want further promotion precisely because it would mean too much commitment and too little time for 'life'.

> There is more to life than work. Work pays the bills. I've got a job that I enjoy and a very responsible job and a demanding job. But it pays the bills. And at the end of the day I've got to keep telling myself there is life outside work. I've got a family, I've got a husband, I've got children. They need me as much as they do in work. And you've got to draw the line somewhere. I don't really want promotion, no I don't want it, I don't want what they expect from people because they expect far too much. *(027A,F,40yrs)*

At Make-a-Lot shift work enabled a different reconciliation of paid employment and unpaid care work and was spoken of in both positive and negative terms. One of the men told us how he was able to share domestic tasks because of being on shifts.

> Because I work shifts, if Lynne's been in work all day and I've been at home I'm getting food and things ready for when she comes home. Or do the washing – the washing machine does the washing – put the

> hoover over... A lot of it has rubbed off from my father. Because he done shift work and he always used to do the food, used to put the hoover over, he may do a bit of washing on a weekend. But he always did something around the house. When the kids were on holidays he'd be the one that made us food and everything else. *(001C,M,39yrs)*

And another man valued having time free during the day.

> I think it's very important because it's allowing me to do what I can do. If it was a position when it's Monday to Friday 9 to 5 then, I mean, I can't take my daughter to school, I can't fetch her from school. Whereas now, maybe 70% of the time, I can take, or bring her back from school. So it gives me that flexibility. *(004C,M,43yrs)*

For others, though, shifts could interfere with family life, particularly if their own and their partner's time off did not coincide. One man, for instance, said that he gets more satisfaction from home than work, particularly

> seeing my boys play football ... when I got to work weekends and I can't do things with the kids then ... I mean at home, you know, I prefer to be with them but I can't, obviously... because I have got to work, so that they can do those type of things. *(036C,M,40yrs)*

The need to provide, together with the fact that he worked shifts, made spending more time with his sons impossible. Thus some saw shift work as offering flexibility in combining work and family commitments whereas others saw it as leaving little room for family life.

Full-time work, particularly in more senior positions, involved long hours. One of the male managers in BigShop described his hours of work.

> On an average day I'm in by half past seven, quarter to eight and I'd probably still be here seven o'clock at night...So, it's a twelve hour day, today shouldn't be too bad, cos I came in at eight o'clock and I should be gone by six. So that's quite a short day. Compared to Monday when I was in at six and I went home at nine o'clock at night. [His wife accepts that] she's got me for six or eight weeks a year anyway, fully... And the other forty-two weeks a year is BigShop's. *(013B,M,36yrs)*

Many of those working full-time felt that a reduction in working hours would enable them to achieve a better balance between 'life' and 'work'.

> I'd like to go job sharing, that would be ideal...if I could afford it that's what I'd love to do. So I'd have more time in the house for the children

you know. ... Simon's always been there and lucky I've got a good husband and a good father to the children, you know, he's wonderful. But I, I miss out, I feel as if I've missed out. (*037A,F,36yrs*)

It was mostly women who voiced these views although some men spoke in similar terms. Other men, however, even though they would like to be able to spend more time with their families, saw no conflict between full-time employment and family responsibilities. The provider role required that they work full-time and this was in itself a reconciliation of work and family life. Men were more likely to express the view that work structures life and makes family life possible. One of the men said that the importance of work was 'to do with providing a structure to your life' (*028A,M,45yrs*). And another said that work was,

as important as the family...It's equally important because you can't do one without the other. Coming to work finances anything you do outside work. It dictates, more or less, how your family lives. What you do with your life. And if you lose one then the other collapses. I can't say that if you lost your family your work would collapse. But if you lost your work your family environment would change dramatically in a very, very short time. (*001C,M,39yrs*)

What comes across in these accounts is a very clear gendering of the work–life balance and evidence that the form it takes differs in the three different workplaces depending on the different hours of work offered and the availability of family-friendly policies.

## Undermining the gendered work–life balance

Most of the women had changed their employment and/or their hours of work in response to changing family circumstances, particularly the need to care for children or other relatives, and the need for income. In contrast men's work trajectories were much less responsive to changing care needs (see also Crompton *et al.*, 2003). This was summed up by one of the women.

I had the impression that you went to do a job and you trained for a job. And then you just progressed through that employment upwards. I think that my father was in the same employment for years and years....but then on reflection, looking back, that's more a man's thing, they do that more than women. Women sort of flit. Bearing in mind they, their children, their responsibilities for the children, getting somewhere and getting back. And fitting everything in with your job falls to the women. I don't know many of my friends whose husbands do that. (*012A,F,35yrs*)

Changing family circumstances did, however, affect the balance of work and life for men in so far as paid employment assumes a greater importance once they take on family responsibilities. It is then vital that they get a steady, well-paid job in order to provide for their families.

> Your priorities do change a lot. I've had a lot of jobs in the past, then I got married and I realised then that I can't really, I used to go from job to job, if I fancied a job I'd go for it. Didn't really worry about consequences because I was only looking after myself basically. But then once you get married then, different things come into it...If I wasn't married I probably wouldn't have applied for the job here. *(005C,M,32yrs)*

These responsibilities can keep men in work even though they may prefer to be doing something else but it is only when the need to provide lessens that it is possible for the balance between 'work' and 'life' to change. Thus, on the whole, men who are fathers achieve a balance between family life and work by working full-time while women who are mothers achieve it by adapting their hours of work and their employment to the needs of their children and their partners.

These gendered patterns were used to explain the different repercussions of job insecurity for women and men.

> I think the majority of men expect to work and be the main provider, obviously, isn't it. But I think they expect to work. Women have time off then with children, you know, they take time off to raise their children, they go back perhaps part time. And a woman can relate more if she's got to give up her, she can go and pick the children up from school herself, she can do things for the children, you know, if they've got children obviously. But I think a woman can handle it [job insecurity] better, if the worst comes to the worst. *(006A,F,54yrs)*

There was, however, evidence that men's job insecurity is undermining this gendering of the work–life balance. Just over half the men in our sample had experienced unemployment or redundancy at some time during their working lives. For some of our interviewees, men's job insecurity had led to a differently gendered work–life balance with women taking on the provider role and men taking on more of the childcare responsibilities (Charles and James, 2003b). Amongst our younger interviewees there was also evidence of more variation in the work–life balance and the gendered pattern was not so clear. This related to younger women's expectations of being able to combine full-time, paid work with childcare responsibilities, their assumption that it was unrealistic to rely on a male partner for financial security and men's realisation that they could no longer anticipate secure, full-time employment.

## Male breadwinner ideology and job insecurity

Despite the impact of men's job insecurity on the gendering of the work–life balance, many of our interviewees felt that the ability to provide was important to men. In particular male breadwinner ideology still informed the way they talked about the impact of job insecurity.

> Men tend to be the breadwinners so, if the men are out of work and the women are working they still feel insecure. Because that means that the women are actually getting the money and they're not. And that's an unequal thing as well. I think men need to, they need to get, they need to have that thing to be the one's working. To be able to be seen to be providing if they've got a family. *(033B,M,22yrs)*

In response to a question about whether they thought job insecurity was more serious for women or men, just under half our interviewees thought that it was worse for men. This was generally because men were assumed to be breadwinners and therefore the loss of the provider's job would be more serious for a household than the loss of a secondary job. But it was also linked to a man's sense of self and the importance of the provider role to masculine identity. In contrast, over half our sample thought that the implications of job insecurity depended not on gender but on who had the provider role, and along with this went a recognition that women's *and* men's wages were vital for families to survive. Despite this, there was still a feeling that men would want to retain the provider role.

> I don't think there's many families that both don't work now and I think everyone here their wives are working and things like that. I think it's equal now at the end of the day, you know, as long as money comes into the house. It doesn't matter where it comes from, personally. [Yes, so do you think that men and women cope the same way with those things?] No. I think a man would be more distressed if he lost his job. ... at the end of the day if I was looking after the baby (laughs) and she was coming through the door with, 'Where's my tea, this that and the other', it would stress me out. *(012B,M,31yrs)*

There was thus a recognition that, while gendered boundaries between paid and unpaid work might be changing and there is now much more equality between women and men, there is still a sense in which the ability to provide is particularly important for a man's sense of self.

Views on the significance of job insecurity for women and men differed in the three workplaces. Thus in BigShop over half our interviewees thought job insecurity would be worse for men with over twice as many women as men thinking so. We suggest that this reflects the fact that part-time working is widespread at BigShop and many of the women regard their wages as secondary while the few men with families were all main providers (Charles and James, 2005). There is a clearly gendered and 'traditional' work–life balance in evidence amongst our BigShop interviewees. In BureauGen just under half our interviewees thought job insecurity was worse for men. This went along with the view that women's wages were secondary, even though most women were working full-time and some of our women interviewees were earning more than their partners. In Make-a-Lot the proportion saying job insecurity was worse for men was significantly lower at a third. Here all were on full-time wages and, as several interviewees commented, many women were providers. Thus it is in the organisation which is most male dominated and where there are no formal family-friendly policies where interviewees are least likely to say that men's job insecurity is more serious than women's. It is also here that women work full-time alongside men, many of them on shifts, and there are no flexible or non-standard hours of work which are taken up more by women than men. This contrasts with BureauGen and BigShop, both of which have policies which enable carers (usually women) to be 'flexible', thereby differentiating them from employees who have no caring responsibilities. Thus in Make-a-Lot, women are seen to be behaving 'like men' in employment terms while, in the other two workplaces, gender differences in the uptake of family-friendly policies and flexible working hours are very much in evidence. In BigShop and BureauGen these gender differences reinforce the view that women's relation to paid work, the significance of job insecurity to them, and the way that they resolve the contradictions between 'work' and 'life' are different from men's.

## Reassessing the work–life balance

Ageing and life events such as bereavement as well as job insecurity or job loss could lead to a reassessment of the balance between life and work. Our interviewees spoke about the changing balance of work and life with age.

> I think the older you get the more you think that there is a life outside of work. And the more the struggle it gets to come in in the morning… I probably see far more of my work colleagues than I do of my husband or the kids, so it is important. And I do, I do like my job… [but] work is not as important as home. Home comes first every time. *(027A,F,40yrs)*

Early retirement was something that was spoken about a lot, particularly by those at Make-a-Lot where it was a means of reducing the workforce in the context of previous rounds of redundancies and the possibility of more in the future. If it was financially viable early retirement was seen as a way of rebalancing work and life in favour of life and providing time to do those things that you'd always wanted to do. Older women who wanted to be able to spend more time with their grandchildren or simply to have time for themselves often spoke about this. One of them told us:

> Ideally I would like to give up work. I enjoy going back to college and doing things, I haven't done it for years now, like. I've got a knitting machine, I enjoyed learning how to work that. And I went and learnt computers, I enjoyed that. I enjoy learning things. I love reading. Ideally I would like to just give up work and be financially secure enough to be me. But I'm not able to be me at the moment. I enjoy the grandchildren and everything ... but I'm just so busy working and so busy looking after grandchildren that I haven't got time to take up the things that I want to do at the moment. *(024C,F,50yrs)*

Several interviewees talked about the way life events, particularly bereavement, could lead to a reassessment of the importance of work and the balance between work and life.

> Again, I think as you get older and you go through important changes, I've lost a few people in the last 10, 15 years and my perspective on life has sort of, well, it has changed.... Time is more important now, to have time. To do the things that you want to do which don't include work...What I want out of life is time and the health to enjoy it and that's all. *(003C,M,43yrs)*

Job insecurity and the possibility of redundancy were seen by some as creating opportunities; young men, for instance, spoke about how being made redundant might enable them to travel and see the world, something that having a secure job would make less likely. They could also lead to a reassessment of the work–life balance. Several men had come into BureauGen having worked in highly competitive, 'macho' working environments and some wanted to reassess the place of paid work in their lives. One man who had been made redundant by a previous employer now wanted to spend more time with his children and give priority to being a father. And women who had become the main provider due to their partner's job insecurity often reassessed the importance of work, becoming more ambitious in career terms and insisting that their partners took on more of the domestic work at home (Charles and James, 2003b).

These comments and the way that the significance of paid work can change in response to non-work-related as well as work-related events show that 'life' is understood as consisting of many activities besides childcare. Indeed many of our interviewees felt that there needed to be a better balance between life and work and that work often encroached too much on life.

> I think you've got to have a life outside work. I mean, you can't just stick yourself to work because you'll just go mental. You will. You'll crack. Because people go drinking after work, Friday and Saturday night, and it's a big relaxer. You think, good, no work for 2 days or 3 days or whatever. And you've got to have that sort of release to get it out of your system. Because otherwise if you just stay in and work Monday to Friday, stay in the house all weekend then back in work, you're not really releasing that pressure. ... And your body builds up so much energy; you've got to really go out dancing on a Friday and Saturday night. *(033A,M,26yrs)*

But, on the other hand, they also recognised that work was part of life and that it provided them with friends and a social life.

> One of the things with BigShop I had a big social life. And that was one thing I missed when I actually went away from my store. That I missed the friends I made. I see one or two now and again. And I'll go out for a drink, but I miss working with them and then go out with them as well. You had a good, you had a good time. *(033B,M,22yrs)*

Indeed, several of our interviewees had met their partners at work and many commented that they saw more of their workmates than their families.

> I probably spend as much time with my workmates as my wife. Probably more. So, you know, I spend eight hours with them. So it's not just being in work. It's communicating with different people. *(036C,M,40yrs)*

And one of the women spoke about how work relations were as close as family.

> I'm here with them more than I am with my family....There is a closeness in a factory that you don't get anywhere else. And a laugh. You get a laugh. *(024C,F,50yrs)*

One way of maintaining a balance was by ensuring work was not too demanding and some of our interviewees had taken jobs at BureauGen precisely in order to escape high levels of commitment and responsibility.

> I can walk out of here and simply not think about BureauGen until the next day...I was in [another job] before I came to work here and I would,

> that job you carry home on your shoulders with black clouds....Sunday night I don't get depressed. I don't wake up at 3, 4 o'clock in the morning stiff with worry and I can't work out what I'm worried about. *(09A,M,60yrs)*

For others, the undemanding nature of the job enabled them to pursue other life interests. These ranged from making a career change through caring for severely disabled children (this had been made possible by family-friendly policies) to surfing and undertaking voluntary work.

> I do voluntary work ... one evening every 2 weeks so the salary side of things isn't by any stretch of the imagination my main motivation. *(028A,M,45yrs)*

Others, however, talked about the way paid employment made it difficult to be involved in activities such as voluntary work and how this was leading to the impoverishment of civil society.

> At one time I did a lot of unpaid work, now again I think that times have moved on because nowadays it is highly unlikely I would consider doing unpaid work. I think if I could afford to stay at home and not need to work, then again I could consider it...There was a time I used to be a person who would attend political or social meetings something like council meetings. I really believe in the good of the community, whereas now I feel far more isolated because I find it hard enough to hold onto what I have got myself. *(016A,F,37yrs)*

## Conclusions

The findings we have presented here support the contention that the work–life balance is gendered but also suggest that this gendering can be undermined by men's job insecurity and their resulting inability to provide for their wives and children. The women and men in our sample balanced work and life differently at different stages of the life course. Most women had changed their hours of work or moved in and out of the workforce in response to changing family and childcare needs, while men had pursued a more linear trajectory with change in the work–life balance only becoming possible once their children were no longer financially dependent. This goes along with men's view that paid work is essential to support family life and therefore has to take priority while women are more inclined to see the balance between paid work and family life as having to be negotiated rather than being fixed. Men's experiences of job insecurity can, however, undermine this gendering of paid work and care work, leading to situations of 'role reversal' with women taking on the main provider role and, amongst our younger interviewees, there is more variation and changeability in the work–life balance negotiated between heterosexual partners. This suggests that the spread of job insecurity to men and the disappearance of jobs for life is undermining the gendering of the work–life balance and leading to more variation in how paid and unpaid work is distributed within households.

Despite these changes there is also evidence of the continuing importance of the provider role for men which is reflected in views on the relative importance of job insecurity for women and men. A little under half our sample thought that job insecurity would be worse for men than women and there was support for the idea that men would suffer if they were unable to provide. At the level of the household both wages were seen as important, albeit one might be more important than the other, but at the level of self identity job insecurity was seen as more significant for men than women. There are signs of change here as well, though, in so far as a little over half the sample did not think there was a gender dimension to the seriousness of job insecurity and talked in terms of gender equality or the fact that nowadays men can be househusbands and women providers.

A comparison of our three organisations shows that they were associated with different ways of reconciling paid employment and family life and with different views on the gender dimensions of job insecurity. Thus, counter-intuitively, interviewees in the female-dominated industries seem to be more traditional in terms of attitudes towards gender roles than those in the male-dominated one. This suggests that part-time hours, flexibility and the fact that taking advantage of family-friendly policies is seen as jeopardising career advancement can reproduce gender divisions of labour and familial ideology by facilitating women's ability to combine paid and unpaid work. This reinforces the idea that it is a woman's role to reconcile work and 'life' while a man's role is to work to make 'life' possible. Conversely, the commitment to gender equality implied by family-friendly policies, and the experience of women and men working full-time alongside each other, pose a challenge to 'traditional' gender divisions of labour and can be seen as undermining male breadwinner ideology.

We commented at the beginning of this chapter on the narrowness of policy and research definitions of the work–life balance which reduce 'life' to unpaid care work. Our material also suggests that defining the work–life balance in this way misses out on many dimensions of life which people regard as important. Several of our interviewees stressed that work is part of life and that life takes place at work. Furthermore work provides the basis for life and enables many interviewees to live what they see as a desirable lifestyle. There is therefore a sense in which work and life should not be seen in opposition to each other but as being interdependent. There is also evidence that men as well as women would like working hours that allow them to spend more time with their children or simply to have more time to do other things such as voluntary work or engaging in political activity. This suggests that too much work is deleterious, not only for family life, but also for people's ability to undertake other socially important activities. We would therefore suggest that the work–life balance is about more than a balance between paid work and family life and that this needs to be recognised in order to ensure the continued vitality of civil society; it is not only parents who need to be able to work flexibly. Moreover it is essential that those who reduce their hours of work or take advantage of other family-friendly policies are not disadvantaged in the workplace in relation to those who do not do so. As we have seen, this has the effect of reinforcing rather than undermining the gendered boundaries between paid employment and unpaid care work.

## Acknowledgments

We wish to thank all those organisations and individuals who so generously gave up their time to take part in this research and Chris Harris whose advice throughout the project was invaluable.

## Note

The research on which this chapter is based was funded by the ESRC as part of its *Future of Work* programme. The project was 'The gender dimensions of job insecurity: an ethnographic study' (L212252012) and was carried out by Nickie Charles, Emma James and Paul Ransome in the Department of Sociology and Anthropology, University of Wales Swansea.

## References

Bell, Alice and La Valle, Ivana (2003) *Combining self-employment and family life*, York: Joseph Rowntree Foundation.

Brannen, Julia, Moss, Peter, Owen, Charlie and Wale, Chris (1998) *Mothers, fathers and employment: parents and the labour market in Britain 1984–1994*, London: Department for Education and Employment.

Burghes, Louie, Clarke, Linda and Cronin, Natalie (1997) *Fathers and fatherhood in Britain*, London: Family Policy Studies Centre.

Charles, Nickie and James, Emma (2003a) 'Gender and work orientations in conditions of job insecurity' in *The British Journal of Sociology*, 54(2): 239–57.

Charles, Nickie and James, Emma (2003b) 'The gender dimensions of job insecurity in a local labour market' in *Work, Employment and Society*, 17(3): 531–522.

Charles, Nickie and James, Emma (2005) 'Perceptions of job insecurity in a retail sector organisation' in Stewart P. (ed.) *Organisational change and emerging patterns of work and employment*, Oxford: Oxford University Press.

Crompton, Rosemary, Dennett, Jane and Wigfield, Andrea (2003) *Organisations, careers and caring*, Bristol: The Policy Press.

Dex, Shirley and McCulloch, Andrew (1995) *Flexible employment in Britain: a statistical analysis*, Manchester: Equal Opportunities Commission.

Drew, Eileen and Emerek, Ruth (1998) 'Employment, flexibility and gender' in Drew, E., Emerek, R. and Mahon, E. (eds) *Women, work and the family in Europe*, pp. 89–99, London and New York: Routledge.

EOC (2003) Equal Opportunities Commission *Fathers: balancing work and family*, Research Findings, March.

Forth, John, Lissenburgh, Steve, Callender, Clare and Millward, Neil (1997) *Family-friendly working arrangements in Britain, 1996*, London: Policy Studies Institute.

Giovannini, Dino (1998) 'Are fathers changing? Comparing some different images on sharing of childcare and domestic work' in Drew, E., Emerek, R. and Mahon, E. (eds) (1998) *Women, work and the family in Europe*, pp. 191–199, London and New York: Routledge.

Guardian newspaper, 2/1/03.

Hatten, Warren, Vinter, Louise and Williams, Rachel (2002) *Dads on Dads: needs and expectations at home and at work*, Manchester: Equal Opportunities Commission.

Hojgaard, Lise (1998) 'Workplace culture, family-supportive policies and gender differences' in Drew, E., Emerek, R. and Mahon, E. (eds) *Women, work and the family in Europe*, pp. 140–149, London and New York: Routledge.

LaValle, Ivana (2002) *Happy families? Atypical work and its influence on family life*, York: Joseph Rowntree Foundation.

Lupton, Deborah and Barclay, Lesley (1997) *Constructing fatherhood: discourses and experiences*, London: Sage.

Morris, Lydia (1990) *The workings of the household*, Cambridge: Polity.

Neathey, Fiona and Hurstfield, Jennifer (1996) *Flexibility in practice: women's employment and pay in retail and finance*, Manchester: Equal Opportunities Commission/Industrial Relations Services.

O'Brien, Margaret and Shemilt, Ian (2003) *Working fathers: earning and caring*, Manchester: Equal Opportunities Commission.

Stevens, J., Brown, J. and Lee, C. (2004) The second work-life balance study: results from the employees' survey, Department of Trade and Industry.

Veenis, Els (1998) 'Working parents: experience from the Netherlands' in Drew, E., Emerek R. and Mahon, E. (eds) *Women, work and the family in Europe*, pp. 182–190, London and New York: Routledge.

Wajcman, Judy (1998) *Managing like a man*, Cambridge: Polity.

# 10
# Workplace Partnership and Work–Life Balance: A Local Government Case Study

*Stephanie Tailby, Mike Richardson, Andy Danford, Paul Stewart and Martin Upchurch*

## Introduction

This chapter explores the links between work–life balance and workplace partnership, principally through a local authority case study. This was one of six organisations studied in our research on 'patterns and prospects for partnership at work in the UK', part of the ESRC *Future of Work* programme.[1] The local authority case study is of particular interest to the concerns of this book. In 2001, the Council introduced a work–life balance policy that was the product of a trade union – management partnership. It was among the 'exemplars' in the local government sector where the employers and trade unions identified workplace partnership as the means of extending flexible working practices to the benefit of employees, local authorities and users of council services. Our interest was in the benefits that employees stood to gain. This section sets the scene by introducing briefly the concept of partnership at work, sketching the public policy context of local government 'modernisation', and identifying the issues that guided our case study investigation.

The government's work–life balance campaign proposes that greater flexibility in working time can be developed to the benefit of employees and employers, and that innovations at workplace level can contribute to advances in social welfare, equality of opportunity and UK economic performance (DTI, 2001, 2003). As such the assumptions are complementary to the 'mutual gains' philosophy that, in the UK, has become distilled in the concept of partnership at work. There is no simple definition of the concept (Terry, 2003: 463), but the principles have been articulated by interest groups such as the Trades Union Congress (1999, 2000) and the Involvement and Participation Association (IPA, 1997). They are based essentially on the idea of a joint worker-management commitment to the organisation, its goals and business success. They include maintaining high levels of trust between workers and managers; promoting flexibility and job security; recognising legitimate differences of interest; ensuring transparency in management decision-making; and providing attention to the quality of working life. The management practices that are presumed to foster this mutuality include the teamwork techniques of 'high commitment management', its human resource management (HRM) policies of employee involvement (via continuous improvement programmes, and structured two-way management communications), together with representative participation – or union involvement in management (e.g. Knell, 1999; TUC, 2003).

In the American literature, studies propose that employers' provision of 'flexible and family-friendly' employment practice is part of the 'high road' of 'high commitment management' (e.g. Osterman, 1995; Berg *et al.*, 2003), although the association has not been found in all analyses of the survey data (e.g. Wood, 1999; Wood *et al.*, 2003). And as White *et al.* (2003: 178) note, the evidence to support the idea that employees gain from the new work and HRM practices is 'mixed at best'. They cite the range of survey and case study evidence that suggests that employees' experiences of 'high road' work practices and associated HRM techniques also include work intensification, increased work stress and reduced job satisfaction. Their statistical analysis of UK survey data suggests that while long working hours are the main source of a reported *negative job-to-home spillover* – the sap of time or energy among employees for involvement in 'family life' – high road management practices contribute similarly. They conclude that the countervailing effect of any employer-given 'flexible and family-friendly' employment practices looks 'feeble in comparison' (2003: 192).

In the UK, there have been successive Conservative and Labour government efforts to reform work, employment and employment relations in the public services. In the 1980s and 1990s, Conservative governments tried to undermine the power of trade unions via restrictive legislation, strict cash limits on public expenditure, the devolution of management authority, and the introduction of compulsory competitive tendering (CCT). These policies led to the casualisation or loss of many women's jobs in local authorities (Colling, 1999; Hegewisch, 1999) and an increase in the intensity of work (Green, 2001).

Since 1997, the Labour government has encouraged the unions to work in partnership with employers to 'modernise' local authority services. As under the previous Conservative government, emphasis has been placed on the interests of service users, as identified in government-set performance targets (Martinez Lucio and MacKenzie, 1999). In local government the key 'modernising' initiative focuses on Best Value guidelines. The previous obligation under CCT was for local authorities to tender contracts for the delivery of a number of services, and to accept the lowest cost in-house or external bids. Best Value eases the prescriptive nature of CCT, but extends the scrutiny of performance to all services (Bach and Winchester, 2003: 291). There is more emphasis on the quality of service provision, but the objectives – namely, to 'secure sustained economies from all authorities, as well as continuous improvement in service quality' (Cmnd 4014, 1998) – are potentially contradictory (Martin, 2000).

Councils are required to undertake fundamental performance reviews of all services over a five-year period. They must 'challenge, compare, consult and compete' (the 4 Cs). The obligation to consult relevant 'stakeholders', especially service users, is constrained by budgetary pressures, and national performance indicators developed by government in consultation with the Audit Commission covering cost, quality and efficiency. Competition and tendering thus remain important features of local authority management. The 1998 White Paper states that 'retaining work in-house without subjecting it to real competitive pressure can rarely be justified' (Cmnd 4014, 1998). Trade union involvement, however, is now actively encouraged to elicit the co-operation and trust of employees necessary to achieve the Best Value targets. The principles of joint working on Best Value were outlined in the 2001 National Joint Council Framework Agreement between the employers and main trade unions (GMB, T&GWU and UNISON). The extent of union involvement at local level is difficult to assess (although see Geddes, 2001), but it almost certainly is uneven.

The relationship between workplace partnership and work–life balance issues in local authorities is clearly influenced by the gender composition of the workforce. Women constitute 71 per cent of the 1.5 million staff whose pay and conditions are determined by the National Joint Council (NJC) for local government services. They are under-represented among chief officer and senior management grades whilst constituting around 90 per cent of the part-time workforce that is over half of total employment in local authorities, and part-timers are heavily concentrated in the lowest pay grades (Thornley, 2003; Local Government Pay Commission Report, 2003). The NJC was established in 1997 when the formerly separate national agreements for manual workers, and for administrative, professional, technical and clerical staff (APT&C) were combined in the Single Status agreement. Working time and holidays were to be harmonised, and a national pay spine based on a jointly agreed job evaluation scheme was designed to encourage local agreements on grading structures that would facilitate equality of opportunity between men and women, and between manual and white-collar staff. Local implementation of the agreement, however, has been slow and uneven, for a number of reasons.

There is ostensibly a large measure of agreement between the two sides of the NJC on issues concerning work–life balance provision. Both sides aspire to achieve more in the area of gender equality and, on the employers' side in particular, there is the imperative of Best Value. A guidance document issued in 2001 states that:

> Within local government, working with in-house employees to provide high quality services that meet the challenges of Best Value is a key area of joint concern. A social partnership approach can support joint ownership of the need to change, and any changes made. (NJC for LGS, 2001)

There is emphasis on the 'importance to local government of developing modern patterns of service delivery', and of 'encouraging working patterns that enable people to get a better balance between paid work and their other priorities'. There is reference to the analysis of the 1998 Workplace Employee Relations Survey data that suggests a link between 'high commitment management practices' and organisational success, and the inclusion of 'flexible and family-friendly' employment practices among the former. And in their evidence to the 2003 Local Government Pay Commission, the employers reported staff survey findings that 'some employees value flexibility above extra pay, often because the opportunity to work particular hours means they can save on childcare costs'.

The above summary of recent developments in local authorities identifies a number of important questions that shaped our case study research. What importance do employees attach to work–life balance provisions vis-à-vis other terms and conditions? How much do they know about the details of management policies and collective agreements? What factors in their daily work-lives do they view as barriers to a better work–life balance? Can service-user preferences and service-provider interests in work–life balance be reconciled? Are the Best Value imperatives for cost and performance improvements compatible with the aim of work–life balance satisfaction? Our research, focused on one local authority in 2001 at the time when a work–life balance policy agreed through partnership working between full-time lay union officials and senior managers was being 'rolled out', allows us to make a preliminary assessment.

Our research used both quantitative and qualitative data collection methods to explore the views and experiences of employees. Interviews were also conducted with managers and lay trade union officials covering a number of issues raised in the debates on workplace partnership. At our local authority research site (hereafter called CityCo) we recorded 89 interviews with an average duration of one hour. Twenty-two interviews were with senior or line managers, five were with lead stewards among the unions recognised locally (UNISON, GMB, T&GWU and UCATT) and 62 were with staff in six departments covering manual, administrative and white collar professional occupations. Also, we distributed a questionnaire to 750 staff in the departments where we conducted research interviews.[2] There were 389 useable responses, a response rate of 52 per cent. In the following section we sketch the local context in which the work–life balance policy was forged and its main provisions, before exploring the employees' evaluations and developing some conclusions.

## CityCo case study

CityCo is a unitary authority, responsible for the provision of the full range of local government services. Excluding education, it employed 10,000 staff in 2001. Women comprised two-thirds of this total, including most of the 4000 part-time staff employed in local government services. CityCo has been Labour-controlled for most of the past two decades, facilitating a broadly accommodative relationship between trade unions and management. When confronted by the threat of jobs losses and casualisation posed by CCT, full-time union officials worked with managers in the most affected departments in an effort to retain contracts and services in-house. The corollary was an acceptance that pay had to be competitive with the private sector, or that costs had to be cut through work reorganisation initiatives.

Union representatives in 2001 believed that there were few differences between Best Value and CCT; as one interviewee argued, 'well it's CCT in another guise'. It was clear that the performance levels and organisational processes set by Best Value reviews forced the local authority to consider outsourcing services if it was unable to secure the requisite service improvements in-house. This realisation nevertheless deepened trade union involvement in the steering groups and Best Value review panel meetings that discussed whether the public would be best served by externalising services or keeping them in-house. Senior stewards explained the logic in terms of insider involvement to gain more leverage in '*leading the debate where we want it to go and achieve what we want to achieve in terms of defending our members'*. Yet there was also an aspiration that partnership with other stakeholders could secure the interests of CityCo employees and those of the local community of council service users. How employee interests were to be articulated in this process was not entirely clear. Full-time lay union officials thought that few of their members were sufficiently informed about the meaning of partnership, or the prominence it had been given in securing Best Value reforms. One shop steward noted that '*I don't think it's been explained enough and I guess we might be as guilty as anybody else'*.

Partnership was described by one union representative as '*a scenario in which unions and management are the joint initiators of policies that are of benefit to the employer and employee*'. As such it remained an aspiration since, in the view of this interviewee, partnership for managers meant 'consultation with the unions over policies that are management initiated'. The exception to this rule, or the area where a 'genuine' partnership had been forged by unions and management, according to most of the union representatives and senior managers who were interviewed, was the Work–Life Balance Policy agreed in the spring of 2001. One policy officer commented:

> That was about trade unions and managers and a councillor being at the same place and having the same level of influence. So it's not like managers developing a policy, going to the trades unions and saying 'you have two days to comment on this, consult your members and come back to us and tell us what you think and we might or might not listen to you'. ... It's 'we're going to sit round the table and talk about how this can work best for the organisation and management and for the trades unions and employees'.

## CityCo's Work–Life Balance Policy

The inspiration for the work–life balance policy was an action research[3] project on flexible working conducted in two departments in the late 1990s. CityCo was one of the local authorities that piloted the principles of 'positive flexibility' – serving employee interests and not simply business needs – that were agreed in a European Union funded study involving the TUC, and trade union confederations elsewhere in Europe. Local government was selected as a site for the research in the UK, and the national Employers' Organization was involved among the partners steering projects at local level. Most full-time union representatives at CityCo were receptive to the initiative, viewing it as a means of promoting gender equality in employment practices and policies.

Departmental and HR managers were centrally involved. Yet the action research project subsequently became the work–life balance policy largely because of trade union lobbying and the political weight lent by a supportive Councillor. Without the latter, one interviewee commented, 'the initiative would probably have withered on the vine'. The champions of work–life balance as an equality initiative used the context of Best Value to make the 'business case' and, once senior managers and the HRM department had been brought 'on board', the parties worked in partnership to draft the new policy.

The written policy refers to the joint recognition of the importance of employees being able to balance work with social, family and caring responsibilities, and a shared understanding that flexible working may serve a range of constituencies. The benefits for CityCo, as an employing organisation, are conceived in terms of improved staff morale and recruitment and retention rates, and an extension of flexible working in the interests of service delivery. The stated aim of the policy is 'to provide a framework for flexible working throughout the Authority to the mutual benefit of employees, the Council and users of the services the Council provides to the local community'. The inherent problem in reconciling different 'stakeholder' interests emerged during the pilot study stage. It was difficult to persuade staff in one of the two selected departments that they shared the interest of service users for the Sunday opening of the facility, despite the guarantee that premium rates for unsocial hours working would be paid.

The work–life balance policy identifies a number of flexible working-time arrangements potentially available to employees. There are separate, longer-standing policies in respect of CityCo's 'family-friendly' provision, up-dated to include parental leave, time-off for family emergencies and so on. Many of the flexible working-time arrangements had been available previously (flexitime, unpaid leave, term-time only working, annualised hours), but only on a selective and contingent basis. A union representative commented that CityCo *'has always had reasonable flexible working in different bits but your face had to fit'*. The policy in principle provided all employees with the right to request flexible working, and for managers to propose such arrangements. There is no automatic employee entitlement to the available working-time practices; the work–life balance policy makes clear that requests have to be assessed by managers at department level to ensure that they are compatible with operational requirements and the working-time preferences of other employees. But employees have a right to union representation and there is an appeals procedure.

The partners involved in the 'positive flexibility' project wanted to dissociate the concept of flexibility from the 1980s and 1990s trends towards employment casualisation in local government by emphasising the potential mutual gains to be achieved through the development of working-time flexibility. CityCo trade union representatives embraced these sentiments, but at the same time articulated some scepticism that mutuality could be attained. There was some lack of trust in individual manager's conversion to a mutual gains philosophy. This was expressed by one interviewee who argued that the danger of the work–life balance policy was that it might be *'used by non-supportive managers in a way that would allow them to just drive down terms and conditions'*. More generally, it was recognised that managers were under pressure to contain costs, boost efficiency and attain performance targets, although such pressures varied in their intensity between departments. Even the most enthusiastic supporters of the work–life balance policy accepted that any moves to flexible working had to be voluntary on the part of employees. That is to say, the policy's contribution to employee welfare was seen as much in the right it apparently gave employees to resist management-led working-time innovation as in the right to attain a preferred pattern of working hours. But the right to resist was not watertight. The policy stipulated that 'Where flexible working does not provide sufficient staffing necessary to meet changes in service delivery, a service review under the Council's existing Managing Change Policy may be appropriate'.

## Work–life balance: an issue for all?

The work–life balance policy was hailed as a valuable outcome of partnership at work by those that developed it; one that offered tangible benefits to employees as well as other stakeholders. But was work–life balance, in the shape and form proposed, of broad interest to employees? The first government sponsored national work–life balance baseline survey showed a 'positive attitude' among employees to the principle that 'everyone should be able to balance their work and home lives in the way they want' (Hogarth *et al.*, 2001: 4; see also Stevens *et al.*, 2004). Our CityCo survey asked more directly whether employees agreed or disagreed with the statement that 'an employer should help its staff balance their work and other aspects of their lives (such as family care)'. More than 80 per cent of all respondents agreed with the principle. The proportion was higher among women than men (90 per cent vis-à-vis 78 per cent), and among white-collar professionals than manual workers (98 per cent vis-à-vis 75 per cent). This did not necessarily mean that employees individually attached much significance to work–life balance provision or, indeed, that they were aware of the policy that had been negotiated on their behalf. Our interviews suggested that knowledge of the policy varied between different occupational groups and departments.

The first national work–life balance baseline survey found a significant 'latent demand' for flexible working-time arrangements, measured in terms of the reported interest among employees in arrangements they did not currently have (Hogarth *et al.*, 2001: 17). Our CityCo survey asked employees to identify which, if any, among a list of ten flexible and family-friendly employment practices, would assist them to enjoy a better work–life balance. As Table 10.1 shows, a significant proportion of all respondents (between 33 and 40 per cent) identified the following practices: home working, for some of the time; a compressed working week; reduced hours; and career breaks. The 'demand' for any of these practices varied by occupation and parental status. Men, managers, manual workers and employees with young children were the most likely to regard reduced working hours as of assistance. Managers, white-collar professionals and parents of young children were most interested in home working for some of the time. Relatively few among all survey respondents (especially men), replied that term-time working would be of assistance, possibly because it affords flexibility with respect to childcare but at the cost of reduced annual earnings.

In contrast, 66 per cent of all respondents identified 'more flexible working hours, or flexitime', as a means to achieve a better work–life balance. In the context of the local government sector, flexitime is not especially innovative, and at CityCo it had been available in areas of white-collar employment for many years. Nevertheless, the survey revealed a much wider interest, with 60 per cent of manual workers identifying it as

*Table 10.1* Employees' views of the types of employer provision supportive of an improved work–life balance (%). N = 389.

| | Flexitime | Job share | Reduced hours | Term-time working | Compressed working week |
|---|---|---|---|---|---|
| All respondents | 66 | 20 | 40 | 17 | 33 |
| Women | 62 | 23 | 33 | 24 | 32 |
| Men | 69 | 16 | 46 | 9 | 33 |
| Managers | 69 | 13 | 49 | 5 | 44 |
| Professionals | 73 | 29 | 36 | 22 | 51 |
| Technical & Administrative | 77 | 15 | 36 | 23 | 38 |
| Clerical & Secretarial | 69 | 20 | 33 | 16 | 35 |
| Manual | 60 | 21 | 50 | 18 | 18 |
| Dependent children | | | | | |
| 0 –4 years | 79 | 38 | 45 | 27 | 41 |
| 5–11 years | 76 | 29 | 48 | 33 | 43 |
| 12–18 years | 65 | 19 | 42 | 16 | 28 |
| No dependent children | 65 | 18 | 37 | 11 | 36 |
| Other caring responsibilities | 50 | 20 | 20 | 20 | 10 |

| | Home working | Workplace nursery | Help with childcare costs | Paid parental leave | Career breaks |
|---|---|---|---|---|---|
| All respondents | 37 | 14 | 17 | 23 | 37 |
| Women | 44 | 18 | 20 | 23 | 37 |
| Men | 30 | 9 | 15 | 23 | 37 |
| Managers | 51 | 5 | 8 | 10 | 26 |
| Professionals | 71 | 25 | 34 | 29 | 58 |
| Technical & Administrative | 47 | 13 | 13 | 21 | 36 |
| Clerical & Secretarial | 45 | 12 | 13 | 18 | 32 |
| Manual | 8 | 12 | 18 | 29 | 40 |
| Dependent children | | | | | |
| 0 –4 years | 55 | 55 | 62 | 72 | 52 |
| 5–11 years | 57 | 33 | 57 | 62 | 52 |
| 12–18 years | 30 | 9 | 12 | 26 | 42 |
| No dependent children | 34 | 6 | 5 | 7 | 33 |
| Other caring responsibilities | 40 | 10 | 0 | 10 | 40 |

of potential assistance. As might be expected, employees with young children showed a relatively strong interest in flexible working and 'family-friendly' provision. Parents of children under the age of 12 indicated that, among other 'family-friendly' provisions, a workplace crèche would be of assistance, but this was not available at CityCo. Despite this, when asked if CityCo could be described as a 'family-friendly employer', parents of young children were the most likely to agree. As Table 10.2 shows, 53 per cent of all survey respondents agreed that CityCo was family-friendly; the proportion was higher among women than men, and higher among managers and white-collar professionals than among clerical and manual employees.

The interviews shed some light on these different evaluations. Flexitime was unevenly available in 2001. Many of the professional, administrative and clerical staff interviewed had access to the arrangement, and generally viewed it as an employment benefit. Some commented favourably on the parental leave arrangements. A female administrator argued that 'family-friendly' provision was:

> one of the things that CityCo was really good at ... if you needed to have time off because your child is sick you get that as carer's leave. If you have to come in later than 9.30 in the morning that's fine.

*Table 10.2* Employees' evaluation of whether the Council was a 'family-friendly employer'
(%). N = 389.

| | Yes | No | Undecided |
|---|---|---|---|
| All | 53 | 18 | 29 |
| Women | 57 | 49 | 31 |
| Men | 49 | 23 | 28 |
| Managers | 67 | 13 | 20 |
| Professionals | 64 | 18 | 18 |
| Administrators | 56 | 10 | 34 |
| Clerical & secretarial | 53 | 14 | 33 |
| Manual | 40 | 25 | 35 |
| Dependent children | | | |
| 0 – 4 years | 72 | 7 | 21 |
| 5 – 11 | 56 | 22 | 22 |
| 12–18 | 60 | 19 | 21 |
| No dependent children | 49 | 18 | 33 |
| Other caring responsibilities | 50 | 10 | 40 |
| Full-time permanent | 51 | 21 | 28 |
| Part-time permanent | 56 | 10 | 34 |
| Temporary | 73 | 0 | 27 |

There was also recognition of the employer's interest in family-friendly management. Another woman in an administrative role argued that *'if somebody's ill, like my daughter was, they have got to see their way to help. Because, I mean, otherwise you're going to go out sick.'* Nevertheless, interviews with manual employees revealed a fairly common view that it was difficult to get time-off for family-related crises, or to attend a doctor's or dental appointment. Many employees apparently had not been 'empowered' with knowledge of their new legal entitlements. Flexitime generally was not available to manual employees, despite the provisions of the national 'single status' agreement that prescribes the harmonisation of hours and conditions. The managers of mainly manual staff at CityCo were sceptical that flexitime could be conceded where service delivery had to be competitive with the rates and hours offered by private sector contractors.

Work–life balance is claimed to be 'an issue for everyone, not just parents', and some studies have suggested that employees often value flexible working above higher pay (Employers Organisation for Local Government, 2003). As reported above, among our CityCo survey respondents there was a widely shared view that flexitime would be of work–life balance assistance, and that such provision was regarded as of benefit among those who had access to it in 2001. There was less evidence, however, that employees thought of work–life balance provision as among the most important rewards of paid work.

Our questionnaire asked employees to identify, from a list of 13 items, the three they regarded as the most important – and least important – aspects of work. As Table 10.3 shows, among all survey respondents there was little affection for long working hours; 'plenty of overtime' was cited

*Table 10.3* Employees' evaluation of the most and least important aspects of work (%). N = 389.

| | Most important | Least important |
|---|---|---|
| Good pay | 55 | 6 |
| Getting on well with colleagues | 45 | 8 |
| Good working conditions | 42 | 8 |
| Job security | 42 | 8 |
| Having an interesting job | 37 | 12 |
| Opportunity to use skills | 18 | 6 |
| A fair work–life balance | 17 | 21 |
| Opportunity to use initiative | 11 | 10 |
| Good relations with supervision | 11 | 18 |
| Good training provision | 9 | 21 |
| Having responsibilities at work | 7 | 29 |
| Good promotion prospects | 4 | 47 |
| Plenty of overtime | 1 | 79 |

most frequently as among the least important aspects of work. 'A fair work–life balance' was included as a most important aspect of work by only 17 per cent of all respondents, and 21 per cent rated it as least important. 'Good pay', 'good working conditions', 'getting on well with colleagues' and 'having an interesting job' were all included more frequently as the most important aspects of paid work.

Women were as (un)likely as men to rate 'a fair work–life balance' among the important 'rewards' of paid work, but parental status and occupation were relevant 'variables'. The employees most likely to attach significance to this item were those with dependent children, managers and white-collar professionals. Thirty-eight per cent of employees with children less than four years old, and 30 per cent with children under 12 years, included 'a fair work–life balance' as a most important aspect of work. Among managers, 29 per cent rated 'a fair work–life balance' positively. Given that managers were responsible for the implementation of the work–life balance policy it is perhaps more relevant to note that 21 per cent included it as a least important aspect of work. Women were reasonably well represented among the relatively well paid professional stratum at CityCo, and full-time working was the norm among this occupational group. Among all white-collar professionals, our survey found that 39 per cent rated 'a fair work–life balance' positively, compared with 15 per cent of administrative staff, 12 per cent of secretarial and clerical staff, and 9 per cent of manual workers. It was only among white-collar professionals that 'a fair work–life balance' came close to rivalling 'good pay' as a most important aspect of work.

## Obstacles to a better work–life balance

Employees may express the desire for a better work–life balance (e.g. fewer hours or, in some circumstance, more hours of paid work) without being confident that the work–life balance provisions of employers offer an effective means to the end. Our survey sought to explore the views of employees on workplace issues that might restrict the attainment of a better work–life balance at CityCo. As Table 10.4 shows, excessive work pressures, the demands of service users, and organisational demands within CityCo were identified by nearly half of the respondents as obstacles to a better work–life balance. These factors are, of course, inter-related. The ideal of securing positive work–life balance gains for all parties – for the organisation, service users, and employees – that do not impose costs on other 'stakeholders' – has to confront potential conflicts of interest. Moreover, the principles of partnership include transparency in decision-making and the involvement and consultation of staff. These principles did not appear to be deeply embedded at CityCo where the work–life balance policy was achieved through a union-management partnership in 2001. More than a third of all survey respondents, and 40 per cent of manual workers,

*Table 10.4* Employees' evaluation of obstacles to a better work–life balance (%). N = 389.

| | Demands of council service users | Organisational demands of CityCo | Excessive working hours | Excessive work pressure |
|---|---|---|---|---|
| All respondents | 48 | 48 | 22 | 49 |
| Women | 37 | 40 | 16 | 42 |
| Men | 58 | 53 | 27 | 55 |
| Managers | 66 | 63 | 50 | 68 |
| Professional | 41 | 52 | 15 | 48 |
| Administrator | 51 | 56 | 18 | 56 |
| Clerical | 52 | 49 | 14 | 39 |
| Manual | 43 | 36 | 26 | 52 |

| | Senior management opposition | Line management opposition | Insufficient consultation | Other obstacles |
|---|---|---|---|---|
| All respondents | 25 | 16 | 34 | 7 |
| Women | 23 | 16 | 29 | 7 |
| Men | 27 | 16 | 39 | 7 |
| Managers | 10 | 18 | 24 | 5 |
| Professional | 33 | 23 | 35 | 5 |
| Administrator | 36 | 11 | 27 | 9 |
| Clerical | 27 | 19 | 35 | 6 |
| Manual | 24 | 14 | 40 | 8 |

reported insufficient consultation as an obstacle to their attainment of a better work–life balance.

The survey showed that white-collar professionals had the most developed 'work–life balance consciousness', in the sense of attaching high value to this among the 'rewards' of paid work. Most were employed in central departments and offices where the work–life balance policy was most easily publicised, and many of those interviewed worked in departments where there had been some involvement with the initiative. They were not, however, uncritical of the policy. One woman articulated a feminist perspective that the idea of work–life balance – and its interpretation at CityCo – was a matter of 'freeing up' women 'to go home and do more housework'. Her male colleague thought it would take rather more than flexible and family-friendly employment practices to encourage men to embrace equality in a dual-earner household, rather than their traditional status as the main breadwinner and occasional household work assistant. A woman who had joined CityCo from another local authority thought that its provision of flexible and family-friendly employment practices were decidedly modest in comparison. Some respondents also argued that the scope left for unequal access to work–life balance provision was the principal problem. One woman suggested that:

> You're really at the mercy of whether your manager thinks it's a good thing or a bad thing, or can be bothered to manage the complexity that may be the result in implementing it.

This point is important. CityCo's work–life balance policy – which in certain respects anticipated the provisions of the 2002 Employment Act – gives individuals a right to request flexible working. Their confidence in putting forward a claim, however, may be undermined by their assessment of the 'work norms' set for a department, or for the organisation as a whole. Table 10.4 shows that as the work–life balance policy was being 'rolled out' from the centre in 2001, more employees regarded opposition by senior management, rather than by line managers, as an obstacle to their attainment of a better work–life balance. Nonetheless, opposition by managers was less likely to be viewed as an impediment than excessive work pressures, the demands of service users and organisational pressures. Thus, many employees recognised that the obstacles arose from the pressures bearing on CityCo and its managers, which in turn increased their own work pressures.

These pressures varied in their nature and intensity between directorates and departments and, as the interview data revealed, shaped managers' receptivity to the work–life balance policy. The contract services directorate employed mainly manual workers, and in 2001 many services were still tied into contracts negotiated under the CCT regime. Managers regarded Best Value as a similar challenge and were nervous about the cost and staffing implications of the work–life balance policy, and most other legislative or collectively negotiated provisions for advancing employee welfare and equality objectives. One manager summarised the view of his colleagues.

> On the one hand we have policies, employment policies such as Single Status and equal pay legislation and that sort of thing, and on the other we have the pull of Best Value which is saying you've got to be at least as good value for money as external suppliers ... Sometimes it's very difficult to balance those two because you're not necessarily comparing like with like.

Several managers argued that it was a matter of social justice that manual workers should be treated equally with office employees in respect of working hours and working-time flexibility. At the same time, they raised objections to the extension of flexitime in their service departments.

> We are a trading company. We are in business and we've got a contract which says we'll be available from 8 o'clock in the morning until 5 o'clock at night, and then we'll have an emergency staff available 24 hours a day, 365 days a year.

In other words, there was anxiety about the consequences of employees asserting their right to request flexible working. Nevertheless, some managers accepted the 'business case' for engaging in some innovation. For example, one manager saw the potential of flexitime as a means of arranging early and late shifts to provide service users with a longer 'trading day'.

This would require 'flexibility' from employees over and beyond that which has been conceded over the past ten or fifteen years. For example, in order to meet CCT requirements, the 'job and finish' bonus payment scheme for construction workers was replaced in the 1980s by a cash-based incentive scheme. Fixed pay rates were set for jobs, payment was dependent on job completion, travelling time was calculated into the rate, and there was no payment for 'void calls' – that is, where the tenant was out when the employee arrived. The rates were tight and with the ceiling on earnings removed, employees had an incentive to be functionally flexible or, as one employee expressed the point, to ignore craft demarcations, so that plumbers, for example, put 'sink units in and whole kitchens and things'. Managers acknowledged that employees had become very flexible in a variety of ways, and noted that they now fixed appointments to the convenience of the 'customer', arranging 'to see that person at 6 or 7 o'clock at night'. The net result, as one manager explained, was that workers

> can earn whatever they like, so I imagine that they do earn an awful lot more money, but they work an awful lot harder, or longer.

Initially in the 1980s, construction workers had resisted the new payment scheme. In the negotiations over the implementation of the Single Status agreement after 1997 they rallied to defend it because, by their reckoning, they would incur a five per cent pay cut in shifting to a 37 hour week at the new pay rates on offer. Elsewhere in contract services, employees noted how current pay rates, rather than a 'work addiction', encouraged long hours:

> People are not always tied to the job because they love it. They are actually working because they need to get the money to pay the bills.

A woman working part-time in the catering department who wanted to work term-time only, in order to manage childcare, felt that she was constrained by the reduction in earnings this would involve. A man in grounds maintenance who wanted to work part-time because he was nearing retirement after forty years in paid work, felt constrained by the implications for his pension payments.

Our research included a department employing mainly women on administrative grades that was 'service user facing' and in the front-line of the Best Value reviews. Flexitime has been available for many years and the employees we interviewed viewed it – and other 'family-friendly' provisions – as positive features of CityCo employment. At the same time, however, they had experienced work intensification. The Best Value review involved an explicit threat of service externalisation. The service improvement plan that formed the basis for keeping work in-house – and to which the unions assented as the means of protecting jobs – involved an acceleration of workflow restructuring that had been in train since the end of the 1990s. This embraced a move to generic working (multi-tasking), the regrouping of staff into 'customer focus' teams, a more extensive use of computerised systems and, in one area, the introduction of call centre technology. Office opening-hours were extended and performance management was intensified through testing and target setting. One employee summarised the view that work had become much more pressurised.

> It's definitely got harder and there's that many tasks to perform that it has become more intense. There's a lot more pressure there to get tasks done within a deadline.

Staff had flexibility in their start and finish times, but were expected to complete more work in the time they were at work. A manager noted that:

> This is the pace at which we must accept we all have to work at because whilst *there is the requirement for continuous improvement that will naturally lend itself to continual change.*

Some of the department's managers were enthusiastic about the work–life balance policy because of this. They envisaged home-working as a means of economising on office-costs, and the introduction of a twilight shift to accommodate service users' preferred times for telephoning bill payments or queries. Relatively few of the employees we interviewed were keen and most were concerned that home-working could be isolating. In the event, the proposals were not pursued, possibly because some among the managerial staff were sceptical that the home provided a good environment in which to meet paid-work targets.

## Work stress

The staff surveyed suggested that excessive work pressure was the principal obstacle to a better work–life balance. As Table 10.5 shows, two-thirds reported that the amount of work they were expected to complete each week had increased in the past three years. The proportion was higher in departments that had been subject to a Best Value review (Richardson *et al.*, forthcoming). Among the various occupational groups, managers were the most likely to report an intensification of work and an extension in working hours. In the interviews many managers reported an expansion of their job roles, for example, where departments had been merged or, for line managers, where there were shortages of staff. Best Value performance-monitoring obligations had added to workloads of senior managers and departmental heads. Managers were the occupational group most likely to report excessive working hours as an impediment to a better work–life balance and they were among the most likely to view excessive work pressures as an impediment (see Table 10.4). If raising women's representation at management level is an objective of work–life balance policies, the context does not seem to be especially supportive at CityCo.

*Table 10.5* Employees' perception of work intensification, by gender and occupational group (%). N = 389.

| | Increased | Decreased | Unchanged |
|---|---|---|---|
| Change in the amount of work I am expected to complete compared to 3 years ago | | | |
| All respondents | 66 | 3 | 31 |
| Women | 61 | 6 | 33 |
| Men | 70 | 1 | 29 |
| Manager | 87 | 0 | 13 |
| Professional | 54 | 9 | 37 |
| Administrator | 56 | 11 | 33 |
| Clerical & secretarial | 66 | 2 | 32 |
| Manual | 68 | 0 | 32 |
| Change in the number of hours I am expected to work each week compared to 3 years ago | | | |
| All respondents | 25 | 5 | 70 |
| Women | 26 | 9 | 65 |
| Men | 23 | 3 | 74 |
| Manager | 45 | 0 | 55 |
| Professional | 15 | 15 | 70 |
| Administrator | 21 | 12 | 67 |
| Clerical & secretarial | 19 | 3 | 78 |
| Manual | 27 | 3 | 70 |

It was reported earlier that white-collar professionals were the most 'work–life balance conscious'; that is, they were most likely to rate 'a fair work–life balance' as an important aspect of work. Among this group the proportion reporting work intensification was a relatively low 54 per cent, and the proportion reporting a prolongation of working hours was only 15 per cent. Were these employees relatively successful in asserting their work–life balance interests? Other survey data suggests perhaps not. There was evidence of workplace stress, including a 'negative spill-over' from work to home. Three-quarters of all respondents reported that they felt very tired at the end of the working day: the proportion was 80 per cent for manual employees; 87 per cent for managers; and 72 per cent for professionals. Professional staff were most likely to rate 'an interesting job' as an important aspect of work, but were among the least likely to agree they felt a sense of achievement from their job. They were also among the most likely to report that they worried a lot about their work outside working hours (40% did so in comparison to 34% of all respondents). Thus, attaching importance to work–life balance provision clearly is not the same as attaining a better work–life balance. A woman working in one of the policy departments commented that *'the work–life balance policy is great ... but I don't think I could use it because we're far too busy; that's the experience of most people ... or what I see quite a lot'.*

## Conclusions

The Labour government's work–life balance campaign proposes that greater flexibility in working time can benefit employers and employees, and that workplace innovations can increase efficiency and fairness at work. These assumptions complement the 'mutual gains' philosophy that has been distilled in the concept of partnership at work. Advocates of partnership argue that by working together in a spirit of trust and mutuality, employees and management can advance their respective interests. From this perspective, attention to the quality of working life and employees' work–life balance aspirations are part of a reciprocal exchange that facilitates employee commitment, flexibility and contribution to greater organisational efficiency.

The government has encouraged trade unions and employers in the local government sector to work in partnership to achieve a 'modernisation' of local authority services. The objectives of the government's Best Value policy are to secure sustained economies from all local authorities and a continuous improvement in service quality.

In this context, the employers and unions represented on the NJC have identified the potential for partnership working on work–life balance at local level to satisfy a range of 'stakeholder' interests. The assumption is that the reorganisation of service provision to meet the Best Value imperatives for cost, quality and efficiency improvements can be achieved in ways that are compatible with employee welfare and policy commitments to gender equality in employment. The CityCo case study findings illustrate some of the tensions and contradictions in this project.

First, it was clear that for many employees work–life balance provision in the form on offer was not among the most pressing of claims. The survey showed that a majority of employees agreed with the principle that employers should assist staff to balance work and other aspects of their lives. There appeared to be a latent demand for some forms of flexible working, notably flexitime which was not universally available to CityCo employees in 2001. Yet relatively few respondents rated 'a fair work–life balance' as among the most important rewards of paid work. White-collar professionals were to some extent an exception, but even among this relatively well-paid group, 'a fair work–life balance' was identified less frequently than 'good pay' as a most important aspect of work. Good pay can afford some control over working hours. Conversely, poor pay restricts employees' options, irrespective of the innovative working-time patterns on offer. Male construction workers worked long hours because their pay rates were 'tight'. Women cleaners held multiple short-hours contracts in their effort to balance reasonable pay with childcare or other domestic responsibilities, and a part-time worker in catering would have preferred term-time only working, but could not afford the loss of earnings.

Second, employees identified other work-related constraints to a better work–life balance. Excessive work pressure, service user demands and organisational pressures were each identified by nearly half of all survey respondents as significant obstacles. These factors are inter-related and highlight the difficulties in attempting to reconcile different stakeholder interests. Contributing to excessive work pressures were inadequate staffing; departmental mergers and management de-layering; and the accretion of work-intensifying changes in working practices. More generally, government pressures for cost savings and efficiency gains impacted directly on management. In the departments that had formerly been subject to CCT, and where successful bidding had kept services in-house, managers argued that the scope to effect economies had been exhausted. Best Value extends the scrutiny of performance to all services. In a department that was 'service user facing' and that was subject to a Best Value review at the time of our research, the threat of service externalisation had encouraged trade union co-operation in the management of change in an effort to retain jobs in-house. Among employees the reported outcome of the new working practices, performance targets and performance monitoring regime was work intensification; the demand for higher work effort in a given number of hours, irrespective of how those hours were configured over the working day. Employees in departments subject to a Best Value review were among the most likely to report work intensification, but the experience was not confined among these.

Two-thirds among all CityCo employees who we surveyed in 2001 felt that the amount of work they were expected to complete had increased in comparison with three years previously. This increase in work intensity produced a negative job-to-home spillover for many; for example, feeling very tired at the end of the working day, and worrying a lot about work outside working hours.

Finally, the moves to extend operating or opening hours in some departments – in order to make better use of premises and equipment, or to compete effectively with alternative service suppliers – were rarely viewed positively by permanent employees. In fact, the difficulties in reconciling organisational efficiency objectives, service-user convenience and employees' work–life balance aspirations had become apparent during the 'positive flexibility' pilot study. Few staff in the department affected could see how they stood to gain from an extension of opening hours to include Sunday working. This was in spite of a guarantee from service managers that premium 'unsocial' hours payments would be made. Managers achieved adequate staffing in the first instance only by recruiting – on temporary contracts – a new shift of Sunday-only workers.

Our findings relate to one local authority only. The local government sector is diverse in terms of authority size, the range of services provided, and the climate of union-management relations at local level. Yet CityCo in 2001 was regarded as an exemplar of the partnership approach to work–life balance prescribed by employers and trade unions represented on the NJC, and it seems likely that the tensions revealed by the case study findings are present elsewhere in the sector. Indeed, they are touched on in the evidence submitted by the trade unions and by the employers to the NJC Local Government Pay Commission in 2003. This was established in the wake of the one-day national strike in 2002 that united local authority workers in protest against low pay. The trade union side argued that few local authorities have been sufficiently active in developing work–life balance provision in the interests of gender equality (NJC Trade Union Side, 2003: 17). The employers articulated their frustration with the slow pace of local negotiations to achieve the 'cost effective flexible working' that, in their view, is essential to meet Best Value efficiency and performance targets (Employers Organisation, 2003).

## Notes

1. ESRC award reference number L212252096.
2. The employee survey included questions taken from the Workplace Employment Relations Survey (WERS 98) to allow some comparison with the national data set.
3. Action research, as defined by Reason and Bradbury (2001), differs from conventional research in that it is intended to contribute to existing knowledge and to social action through the active involvement of the researchers as participants in the social system.

## References

Bach, S. and Winchester, D. (2003) 'Industrial Relations in the Public Sector', in Edwards, P. (ed.), *Industrial Relations: Theory and Practice*, 285–312, Oxford: Blackwell.

Berg, P., Kalleberg, K. and Applebaum, E. (2003) 'Balancing Work and Family: The Role of High-Commitment Environments', *Industrial Relations*, 42(2): 168–88.

Cmnd 4014 (1998) *Modern local government: in touch with the people*, London: The Stationary Office.

Colling, T. (1999) 'Tendering and outsourcing: working in the contract state?', in Corby, S. and White, G. (eds), *Employee Relations in the Public Services*, 136–55, London: Routledge.

DTI (2001) *Essential guide to work-life balance*, September. London: Department of Trade and Industry.

DTI (2003). Balancing work and family life: enhancing choice and support for parents, January, www.dti.gov.uk/er/workingparents

Employers Organisation for Local Government (2003) Evidence to the Local Government Pay Commission, April, www.lg.employers.gov.uk/conditions/commission/evidence

Geddes, M. (2001) 'What about the workers? Best Value, employment and work in local public services', *Policy & Politics*, 29(4): 497–508.

Green, F. (2001) 'It's Been a Hard Day's Night: The Concentration and Intensification of Work in Late Twentieth-Century Britain', *British Journal of Industrial Relations*, 39(1): 53–80.

Hegewisch, A. (1999) 'Employment flexibility: push or pull?', in Corby, S. and White, G. (eds), *Employee Relations in the Public Services*, 114–35, London: Routledge.

Hogart, T., Hasluck, C. and Pierre, G., with Winterbotham, M. and Vivian, D. (2001) Work-Life Balance 2000. Results from the Baseline Study. DfEE Research Report. London: Department for Education and Employment.

Involvement and Participation Association (1997) *Towards Industrial Partnership*, London: IPA.

Knell, J. (1999) *Partnership at Work*, Department of Trade and Industry (DTI) Employment Relations Research Series No. 7.

Martin, S. (2000) 'Implementing 'Best Value': local public services in transition', *Public Administration*, 78(1): 209–27.

Martinez Lucio, M. and MacKenzie, R. (1999) 'Quality management: a new form of control?', in Corby, S. and White, G. (eds), *Employee Relations in the Public Services*, 156–74, London: Routledge.

NJC for Local Government Services. (2001) Finding the Balance. Work-life Policies in Practice, September, www.lg-employers.gov.uk/documents/publications

NJC Trade Union Side Submission to the NJC Local Government Pay Commission, May 2003.

Osterman, P. (1995) 'Work/Family Programs and the Employment Relationship', *Administrative Science Quarterly*, 40, December, 681–700.

Reason, R. and Bradbury, H. (eds) (2001) Handbook of Action Research, London: Sage.

Report of the Local Government Pay Commission, October 2003.

Richardson, M., Tailby, S., Danford, A., Stewart, P. and Upchurch, M. (2003) 'Best Value and Workplace Partnership in local government', Forthcoming in *Personnel Review*, 34(6): 2005.

Stevens, J., Brown, J. and Lee, C. (2004) *The Second Work-life Balance Study: Results from the Employees' Survey*, DTI Employment Relations Research Series No. 27.

Terry, M. (2003) 'Can "partnership" reverse the decline of British trade unions?' *Work, Employment and Society*, 17(3): 459–72.

Thornley, C. (2003) *More Cold Comfort. A UNISON briefing document for the NJC Local Government Pay Commission*, London: UNISON.

Trades Union Congress (1999) *Partners for Progress: New Unionism at the Workplace*, London: TUC.

Trades Union Congress (2000) *Partnership. A boost to business*, London: TUC.

Trades Union Congress (2003) UK Productivity. Shifting to the high road. TUC Economic and Social Affairs Department, August.

White, M., Hill, S., McGovern, P., Mills, C. and Smeaton, D. (2003) 'High-performance', Management Practices, Working Hours and Work-life Balance', *British Journal of Industrial Relations*, 41(2): 175–96.

Wood, S. (1999) 'Family-Friendly Management: Testing the Various Perspectives', *National Institute Economic Review*, 168 (April), 99–116.

Wood, S.J., de Menezes, L.M. and Lasaosa, A. (2003) 'Family-Friendly Management in Great Britain: Testing Various Perspectives', *Industrial Relations*, 42(2): 221–50.

# 11

# Multiple Burdens: Problems of Work–Life Balance for Ethnic Minority Trade Union Activist Women

*Harriet Bradley, Geraldine Healy and Nupur Mukherjee*

> I am a full-time mum, I work, I am a taxi driver, I am a banker, I am everything at the moment that's how I feel, plus I am a first aider, plus I am a union rep, so at the end of the day when I go home I am absolutely whacked. But my job does not stop there. I have to carry on and cook and clean and spend time with the kids and that, but sometimes it would be nice if I had somebody to offload on... . I do not get on very well with my area organiser at the moment so it doesn't help that I haven't got that support there. (*Anita, Indian, 30s, widow, children*)

While much has been written about work–life balance, the parameters of the debate, both policy-oriented and academic, have been rather limited. The focus of the debate has been on working mothers and how they can reconcile the burdens of looking after their children and homes with the demands of employment, particularly in contemporary Britain with its intensified 'lean' production systems, stressful management regimes and long hours' culture. What else might lie in the largely unpicked 'life' side of the equation is often unquestioned, while 'work' is typically viewed in line with New Labour thinking as the chief mechanism of social inclusion (Levitas, 1998). The work–life balance, then, in New Labour terms is about finding solutions to a major contradiction in Blairite policy: the imperative of securing full citizenship by means of getting as many as possible of the population into the labour market and out of state dependency, while at the same time securing social order by improved parenting and highlighting parental responsibility for their offsprings' future as adult worker-citizens. What a more satisfactory work–life balance might be in terms of a whole range of wider social activities and relationships is rarely considered. But people interviewed by the authors of this chapter have tended to see the issue in these broader terms: how to pull together paid work and career development, family life and friendships, leisure, education and training, voluntary work and community activities to achieve a rich full life but retain health and sanity.

Thus, one little regarded aspect of the long hours' culture and the problems it poses for work–life balance is its impact on voluntary and community work and political organisations. Older women who are not in employment have in the past been the backbone of the voluntary labour force and of local community associations. The increase in women's labour market employment, especially that of mothers (even if that is largely part-time) clearly jeopardises women's continued involvement in such activities. Hochschild (1989) has pointed to the fact that women not only face a double burden or 'second shift' of housework, but also are responsible for a 'triple shift', the labour of emotional maintenance of their households and (extended) families. What time, then, is left for working women for community activism or political participation?

Our chapter considers this problem in relation to women's trade union involvement. Previous research has continually highlighted the barriers posed by women's household duties to their full participation in their unions' activities (Stageman, 1980; Coote and Kellner, 1980; Bradley, 2000). Here we consider these problems in relation to a particularly under-represented grouping, minority ethnic women, with a focus on the experiences of women of South Asian, African and Caribbean origins living in Britain, who are active union members. The chapter draws on data from a project entitled 'Double Disadvantage' which was part of the 'Future of Work' programme. It is perhaps the first piece of systematic British research focused entirely on minority ethnic trade union female lay activists. Semi-structured interviews were carried out with 57 women activists in 2001–2; 52 of these interviews form the basis of this chapter.

It is pertinent that the women in our study are trade union activists since research demonstrates that family-friendly policies are more common in organisations where *inter alia* there are recognised trade unions (Dex and Smith, 2002; Bond *et al.*, 2002). The black and Asian women in our study are part of the voice of trade unions in the workplace and are seeking to make that voice more responsive to their needs. Their roles as volunteer workers and committed political activists are therefore inextricably linked to their workplaces and as such provide both opportunities and constraints. We would also argue that the factors that enable women trade unionists to balance the 'triple shift' (work, family and voluntary activities) have much in common with those that come into play in other forms of work–life balance. The difference lies in the degrees of freedom that surround the 'choice' to become active in the union and the multiple effects of additional union activities on work–life balance, and in this particular case, the intersection with ethnicity and racism.

In Britain, black and minority ethnic workers were more likely to become union members, particularly African-Caribbean workers (Modood *et al.*, 1997), although recent Labour Force Survey data suggest that this has been sustained for women but not for men (Brooke, 2002). From Table 11.1, it can be seen that black women, of all minority and majority ethnic women, are most likely to be trade union members with a density of 33 per cent, followed by white women (28%), mixed race (27%) Asian or Asian British (26%) and Chinese and other ethnic groups (24%).

Part of the explanation for differences may lie in sectoral employment characteristics. Women are more likely than men to work in the public sector and this tendency is greater for black women and those from ethnic groups (except Indian women) (Hibbett, 2002). Trade union attachment may also reflect black women's awareness of their greater vulnerability at work, but as we shall seek to show in this chapter, it also reflects their strong commitment to civil society and community. Likewise, American research has reported the very important role minority ethnic women have filled in voluntary and community associations (Newman, 2000; Chow *et al.*, 1996). Many minority women are also involved in church or religious group activities.

Yet at the same time, African-Caribbeans are more likely than other women to be bringing up children alone. Modood *et al.* (1997) reported that among their respondents, 47 per cent of Caribbean never married women had dependent children as opposed to 16 per cent of white women and virtually none among South Asian groups. It is also of interest that among formerly married women (widowed, divorced or separated), Pakistani/Bangladeshi and Indian women were the most likely to have dependent children (67% and 58% respectively) than white (51%) and Caribbean (50%) women. The data suggest that white women are more likely to be free of the tasks of caring for children than black and Asian groups.

*Table 11.1* Union density by ethnicity: United Kingdom, autumn 2001

| Ethnic group | All<br>% | Men<br>% | Women<br>% |
|---|---|---|---|
| White | 29 | 30 | 28 |
| Black or Minority ethnic | 26 | 24 | 28 |
| *Of which* | | | |
| Mixed | 25 | 22 | 27 |
| Asian or Asian British | 25 | 25 | 26 |
| Black or Black British | 30 | 27 | 33 |
| Chinese and other ethnic Groups | 22 | 20 | 24 |
| **All employees** | 29 | 30 | 28 |

*Source*: Labour Force Survey (Brooke 2002).
This table uses the National Statistics classification of ethnic group consistent with the 2001 Census.

Many Caribbean families are female-headed and there is a characteristic pattern of early motherhood which contrasts with the delayed family-formation patterns of the white majority population and, as we shall see, is reflected in our study. On the other hand, there has also been a strong tradition in the Caribbean diaspora of female relatives pooling resources and collaborating in childcare. South Asian families, too, tend to have stronger links with the wider kin, therefore offering potential childcare support; however socio-cultural rules may limit the options of type, timing and location of jobs especially for Muslim wives. There are also what we might call 'migratory families' among Asian, Caribbean and African communities, where family members may be scattered widely around the globe, thus adding complexities to women's lives. In migratory families, children may be moved between countries and relatives for purposes of schooling and/or caring. Unsurprisingly, the demand for extended leave rights has come from migratory communities and, where provided, contributes to solving some problems of balancing work and family. Such leave allows women to make periodic visits to their children while having them brought up by family members in Jamaica or Nigeria; thus the mothers can concentrate on their full-time work while children are very young.

Of interest to this paper is whether the incidence of lone parenthood among these groups affects their ability to become active within their unions. This question highlights a deficiency of the literature and debates on work–life balance. It may be argued that behind much of the discussion is an ethnocentric assumption about the nature of household/family relationships. Implicit in the discussion of 'the family' is a model of the two-parent white nucleated family, which, as we know, is increasingly likely to have two earners, although men still tend to be the major earners (Bradley *et al.*, 2002a; Hakim, 1995). Yet families reflect complex patterns many of which pose special problems of 'balance' between employment and other aspects of life.

This chapter, then, looks at the specificities of work–life balance in the lives of black and minority ethnic women and how this impacts on their trade union involvement. It reveals the 'multiple burdens' faced by many of these women, the constraints that face them and the solutions they have adopted. Respondents' accounts stress the difficulties they encounter in coping with childcare and other domestic demands, while they often face tremendous pressure to participate as representational black women on a range of bodies. Our respondents show remarkable commitment and enthusiasm for their work within unions and for ethnic community organisations, yet are frustrated by the constraints of time. The chapter explores the ways in which these women contrive to juggle the demands of their jobs, their families and their union and community roles; and suggests ways in which unions might facilitate their further involvement.

## The study and the respondents

The Double Disadvantage project employed qualitative methodologies, based on case studies of four unions, which represent workers in a broad range of occupations, CWU (communication workers), NATFHE (the lecturers' union), UNISON (the major public sector organiser) and USDAW (shop and allied workers). The first phase of the research involved interviewing national and local level officers from each of the four unions. Documentation was collected from the four unions and the TUC and the research team attended a large number of conferences and workshops for women and black union members.

The core of the project was the second phase which involved semi-structured, in-depth interviews with 57[1] minority ethnic female activists from the four unions, including three pilot interviews. The target was 15 in each union but it proved hard to locate or access black women activists in NATFHE and CWU. The interviews were transcribed and analysed using a thematic approach based on iterative readings. The interviews covered women's educational background; employment histories; history of union participation and experience of activities within the union; family background and circumstances; and the needs and priorities of minority women as they themselves defined them. The researcher who carried out the interviews was Asian and was able to build up a rapport with the women which produced remarkably frank and detailed accounts of their experiences: often the interviews ranged widely across their life and work histories. This was true with both Asian and African-Caribbean respondents, possibly reflecting their commitment to a politics of 'black solidarity' in the unions across minority ethnic groups. The two main researchers were white women academics and we were concerned that this might prove a barrier to the project's development. However, this did not prove to be a problem. All the women we encountered were welcoming, helpful and enthusiastic and there was a genuine desire for the voices of black and Asian women[2] to be listened to and publicised.[3]

The women interviewed were shop assistants, post office and British Telecom workers, nurses, social and community workers, council employees, lecturers in further and higher education and teachers in adult education. Although they portrayed their own ethnicity in a wide range of terms, for the purpose of presenting the data clearly we categorised them on the basis of their parents' areas of origin, as African-Caribbean (33), African (10) and Asian (12). 36 lived in London, eight in the South West and 11 elsewhere. The characteristics of our interviewees echo Modood *et al.*'s (1997) findings on lone parenthood. Among our 52 interviewees 21 were lone parents (either single mothers or separated/divorced); of these all but four were African-Caribbean or African. Another 19 were married with children and only 12 had no children (six of these being single). Our interviewees were interesting in they do not fit the conventional view of women trade unionists as either older or younger; our group were primarily in the middle range in their thirties and forties. Eight were in the fifties, 20 in their forties, 22 in their thirties and two in their twenties.

We called the project 'double disadvantage' because that term, along with 'making women visible', had been the twin themes of a seminar for black women unionists held by the TUC, which one of the team attended prior to the commencement of the research. While there are perceived problems with the term in its implication that minority women may be presented as victims and that other aspects of disadvantage (notably class) may be ignored, we found that many of the interviewees did respond strongly to the term in that they had found themselves the target of both racist and sexist practices. In particular, they reported high levels of racism, especially in issues around promotion; many had experienced racist abuse from customers, colleagues and managers, along with more subtle intimations of difference and 'otherness' from workmates which we have referred to as 'everyday racism' (for detail see Healy, Bradley and Mukherjee, 2003). Since women may be able to resist such practices and emerge triumphant, we now find it more accurate to speak of 'double' and indeed 'multiple discrimination' rather than disadvantage. Women listed other aspects of discrimination such as age, nationality, level of education, motherhood and religion.

The experience of the women in our study reveals an aspect of 'work–life balance' that is frequently ignored in the narrow nature of the debates. Work is not assumed as being the core of the problem, rather the reconciling of the demands of time and children are perceived as the problem. However, for many black and Asian women the negative experiences of racism at work may make such a reconciliation harder to achieve. Studies on work–life balance have emphasised the importance of managerial discretion (Bond *et al.*, 2002; Dex and Smith, 2002). In our study, managerial discretion was given as one of key causes of discriminatory treatment. Work–life balance strategies are part of the raft of policies designed to improve women and men's working lives, but their implementation is often subject to managerial whim rather than consistent interpretation of policies. Women from minority groups may be particularly at risk from discretionary behaviour, which may be imbued with racist and sexist bias, and may negatively prejudice decision-making.

The experience of discrimination was of particular significance in considering the lives of our respondents, as many of them had become active in the union specifically because of the frustration they experienced when their aspirations were blocked. Women joined the union and became active because they themselves had experienced discrimination, because other women had suffered or because of a general strong affiliation to the anti-racist cause. Many of them were already active within their own community organisations. Once they became involved in the union many found a new outlet for their energies and talents in taking on more formal union roles; and a number developed aspirations to become full-time workers for the unions. The union then became an 'alternative' career for these women, many of whom had already made career switches in their lives as a result of blocked aspirations (see Bradley, Healy and Mukherjee, 2004).

However, if women are to develop union careers, the demands on their time will be considerable. Apart from the time required within the workplace to deal with problems and negotiations, union activists will be expected to take part in training courses and summer schools, attend conferences and rallies, sit on various committees at local, regional and national level. How did women manage to cope with a third set of duties and responsibilities when many were already shouldering the 'double burden' of employment and household management?

## Balancing lives: carers, second chancers and 'exceptional women'

The story and comments of Tania may stand as a typical case among our respondents. Tania is African-Caribbean, in her thirties, a single parent with two children, one aged 14 and a little one aged three. She is a Londoner and works as an office manager. When asked why with her long experience of her organisation she had not gone for higher management her reply highlighted family commitments:

> I just don't fancy it, I don't fancy the added stress, the added pressure, I've got two children at home and I wouldn't want to go home and take it out on them or have no time for them, if I knew it wasn't stressful or demanding, I suppose I would have gone for it ages ago, but erm, I've seen some managers and they go off with stress.

Tania made clear that family came first for her;

> My children are my first priority, then my family, my friends, and that's about the lot. So you, you don't want work to take over your life, like some of them in there, because they have to take work home, they are stuck on that laptop until about seven o'clock.

Yet despite her resistance to the long hours' culture, Tania works for her local residents' association and is becoming active in her union, holding a branch post. She is typically enthusiastic about her union work, telling us that she wanted to 'delve deeper into her role', that it was 'exciting to be part of it.' How, then, did she manage the balance?

> when I take my foot out of here and go through the gate, I don't think about work, I go home, I go pick up the little one (from nursery), big one normally at home, and it's sort out dinner, then Lucy will be in her room, Josie will be in the corridor playing with her friends, I'll be sorting out dinner, and whatever, six o' clock we sit down to eat and then I chill, I chill out.

It is clear here that the network of female family support, characteristic of Caribbean culture, comes to her aid. Her elder daughter Lucy helps out with chores and when she has to go away for conferences and training, her sister or her mother looks after the children: 'yeah and it's like a miniature holiday because I haven't got them (laughs) so I get a childfree day'.

It is instructive that Tania has put work for two voluntary agencies, the union and the residents' association, before any kind of personal work-based ambition. This was typical of our respondents, relating, as we have said, partly to their ambitions being blocked in their jobs, but also, as in Tania's case, because of their commitment to equal opportunities and supporting their own ethnic communities. However, like Tania, all must weigh up options. We can distinguish three rough patterns of response here. For some people caring responsibilities clearly dominated and limited the amount of time they were prepared to give to their voluntary activities; a second group who we might call 'second chancers' tended to discharge their caring duties until children were grown up enough to be independent and then take up union activism, often with an extraordinary level of commitment. Finally there was a small group of 'exceptional women' who seemed to be able to juggle an amazing array of activities without flagging.

### Constrained carers: family as primary orientation.

We are uncomfortable with the position that some women put family first and others by implication do not. This is not a discourse used for the relationship between men and their families. Nevertheless we know that in the UK women take primary responsibility for children and family. Equally we know that we were by definition talking to women who had been able to take on a degree of activism; few of our sample could straightforwardly be described as 'family-oriented' in the way Hakim (1995) has implied. However, such an orientation was often used to explain why relatively few women, especially minority women, became active in their unions:

> Women don't want to get in anything that is too heavy, you know, some women just feel they've got enough problems at home. (*Amina, African, 30s, single*)

> Asian women do suffer a lot because generally their timing is not easy. You know, they have to be home in the evenings to make the dinner, be with their husbands, be with the children. (*Neera, Asian Sikh, 20s, married*)

Others suggested that the attitudes of Asian husbands about propriety and women's roles were a restraint to their involvement in unions. Evening meetings held in pubs and such places were also said to deter the involvement of some, especially older, Asian women. This has long been considered a barrier to women's participation in unions and it is unfortunate that women are still reporting that they are alienated from meetings that are held in pubs.

Some of the women, whose involvement with the union was limited, explained that family responsibilities were too great: Meryl, who is Caribbean, 26 with three children, splits shifts with her husband who does the 'earlies' before picking the kids up, thus allowing her to do the 10 to 7 shift. But she feels that it would be 'unfair to the kids' to become more active. Others reflected the long-term importance of investing time in the family:

> Of course you're gonna start pushing towards your family because they're the most important thing in your life. The job might not always be there, hopefully your family will. They've got to be your first priority. (*Jane, African-Caribbean, married, children*)

A few women had experienced pressure from families to give up their union work:

> It is difficult because my partner wants me to give up. I mean, I might be actually leaving the company, but he wants me to give up the union because he feels it's taking time away from him and Sarah (two-year old daughter). (*Mona, African-Caribbean, 30s*)

### Second chancers: 'this is my time'

Rita has worked for a retailer for 25 years, but refused promotion because it involved working Saturdays and she felt she needed that time with her two children. Now she has become active as a steward and a regional delegate, since her children are at university:

> You know, being a mother, a wife, working. You just concentrated on the family. That's all I was doing. And then the family was growing up and they were leaving off to university and I started to find my own interests… . I'd reached a certain age and I thought 'this is my time now'

> because I hadn't done anything for myself and I'd always done it for him (her husband). So this was for myself. To fulfil myself ... This is my time and I'm enjoying what I'm doing. *(African-Caribbean, 50s, divorced, children)*

Rita's strategy was the opposite from that employed by many young women today who attempt to establish a career before starting a family (Hewlett, 2002)[4] and she muses on this difference:

> I suppose I've had my clock the other way round. I should have done it first and then concentrated on family.

Lois, a lecturer who is married with three children, also sees herself as regenerating her career, though her aspirations lie in management rather than union work.

> Now I'm going into my forties and seeing life differently. ...gosh, I do need to move on. I've got all this expertise, all these strengths and skills and energy. I've said 'no I'm not ready because I have a lot of commitments you know, with my family and all sorts.' Well I'm thinking differently now. *(African, 40s)*

Lois was one of a number who told us that they had had to turn down opportunities which came up when their children were born, because they felt they hadn't the time or because they felt it would be unfair to their children. We have here a familiar picture of maternal altruism. When children get older, though, there is often a shift in how women perceive the world and their place in it, as Candy's comment shows:

> My priority is myself... For years I've put other things and other people first in my life and now I am getting to a stage where I am getting old, I'll be 50 next year and I, I think I need to put myself first. *(African-Caribbean, married, children)*

**Exceptional women:[5] doing it all**

Carole, who is married with three children, chose a different strategy:

> I have always worked full-time. I've had maternity leaves and went back straight to work. So I've been working since the age of 16 ... I've committed myself to being a working mother. *(African-Caribbean, 40s)*

Miranda also was committed to being a working mother. Definitely something of a 'superwoman', she started as a nurse, had two children on her own, found nursing incompatible with motherhood so started a second career in teaching:

> I was working, doing a degree, looking after the children, so busy, was part-time work of course. (*African-Caribbean, 50s*)

She worked in the evenings while others looked after her children and steadily constructed a teaching career, starting as a volunteer, then a part-time visiting lecturer until she had her degree and could work full-time. Now she has added union activism to her busy life:

> I went to the branch meeting and they were asking for volunteers and I thought because I seem to have more time, perhaps I'm not so pressed now so I says well yes I'd volunteer for black staff. (*African-Caribbean, 50s*)

Shahnaz was one of the most extraordinary women we interviewed. As well as being a leading union activist, she had an array of other activities, including being a magistrate, a Labour Party activist and local candidate, and a housing association officer. She also had two children, and stated that she would not be able to manage without a very supportive husband. She put down her incredible level of energy to ambition to be the best at what she does:

> It's hard. I think we work a lot harder than our mothers did. Because they knew exactly what they were doing and we're trying to be superwomen. And I suppose I still have this thirst, this hunger. I just want to get to the highest point until I decide I've burned out and I just want to sort of crash and chill out completely. (*Pakistani, 40s*)

Shahnaz is relatively young, but Gita and Shelley who are older with grown-up children seem to have escaped from 'burnout'. Gita has a major union post and does voluntary work for the homeless as well as looking after grandchildren. She reflects on the mental strains of it:

> It's very hard, very difficult indeed ... because you're thinking of ... say for instance in the union you've got a case, you're dealing with that. Then come Friday you have to leave it. Monday, you've gone to your other job, you're carrying all the work with you. You're taking the union work with you, back to the other office, so you're always thinking. (*African-Caribbean, 40s, widowed, children*)

But, when asked how she copes, her reply is indicative:

> I don't know how I do it really. But if you really want to you can.

Shelley is also incredibly active in the union with ambitions to rise to the very top. She describes herself as a traditional wife whose life has been changed and invigorated by her union involvement. Two of her children (by her former husband) are grown, but the third is three years old. How does she cope?

> Oh! Juggle! To be honest I couldn't do it unless my husband was as supportive as he is. (*African-Caribbean, 30s*)

Nonetheless she has had to turn down the chance of becoming a tutor in race awareness because it would involve residential work and long absences from home which she considered incompatible with having a young child.

## Having it all? Coping with multiple burdens

The reality behind 'having it all' is a complex myriad of strategies and resources that enabled the women to contribute their talents so widely. The strategies of juggling and organising worked hand in hand with personal, family and institutional resources.

### Juggling and organising

As the comments above indicate, 'juggling' was a common theme. We asked Neera how she managed to juggle her job in retail with doing a degree in marketing and being a union rep:

> It's all about priority making. It might sound bad but if I have an exam during the week I generally put work aside till I've done it. Then I concentrate on work again. (*Asian, 20s, married, no children*)

So how do the really active women manage this juggling? Energy was stated to be important, but organisation and firmness were mentioned by some of the jugglers. Bella's children are grown up now but since she set out to build her new lifestyle she still portrays a life of extraordinary activity: along with her job she actually started her own USDAW branch, is an activist and branch secretary, who would like a union career, is a school governor, a councillor and active in her local Race Equality Council, attends evening classes. How does she cope?

> I don't know! I'm just extremely organised … I have a big board in the kitchen, on the kitchen wall. Everything is plastered on there highlighted and then keyed so I can organise them. (*African, 40s, married, children*)

Shelley gives a similar account:

> It's very much a case of juggling. Because some nights we have to sit down with our diaries and say, right you do this, you do that. We spend a lot of time trying to juggle, slot things in. (*African-Caribbean, 30s, married, children*)

Mona, whose partner wants her to give up work and union activity nonetheless feels she can just about cope:

> I feel that I can do both, but it is difficult. You have to be very ordered and, you know, everything sort of structured. If work's going OK, if you've got no problems, then, yeah, you can juggle it. As soon as there's problems, then you've gotta let something drop. (*African-Caribbean, 30s, married, child*)

Similarly Gita emphasises the need for self-reflexivity and self-control as a way to avoid stress and burn out:

> I try to discipline myself, to say, right, when it's getting stressful take a break. You know, just stop, count to ten and start again basically. (*African-Caribbean, 40s, widowed, children*)

She does confess however, to having passed nights with only three or four hours of sleep, sitting up drinking cups of coffee to keep her awake while she pored over documents for her casework.

Indeed, the balance is often fragile. Joanne's biography has a clear 'exceptional woman' feel. With four children she worked part-time when they were young, worked as volunteer for Women's Aid, at a nursery and with the elderly, did an NVQ as a gym trainer, a counselling course, a university degree, and did a variety of jobs including as a trained hairdresser. However, now she has a problem with her teenage son, which requires her to look after him, and she has no childcare assistance, and this is currently blocking her union activity:

> I'd love to go ... but can't attend all the courses so I don't feel I want to represent the union anymore. Because there's so much going on that you need to be spot on with everything. And I'm a bit of a person if I can't do it the whole way, I don't do it at all. (*African-Caribbean, 40s, divorced, children*)

Reading the women's stories leaves one often gasping with admiration for the energy that is clearly being deployed. Miranda's account of her involvement with the black women workers' movement gives an insight into how the 'empowerment' felt at being involved in something constructive and that the sense of support and solidarity can in itself be an energising force:

> I found it was useful, I mean just stimulating the fact that you tend to feel less isolated and I think it reduced the idea of me being isolated. (*African-Caribbean, 50s, single*)

Candy demonstrated the incremental nature of such events and how they transfer into strategies at the local level.

> I've got my sort of feeling about trying to resurrect a group here, a black and ethnic minority group within the college, that's how I, I've got this bug that I think I need to know more about what's going on and see if I can do something in terms of that and I think that came about from my attending conference and I think maybe I'm hoping that when I attend sort of this next one it will inspire me a bit more to do, to really get it together. (*African-Caribbean, 40s, married, children*)

### Networks of support

Support from various sources is another key resource, and, as previous quotations have indicated, partners are a crucial source of support for some of these women, as for white women. Bella highlighted this:

> Most important, people forget that you need the support at home. I've got a very, very good supportive husband.

Shahnaz also put her success down to a supportive husband and parents, noting that the latter often cooked for them and baby-sat, while 'my husband takes the kids to school and my father picks them up.' Other women noted help from siblings, friends and neighbours, reflecting the strengthened female support networks typical of African-Caribbean societies and diaspora. For example Miranda praised her friends:

> I have been very fortunate in the fact that I have had support, there have been people there for me when I needed help and also in the fact that I was able to get my children into full-time nursery ... put them in at 8 o'clock and pick them up again at 5.00. (*African-Caribbean, 50s*)

Sometimes the ethnic community itself provides help as it did for Shelley in her volunteer role:

> Family workshops as well, especially during the summer periods when school was off you could take your children with you... So my daughter

> was always with me a lot of the time. Because there was a crèche facility so that she could get included. So it wasn't like putting my child away somewhere, I had her with me, you know.

Support from the family remains perhaps the key factor for many women, but it should be remarked that this can sometimes provoke other problems. Amina was from a Nigerian migratory family. When she came to England as a single parent her mother took on the task of looking after her child, but her disapproval of Amina's situation led to constant conflict:

> I would say the first four years my mum and I were falling out basically nearly every day, Monday to Sunday 24/7 if I was at home, so I tried to avoid being at home so I worked a lot, I mean there was one time I had like four jobs just to be out of the house ... So I left her to my mum, my mum and her formed a bond but I was still like the outside person.

To the Nigerian mother, Amina's mistake of having a child 'out of wedlock' was exacerbated by Amina's desire to study rather than simply work to support her child. Things subsequently stabilised however and Amina's mother takes the child, now eight, to and from school, enabling Amina to do her jobs and take a degree.

## Institutional support

There are also institutional arrangements which can enable women to fit the different strands of their life together. Several women mentioned understanding bosses and line managers who allowed them to go off to union meetings, indicating that managerial discretion underpins this permission. Proper time-off arrangements for union duties had helped a few women to develop union careers. But others complained that the policies of unions and employers acted to block their chances of participation. Mona, for example, stated that 'if the union and the company were serious' in wanting to support black workers' networks 'they'd insist it's done on a weekday'. This was a common complaint, as the requirement to spend weekends away from home pushed the jugglers' skills to the limit. Union paid officials need to give more thought to diverse ways of delivering training and networking options. This is of course importantly an issue of gender as white women too face problems of going to weekend events because of domestic responsibilities, and in some cases through husbands' disapproval. Nevertheless, Kirton and Healy's (2004) study of residential women-only union education demonstrated a diversity of respondents with regard to family responsibilities.

There are clearly also ways in which organisations can help employees although the more radical forms of 'family-friendly policy' were not much mentioned here. Flexitime and the availability of part-time work did, however, get mentioned in the women's stories. Carole takes advantage of the flexible hours which are available in retail to manage her childcare commitments. These are especially crucial for single parents and mothers of very young children. Shelley had held a variety of part-time jobs when her children were young and while she was a lone mother after her divorce. She joined her current company because of its family-friendly culture:

> What really sold it to me was a flexible hours' contract within which I could work flexitime. So if I wanted to take the kids to the doctors, dentist, that sort of stuff I could take them and then make the time up. (*African-Caribbean, 30s, married, children*)

However, many women reported contrasting experiences of unsympathetic managers who had penalised them for union work or blocked their career moves, reiterating our earlier point about the significance of management discretion.

## Conclusions

> Candy: One of the union reps was sort of I mean you've got such a voice why don't you be a rep and I think well I haven't got the time, haven't got the energy you know to commit myself ... if I'm not able to commit myself sort of at least 90 per cent it's not worth it.
> Interviewer: Is it that if you weren't overloaded with work and with domestic commitments...?
> Candy: Yes, yes, I would, you know I would, yes.

We have given examples of 'exceptional women' who, through energy and commitment, juggling and organisation, and support from partners, kin or community, have succeeded in coping with a 'triple burden' of union work. However, for some, like Candy, the double burden of home and work precludes developing a more active union role. This chapter has surveyed problems of work–life balance for black women trade union activists and tried to tease out the specificity of their experiences. As women, subject to the dynamic of gender (Bradley, 1996), they continue to be the main performers of domestic labour and perhaps even more importantly the main bearers of family welfare and values. Thus, just like all women, the black activists find their choices constrained when their children are young, and struggle to keep their careers going. This means sacrificing opportunities, making tough choices and relying where it is available on family support and institutional flexibilities. In common with white women, most black mothers stress the prioritisation of family needs.

However, ethnicity combines with gender to create specific circumstances which differ from the majority. Studies of white union activists have tended to suggest that such women are more likely to be single or at least to have grown-up children (Colgan and Ledwith, 1996). Like Kirton and Healy's study (2004), this was not the case among our black and minority ethnic women activists. The majority of our sample, nearly two-thirds, was of Caribbean origin. These women are more likely to be currently or at some time in their lives bringing up children without a present male partner, which makes their burden of domestic work greater. The small number of South Asian women we interviewed makes it unwise to generalise about their experience, but we suspect that, while divorce, separation and single parenthood are less common among those of South Asian origin, cultural expectations about the wife's role also put constraints on South Asian married women's time.

Thus we might hypothesise that their 'double burdens' will be such as to inhibit their involvement in political, voluntary and community activities, such as union work. Against this, it seems that many minority ethnic women are able to tap into extensive networks of support. This reflects the characteristic child-raising patterns of Caribbean societies which are strongly based in communality and sharing and also the typical 'moral economy' of migratory families in which kin obligations and duties are still strongly held (Rapaport *et al.*, 1982; Chamberlain, 1997). This contrasts with the 'privatisation' and 'disembedding' of Western families commented on by so many sociologists, from Parsons and Bale (1956) and Goldthorpe *et al.* (1969) to Giddens (1998) and Beck (1992).

Whilst struggling to handle the demands of family and work, the black and Asian women in our study also suffered the multiple effects of racism and sexism first hand. This experience shaped their willingness to get involved in trade unions and also provided the conditions, which led to a strong sense of social justice in the workplace and in their local communities. Thus the attachment of these women to voluntary work, especially within the ethnic communities, was a key issue emerging from the study. A clear difference from white women activists is that the route into activism is through commitment to anti-racist politics and equal opportunities (see Bradley, Healy and Mukherjee, 2002b; Healy, Bradley and Mukherjee, 2004). One of the 'tough' choices these women have to make is between not just family and career, but also between family, career and volunteer work, that is, whether to take on another 'shift' – the starting point of this chapter. While women spoke of having to put family and/or paid employment before voluntary or union work because of caring and economic requirements they did so often with regret. Miranda expressed her preference as follows:

> Because it involved bringing communities together, working with communities, working with people and that's what I really enjoy doing ... A real strong community of different cultures.

It is this commitment and passion for racial harmony and justice that fuelled these women activists' ability to handle their multiple burdens. Thus we may conclude that for this group of women at least voluntary work has not been squeezed out of the work–life balance calculation.

## Acknowledgments

We are grateful to the ESRC for funding for the project *Handling Double Disadvantage: Minority Ethnic Women and Trade Unions* (No. L21225,2061), to the TUC and the collaborating unions for their involvement. We are also indebted to the women who took part in the project and gave freely of their time.

## Notes

1. Whilst a total of 57 interviews was carried out, three were pilot interviews and two failed to record. The analysis in this chapter is therefore based on the remaining 52.
2. In this project we followed the terminological practice of the group we are studying. Black is the favoured term in the union movement, but given that this term is felt by some Asian women (not on the whole the activists) to be irrelevant to them and thus to exclude them we have tended to refer to black and Asian.
3. The research team saw dissemination of the findings to user groups as a key priority and we have spoken about the research to a number of black women's groups.
4. This tendency has been noted in work carried out with young women in Bristol by Steve Fenton, Harriet Bradley, Jackie West, Will Guy and Ranji Devadason and by Lucy Collins.
5. In many ways, all the women in our study were exceptional. The women we choose here to label 'exceptional women' were those who consistently dealt with multiple burdens throughout their working lives.

## References

Beck, U. (1992) *Risk Society*, London: Sage.

Bond, S., Hyman, J., Summers, J. and Wise, S. (2002) *Family-friendly Working? Putting Policy into Practice*, York: Joseph Rowntree Foundation.

Bradley, H. (1996) *Fractured Identities*, Cambridge: Polity.

Bradley, H. (2000) *Gender and Power in the Workplace*, London: Macmillan.

Bradley, H., Erickson, M., Stephenson, C. and Williams, S. (2002a) *Myths at Work*, Cambridge: Polity.

Bradley, H., Healy, G. and Mukherjee, N. (2002b) 'Inclusion, Exclusion and Separate Organisation – Black Women Activists in Trade Unions'. *ESRC Future of Work Working Paper Number 25*.

Bradley, H., Healy, G. and Mukherjee, N. (2004) 'Union influence on career development – bringing in gender and ethnicity'. *Career Development International*, 9(1): 74–88.

Brooke, K. (2002) Trade Union Membership: an analysis of data from the autumn 2001 LFS. *Labour Market Trends*, July.

Chamberlain, M. (1997) *Narratives of Exile and Return*, Warwick: Warwick University Caribbean Series.

Chow, E., Wilkinson, D. and Zinn, M. (1996) *Race, Class and Gender: Common bonds, different voices*, London: Sage.

Colgan, F. and Ledwith, S. (1996) Sisters Organizing: Women and their Trade Unions in *Women in Organizations*, Basingstoke: Macmillan.

Coote, A. and Kellner, P. (1980) *Hear This Brother*, London: New Statesman Books.

Dex, S. (1987) *Women's Occupational Mobility: A Lifetime Perspective*, London: Macmillan.

Dex, S. and Smith, C. (2002) *The Nature of Family-friendly Employment Policies in Britain*, The Policy Press and Joseph Rowntree Foundation.

Giddens, A. (1998) *The Third Way*, Cambridge: Polity.

Goldthorpe, J., Lockwood, D., Bechhofer, F. and Platt, J. (1969) *The Affluent Worker in the Class Structure*, Cambridge: Cambridge University Press.

Hakim C. (1995) Five feminist myths about women's employment. *British Journal of Sociology*, 46(3): 429–45.

Healy, G. (1999) Structuring Commitments in Interrupted Careers: Career Breaks, Commitment and the Life Cycle in Teaching. *Gender Work and Organisation*, 6(4): 185–201.

Healy, G., Bradley, H. and Mukherjee, N. (2003) Voicing A Double Disadvantage? The workplace and union experience of Minority Ethnic women. *Equal Opportunities Review*, September.

Healy, G., Bradley, H. and Mukherjee, N. (2004) Inspiring Activists: the experience of minority ethnic women in trade unions, in Healy, G., Heery, E., Taylor, P. and Brown, W. (eds), *The Future of Worker Representation*, London: Palgrave.

Hewlett, S. (2002) *Baby Hunger*, London: Atlantic Books.

Hibbett, A. (2002) Ethnic Minority Women in the UK. http://www.cabinet-office.gov.uk/womens-unit/research/genderbriefing/home.htm

Hochschild, A.R, (1989) *The Second Shift*, New York: Viking.

Levitas, R. (1998) *The Inclusive Society?* London: Macmillan.

Kirton, G. and Healy, G. (2004) Shaping Union and Gender Identities: a Case Study of Women-only Trade Union Courses. *British Journal of Industrial Relations*, 42(2): 303–23.

Modood, T., Berthoud, R., Lakey, J., Nazroo J., Smith, P., Virdee, S. and Beishon, S. (1997) *Ethnic Minorities in Britain: Diversity and Disadvantage*, London: Policy Studies Institute.

Newman, K. (2000) *No Shame in My Game*, New York: Vintage Books.

Parsons, T. and Bale, R. (1956) *Family, Socialisation and Interaction Process*, New York: Free Press.

Rapaport, R.N., Fogarty, M. and Rapaport, R. (1982) *Families in Britain*, London: Routledge Kegan Paul.

Stageman, J. (1980) *Women In Unions*, Hull: Industrial Studies Unit.

# 12

# Combining Family and Employment: Evidence from Pakistani and Bangladeshi Women

*Angela Dale*

## Introduction

Pakistani and Bangladeshi women in Britain are characterised by low levels of labour market participation and, amongst the economically active, high levels of unemployment. Small-scale studies (e.g. Allen and Wolkowitz, 1987; Brah and Shaw, 1992; Phizacklea and Wolkowitz, 1993) suggest a relatively high level of home working although this is not captured in survey data. National figures for 1998/9 show economic activity[1] rates of 30 per cent for Pakistani women and 20 per cent for Bangladeshi women aged 16–59. This contrasts with 74 per cent for white women (Labour Market Trends, Dec. 1999). In particular, low levels of economic activity are particularly associated with marriage as well as responsibility of children (Dale *et al.*, 2002). The 2001 Census found that, amongst women aged 16–74, 36.4 per cent of Pakistanis and 40.1 per cent Bangladeshis were categorised as looking after the home and family by comparison with 11.9 per cent white women. However, Pakistani and Bangladeshi women with higher educational qualifications are much more likely than others to be economically active and a crucial question is how family formation influences labour market participation amongst these women. In this chapter we ask, in particular, what changes we can expect amongst younger Pakistani and Bangladeshi women who have grown up in the UK.

We use data from interviews conducted in Oldham supported by analysis of national level survey data from the PSI Fourth National Study and data from UCAS (University and Colleges Admission Statistics) and HESA (Higher Education Statistical Agency). First we provide some contextual information about Oldham.

## The Pakistani and Bangladeshi communities in Oldham

The geographical distribution of Pakistani and Bangladeshi communities in Britain tends to reflect the reasons for their migration. Oldham, an industrial town north of Manchester, was once the centre of the world's cotton industry. The industry peaked in the 1920s with 320 mills, reducing to only 12 by 1991 (Kalra, 2000). In the 1950s there were attempts to revive the industry through the installation of better technology and the use of night shifts to maximise the benefits of the expensive machinery. The recruitment of male workers from South Asia was specifically designed to fill these poorly paid night shifts that were not attractive to local men. These migrants, mainly from the rural areas of Mirpur in Pakistan and from the Sylhet region of Bangladesh, came to Oldham with few formal educational qualifications and little English. Once they were established in a job they were joined by their wives and families and moved into the terraced housing built for earlier mill workers.

Despite the introduction of new technology, the cotton industry was still contracting and the recession of the early 1980s saw its near total collapse. This loss of jobs was not compensated by the growth of new manufacturing industries and resulted in very high levels of unemployment. The more recent migrant groups took most of the impact. Access to alternative work was hampered by the lack of growth in the local economy, particularly in semi and unskilled manufacturing; the limited skill base and lack of formal education of the initial migrants; and the hostility and discrimination which South Asian workers faced in trying to find work. Oldham still remains a relatively depressed labour market although white women's levels of employment are higher than the national average, reflecting the tradition of female employment in the cotton mills.

The largest minority ethnic group in Oldham is Pakistani comprising 6.1 per cent of the population of the Borough in June 1999, followed by Bangladeshis at 3.9 per cent. These communities are also almost entirely Muslim. Because of the young age structure of the Asian population in Oldham, projections show that the ethnic minority population is expected to reach 19 per cent by 2011 (Oldham M.B.C., 1997). A high proportion of this group will have been born and educated in the UK.

Oldham is a relatively poor borough. Seven of its 20 wards are in the worst 10 per cent nationally, according to the 2000 Index of Deprivation produced by the Department for Transport, Local Government and the Regions. A further three are in the most deprived 1 per cent. The Oldham labour market offers mainly semi and unskilled work at low wages and educational attainment is below the national average. This social and economic context was seen by the Borough Council as an important factor behind the disturbances of summer 2001,[2] exacerbated by the educational and residential segregation of the white and Asian communities (Oldham Independent Review Report, 2001). The Denham report (Ministerial Group on Public Order, 2001) concluded that there was 'fragmentation and polarization of communities – on economic, geographical, racial and cultural lines – on a scale which amounts to segregation, albeit to an extent by choice.' Although the research reported here took place before summer 2001, the social and economic backdrop to the disturbances has been present for many years.

## The research questions and the data

In the preceding sections we have set out the context in which we now explore the factors that influence Pakistani and Bangladeshi women's labour market participation. In particular, we ask what changes we can expect amongst younger Pakistani and Bangladeshi women who have grown up in the UK? How do we expect educational qualifications and family formation to influence labour market participation amongst these women? What barriers do these women face in obtaining qualifications and paid employment? To what extent do the family and community impose these barriers and to what extent are they imposed by the local labour market?

Our empirical evidence combines national level quantitative data with qualitative data from local interviews and group discussions. National-level UCAS and HESA statistics provide information on the extent of applications for higher education from Pakistani and Bangladeshi young people and their subject preferences, over time, by comparison with other ethnic groups. Detailed individual interviews were conducted with Pakistani and Bangladeshi women in Oldham, selected to represent different stages of the lifecycle, different levels of labour market participation and different educational levels. All the women in this group had left full-time education. The economically inactive – who were at home – were recruited by calling at dwellings in two different neighbourhoods, both identified from the 1991 Census as having a high proportion of Pakistani or Bangladeshi residents. A group of young unemployed women were contacted through the local job centre. Women who were in employment were recruited by a range of methods which included contacts through our consultation forum (see below) and through local volunteer organisations. The women interviewed, therefore, included young women born or educated in the UK as well as older women who were able to provide some insights into their preferences for their own children's education and employment. In total, 43 interviews were conducted and group discussions were conducted with a total of 37 boys and 35 girls. All interviews were taped and fully transcribed.

We also established a 'consultation forum' which comprised about 12 Pakistani and Bangladeshi women who were working in local government or voluntary organisations in Oldham. We held regular meetings of this forum at which we discussed the project design, enlisted help with access and reported initial findings. We include here some of the views offered by these women.

We cannot claim that our interviews are representative of the Pakistani and Bangladeshi population of Oldham and neither is Oldham representative of Britain more generally. Therefore we also use national-level data from the PSI Fourth National Ethnic Minorities Survey (Modood *et al.*, 1997), designed specifically to capture the experiences of minority ethnic groups in Britain. This therefore provides the best available source of quantitative data for modelling the variation in women's labour market participation. As it contains a representative sample of white women it allows comparisons to be made between Pakistani and Bangladeshi and white women.

The PSI survey was conducted in 1994 and was drawn from a sample of wards selected on the basis of the proportion of the population who were from ethnic minorities. A sample of addresses was drawn from each ward and focused enumeration was used to locate ethnic minorities. The numbers of adults interviewed were: 1232 Pakistanis with a response rate of 73 per cent; 598 Bangladeshis – 83 per cent response rate; and a white sample of 2867 with a 71 per cent response (Modood *et al.*, 1997). By using weights a nationally representative sample can be obtained for each ethnic group. All the analyses reported in this paper have been restricted to women aged 18–59 inclusive and omits those in full-time education.

## The employment context for Pakistani and Bangladeshi women

Women's employment choices are influenced not just by structural and human capital factors but also by cultural expectations and family and community pressures. Therefore an understanding of the perceptions of community values and the general context in which a woman makes decisions about marriage, family formation and employment is relevant and important.

Amongst the older generation of women there was often an acceptance of their role within the home to the extent that questions about paid employment seemed inappropriate and irrelevant. Many women also had heavy family responsibilities often without access to a car or to convenience foods. As one young women said:

> I think that a lot of women don't work because they have too many responsibilities towards their families and they haven't got the time. It can be difficult especially with children, in-laws and housework. My mum, aunts, friends' mothers, you see them working so hard in the home, they would never have time for a job even if they wanted to... (*Pakistani woman 22, single, working full-time*)

Taken together with a lack of formal qualifications and, often, little English, these factors placed considerable barriers to employment in the formal labour market and contribute to the low levels of recorded economic activity amongst older Pakistani and Bangladeshi women.

Traditionally, Pakistani and Bangladeshi women marry at a young age, with 16 or 17 being not unusual, although, as we see below, many women married later. However, those women who remain single into their 20s are, almost by definition, from less traditional families. Many of our respondents had marriages arranged by parents, although usually with their consent and having met their prospective partner beforehand. Amongst the Pakistanis in particular, marriage was usually to a member of the extended family, often with a marriage in Pakistan and the husband migrating to live with his new wife in Oldham. After marriage, a woman traditionally joins her husband's family and both her parents-in-law and husband play an important role with respect to her employment decisions. However, it is not possible to make simple generalisations and, particularly amongst younger women, there was considerable variation in attitudes and expectations on both sides. These are discussed in more detail below.

## Post-compulsory education for Pakistani and Bangladeshi girls

Choices over the uptake of post-compulsory education for Pakistani and Bangladeshi young women were much more complex than for their male counterparts or their white counterparts.

For much of the Asian community in Oldham it was important that girls should avoid any behaviour that might damage the family honour (*izzat*). As Brah (1993: 143) explains, 'a young woman working away from home unchaperoned is understood as providing fertile ground for malicious gossip'. If the girl behaved in a way that damaged the family honour, for example by being seen in public smoking, drinking or out with a boy, her family would suffer in the community and she would no longer be seen as an acceptable marriage partner (Afshar, 1994). This had implications for the continuation of post-16 education for girls in situations where parents were not able to police the activities of their daughters. However, no similar restrictions were mentioned for boys.

Whilst the notion of honour was widely accepted, there were considerable differences in the ways in which it impinged on girls. For the most traditional families it meant that girls were not allowed out on their own and going to further education (FE) college or university was forbidden. By contrast, in other families, girls were encouraged to go to university, even if it meant living away from home, and parents trusted their daughters to behave in an appropriate way. One particularly liberal parent argued:

> Education will never make you immoral. Education makes you strong and it will teach you good and bad. Without education you've got nothing.

Nevertheless this mother had to withstand considerable pressure and gossip from the more traditional members of the community. In her interview, however, she strongly emphasised the importance of *izzat* and drew explicitly on the teaching of Islam to defend her views, in particular citing the need for hard work and self-help:

> So if you work hard and get well educated and help yourself then you'll have your parents' blessings as well as Allah's blessings. (*46-year old Pakistani, 7 children, most university-educated in professional jobs*)

In contrast, other mothers used the teaching of Islam to justify much greater restrictions on their daughter's movements. The most extreme case was an interview with a woman in her mid-40s from rural Pakistan who explained that Islam recommended that a girl should not go out of the house. Another Pakistani woman explained why she felt that girls should not be educated:

> Because then girls get freedom ... I am not against education but freedom, then girls get influenced. (*Pakistani woman, 4 children; born in Pakistan, been in England for 20 years*)

Many of our interviewees quoted teachings from the Quran to justify or explain their views. These were deployed selectively, however, to support quite different positions.

Some of the younger women interviewed had experienced severe restrictions and were determined that they would not impose them on their own children. A Pakistani woman in her early 30s, now working full-time, recalled with bitterness how her parents stopped her from going to college because it was co-educational, although her younger sisters had been allowed to go.

If a girl remained at home under the supervision of her family there was less risk that she would engage in activities which could damage the family's reputation. For a girl to continue in post-16 education it was necessary for parents to be confident that this would not bring dishonour on the family. Girls often engaged in a process of negotiation with parents that, at least for some, resulted in being allowed to continue in education. Continuing FE education in Oldham posed less of a threat than going outside Oldham; the FE and 6th Form college are both in the centre of Oldham and parents would quickly hear if their daughters stepped outside accepted norms of behaviour.

Girls reported that their parents were concerned if they saw Asian girls wearing western dress to college. Traditional Asian dress signified that a girl subscribed to the values and codes of behaviour of their community. It thus provided an assurance to parents and could be used in negotiating permission to attend college. Both young people and women referred to the way in which disapproval within the community acted as a powerful force on conduct of behaviour.

Greater concerns were felt when higher education meant travelling outside Oldham because it was harder for the family to retain control over the girl. Also, girls living away from home could not be given family support and help if they faced difficulties. Role models were frequently mentioned as providing parents with reassurance. For example, if an older cousin had successfully completed higher education this often gave parents much more confidence. The girl's achievements brought status to her family with the result that other parents were more likely to allow their daughters to follow a similar route. Whilst there is obviously scope for conflict between children and their parents, a number of girls still in education had been able to reach a resolution with their parents. Our interviews with married women, however, included several instances where they had been prevented from continuing their education.

## Uptake of higher education

Our Oldham interviews suggested, that there was an increase in uptake of higher education amongst young Pakistani and Bangladeshi women and this view was reinforced by the views of the consultation forum. In order to assess whether there is statistical evidence to support this assumption we have examined national-level data. Labour Force Survey figures for 19–24 year olds studying for first or higher degrees in 1995 (ONS, 1996) show very similar national levels for white and Pakistani and Bangladeshi young people – about 13–14 per cent – but much lower than the 30 per cent of Indians in this age group.

Applications for degree courses, however, indicate a marked increase amongst South Asians, especially for Bangladeshi and Pakistani women – for example an increase of 83 per cent for Bangladeshi women and 60 per cent for Pakistani women between 1994 and 1999 (home students). By comparison, there was a fall in applications from white men over this time period and only a small increase amongst white women. Figures from the Higher Education Statistics Agency (HESA, Table 10A) give the numbers of UK domiciled full-time first-year students on degree-level courses by ethnic group. This shows an increase of 95 per cent for Bangladeshi women and 71 per cent for Pakistani women between 1994/5 and 1998/9. The increases for Bangladeshi and Pakistani men, for the same time period, are 21 per cent and 44 per cent respectively. These increases for Pakistani and Bangladeshi young people are likely to far outweigh the growth in the student-aged population over the four-year time period.

There is also an indication that young Pakistani and Bangladeshi women are narrowing the gender gap in the uptake of higher education.

Amongst first year UK domiciled full-time degree level undergraduate students for 1994/5, girls represented 38 per cent of both Pakistanis and Bangladeshis. By 1999/2000 this had risen to 44 per cent and 46 per cent, respectively (HESA, Table 10A). There is no sign that the increase in applications by Pakistani and Bangladeshi girls in recent years is slowing down. It is, of course, only a decade or so ago since white women, also, were significantly less likely than men to take an undergraduate degree course.

The statistical evidence therefore suggests that there are very real gains being made by Pakistani and Bangladeshi young people and that women, in particular, are narrowing the lead held by men in terms of entry to degree-level courses. This is consistent with the expressed determination of many young people interviewed to succeed against the odds and the encouragement and support given by parents and family. This level of attainment needs to be viewed against the lack of economic resources available to many of these students. Pakistani and Bangladeshi communities in Britain are characterised by high levels of unemployment and economic inactivity, very marked geographical segregation (Peach, 1996) and considerable material poverty (Blackburn *et al.*, 1997; Karn *et al.*, 1999). South Asian students also tend to have lower than average A level scores for the degree-level courses to which they are applying, and are more likely to have achieved these scores after a re-sit (Modood and Shiner, 1994).

## The role of qualifications in the labour market

From our interviews we found that young single women who had left education (all educated in the UK but with a range of qualifications), saw paid work as bringing positive benefits. It was something which, at this stage of their lives, they wished to pursue. They felt that they gained independence and self-esteem from a job and some also saw a job as giving freedom and the ability to 'get out of the house'. This can be understood in relation to the 'traditional' view that women should not take paid-work outside the home. A woman whose father had opposed her taking paid work said:

> My father's comment was – why do you need to work when I can give you the money? (*Pakistani woman, 31, married, 3 children*)

It is noteworthy that all the young women interviewed accepted without question that they would get married and have children. They also foresaw that marriage was likely to lead to some compromises and they would lose some of their individual freedom, particularly if they moved into the household of their parents-in-law. These women all spoke fluent English with qualifications gained in the UK educational system. This removed many of the obstacles to employment faced by older women and more recent migrants without fluent English.

The interviews provided overwhelming evidence for the role of educational qualifications gained in the UK in promoting labour market participation. The influence of qualifications is apparent in two ways. Firstly, as for white women, qualifications provide the entry requirements for many jobs, particularly in the non-manual sector. However, for Asian women (and men) this had a particular significance because of the widely held view (amongst interviewees and members of our consultation forum) that an Asian applicant has to be much better qualified than a white applicant to stand a similar chance of success. Secondly, the *traditional* view amongst the Asian community in Oldham is that women should not work outside the home. Again, this was often reinforced by calling on the teachings of Islam:

> But in our Islam, working outside the home for women is not allowed; as much as they can stay in the home, it's better for them. (*35 years, Pakistani with 5 children*)

Therefore women who wanted to work often found themselves having to justify that decision. Those with higher qualifications appeared more confident and more motivated to argue against this traditional view – also using the Quran to justify their decision. Some of these women will also have had to show considerable resolution and determination in order to have achieved their qualifications. Women with few qualifications often felt defeated by the labour market:

> ...like I said I didn't go to school much and I got married at a young age and to me I think I'm not really good for any job, that's what I think. (*30-year old Bangladeshi, married, 3 children, no qualifications*)

This suggests that the role of qualifications may have a greater impact for Asian women than for white women and, indeed, analysis of the Fourth National Survey of Ethnic Minorities (Dale *et al.*, 2002) shows that this is, indeed, the case. Almost all Pakistani and Bangladeshi women with qualifications at A level and above were economically active by comparison with only 13 per cent of women with no qualifications. However, we need to remember that those Asian women getting higher qualifications are unusual and therefore likely to display other characteristics – for example, considerable determination and strength of character. As more women go into higher education – and there is less resistance to this from the community – we may expect the association between level of qualification and economic activity to weaken.

Generally, analysis of the PSI survey shows that Pakistani and Bangladeshi women who have experienced the same educational system as white women are achieving similar or higher levels of qualification and showing similar or higher levels of economic activity (Dale *et al.*, 2002). However, these figures do not control for the effects of marriage and childbearing. We consider these factors in the following section.

## Marriage and family

In our interviews we were told on many occasions that, by comparison with the white population, Asians give much more priority to their family. We were therefore interested in the role that educational qualifications and employment potential played in relation to decisions about the priorities of family and paid work after marriage and childbearing.

### Younger single women

Amongst the younger, single women there was a general consensus with the view expressed below by a 21-year old Bangladeshi woman with qualifications at GNVQ level, who, in response to being asked what work meant to her replied:

> Freedom and being a person, an individual. When you are in work you are seen as a different person than at home ... At home you have to listen to others and you are like a child obeying orders, at work you can be professional and mature ... work means socialising and making new friends ... it's good when we have meals and go out and have a good gossip...

However, when asked specifically whether she wanted to work after her marriage which was planned for the following year she replied:

> I would like to, I have talked to my future husband about this and he says that this is alright and that he won't mind if I have a job as long as I don't neglect him and the duties of being a wife ... after I get married I will be moving into the family house and I will have to look after their needs, I think it is going to be tough at first, you have to learn how to live again and accustom yourself to this new house and these new people... I hope it isn't going to be too bad. (*Bangladeshi, 21, engaged, working full-time*)

Other respondents made similar comments, which on the one hand asserted the importance of paid work in giving them recognition as an individual and, on the other hand, accepted that after marriage individuality may be subsumed within family life which often included living with parents-in-law.

Thus these young working women enjoyed the freedom that came with a paid job but also accepted that they would get married and have children.

They also foresaw that this might lead to some compromises and loss of their individual freedom, particularly if they moved into the household of their parents-in-law. This may, perhaps, be seen as westernised ideals of 'individualisation' confronting Muslim ideals of prioritising family life over individual desires.

Unlike the Muslim women interviewed by Afshar (1994) in Bradford, these women did not appear to see marriage as giving them independence from their own parents, but as a potential threat to an independence they had achieved through paid work. However, we must remember that the views reported above were from a group of young women who already had the freedom to take paid work. Not all young women – or their parents – held these views. Women from traditional families were likely to get married very soon after leaving school without having worked outside the home.

### Younger married women

Younger married women whom we interviewed varied not just in the extent of their labour market participation but in whether this was represented as their own choice, a negotiated outcome, or the result of family or community pressures. It is significant that those women who had higher level qualifications and the prospect of a 'good' job appeared to be in a much stronger position to choose whether to take paid employment. They had confidence in their own abilities and were also more likely to have married a man who accepted their views on working.

These women were also keen to distinguish between tradition and religion and thereby demonstrate that there was no incompatibility between being a devout Muslim and taking paid work. This was extremely important for women who wished to affirm their adherence to Islamic values – and to uphold the honour of their family – but who did not want to be bound by the traditional values of what was seen by some as a rather old-fashioned and narrow-minded community. A Pakistani law graduate had maintained her career and worked full-time despite having a young child and facing very strong opposition from her parents-in-law. She was strongly opposed to 'sitting at home' and being dependent on her husband. In defining her position she stressed that her opposition was to tradition, not religion:

> I'm not attached to the tradition; I'm concerned with my religion which is a totally different thing. (*Pakistani, 27, law graduate, married, one child*)

Other women found themselves much less able to resist traditional expectations. The parents of a 22-year old Bangladeshi woman did not want her to continue her education or to take paid work. Whilst she had come to the UK when aged 9 and had obtained GCSEs, she married at 17 and had two children at the time of the interview. She found herself unable to resist the control which her parents-in-law exercised over her movements. This meant that she saw paid work outside the home as an impossibility. By contrast, her sister-in-law, who had a university education and was in employment, appeared to have considerable independence.

However, not all women had mothers-in-law who wanted them to stay at home. A number of women whom we interviewed found their mothers-in-law supportive and helpful. It is clear that the power exercised by parents-in-law is negotiated and that education and employment are both significant in giving daughters-in-law bargaining power and confidence.

The graduates in the sample, all from UK universities, were highly committed to their careers but were also committed to a role of wife and mother. Ways of combining work and children were actively explored and, for many, part-time work seemed to offer the preferred balance with mothers or mothers-in-law providing childcare – a pattern reminiscent of that of many white women.

## Analysis of fourth ethnic minority survey

Turning to our national level data from the PSI survey, (reported more fully in Dale *et al.*, 2002) Pakistani and Bangladeshi women without children show similar levels of economic activity as their white counterparts (over 90% are economically active). However, amongst Pakistani and Bangladeshi women with a partner but no children, economic activity is 66 per cent – considerably less than for white women in this category (83%). But it is amongst Pakistani and Bangladeshi women with a partner and children that economic activity is lowest – about 10 per cent – and contrasts most sharply with white women (72%).

This suggests that family responsibilities are a much more important influence on Pakistani and Bangladeshi women's economic activity than for white women. However, unmarried Pakistani and Bangladeshi women are disproportionately likely to be non-traditional women who have delayed marriage. Similarly, those married with no children represent women who have delayed childbearing following their marriage. Women who follow the more traditional way of the community get married at an early age and have children soon after marriage. Thus marriage and presence of children are conflated with age, generation, fluency in English and educational qualification.

### Multivariate analysis

Models of employment behaviour generated for white women show that increased educational attainment leads to a sharp rise in levels of economic activity, particularly amongst women with young children (Macran, Joshi and Dex, 1996; Dale and Egerton, 1997). However, we cannot assume that the factors that influence white women's employment behaviour will be the same for Pakistani and Bangladeshi women who clearly enter the labour market in very different circumstances (Brah and Shaw, 1992; Brah, 1993, 1996).

We have therefore used evidence from our interviews to construct some models which are applied to the national level survey data and which can help to disentangle the range of influences on women's labour market participation.

The explanatory variables in the model include educational qualifications; fluency in English; partnership status; dependent children; age and household size. The population used was women aged 18–59, excluding full-time students.

The variables with a large significant impact on Pakistani and Bangladeshi women's economic activity (by comparison with the reference category) were:

- UK qualification at A level or above and fluency in English – both with large positive effects
- Having a partner; and having young children – both with large negative effects.

Each variable contributed an effect independent of the others, with higher qualifications and children under 12 having the most powerful influence.

As successive cohorts of Pakistani and Bangladeshi women are born in the UK and have fluent English the negative effect of language will apply to fewer and fewer women. The increase in numbers of Pakistani and Bangladeshi women taking degree-level courses, discussed above, is likely to lead to a sharp increase in economic activity amongst future cohorts, although tempered by the strong negative impact of young children. The opposing effects of qualifications and the presence of young children pose the crucial question of how this will be reconciled by younger cohorts of Pakistani and Bangladeshi women.[3]

The results for white women are broadly similar to those for Pakistani and Bangladeshi women but with a key difference – the positive effect of qualifications was smaller whilst the negative effect of young children was also less. Thus we see much less variation amongst white women's economic activity in relation to individual characteristics.

Our interviews provided some tentative evidence that Pakistani and Bangladeshi women might reconcile a desire for paid work with a commitment to family life by seeking part-time employment. For example, when asked about children these two respondents, both with degrees, married and working full-time, replied:

> Well, I would want to work but I don't think I, I wouldn't work full-time, I would like to go on a part-time basis or if I did work full-time I

> would have to work round the hours my husband worked. I don't think that would be possible though I think, it would have to be more of a part-time role for myself, but we have even discussed my husband going part-time and me staying full-time, which doesn't sound right from a cultural point of view. (*Married Pakistani, 23, no children, degree, currently working full-time*)

> I think I would like to give my children the best as well and with that comes financial security and I think as well as my husband earning I would like to do part-time work, therefore my children will get the best, so yes I will work but I won't work to the same degree as now. (*Pakistani pharmacist, married, aged 26, no children*)

So far our analysis has suggested an increasing number of young Pakistani and Bangladeshi women with higher qualifications who will expect to work full-time, at least until they have children. However these women are likely to face additional problems in achieving this goal. Firstly, levels of unemployment are much higher for Pakistani and Bangladeshi women than for white women and this is particularly significant for those younger women with qualifications who have high levels of economic activity. Even when a job has been obtained, however, women may face family pressures that add an additional layer of complexity to the work-family balance. Evidence from our consultation forum (composed largely of well qualified Pakistani and Bangladeshi women in paid work) highlighted cultural expectations that may come from family members. These included attendance at family events such as weddings and funerals – which might include not just immediate, but extended family members – as well as providing hospitality to visiting friends and family. An added complexity in balancing family and work was the fact that Muslim festivals and Christian festivals do not coincide and this may add additional difficulties in terms of planning time away from work.

## Conclusions

There is very clear evidence of change across generations. By contrast with their mothers' generation, where family took priority and there were few opportunities for paid work outside the home, younger women who had been educated in the UK saw paid work as a means to independence and self-esteem. Whilst employment was not something which was taken for granted and many women had to argue with their families to be allowed to work, nonetheless, all the women interviewed expected to get married (if they were not already) and assumed they would have children. They also accepted that this would require some adjustments. Women with higher-level qualifications often showed considerable determination in wanting to combine paid work and childcare. Whilst most women subscribed strongly to the centrality of the family, it is clear that the majority will follow very different routes through the life-course from their mothers. However, there are important questions not yet answered as to how these women will combine the competing demands of work and family. By comparison with their white counterparts, Pakistani and Bangladeshi working women face many more difficulties in reconciling work and family. These include a cultural context where, traditionally, a woman is still expected to give priority to family and domestic life and a workplace culture that, typically, makes few concessions to requirements for prayer facilities or for holiday during Eid celebrations or for Haj, for example. These women therefore experience additional constraints both at home and at work.

## Acknowledgements

This chapter is based on a paper first published in Sociological Research Online.

Angela Dale (2002) 'Social Exclusion of Pakistani and Bangladeshi Women' Sociological Research Online, vol. 7, no. 3, <http://www.socresonline.org.uk/7/3/dale.html>

I would like to thank Nusrat Shaheen who conducted the interviews and Ed Fieldhouse and Virinder Kalra who were colleagues on the project.

I also wish to thank Oldham Metropolitan Borough Council for allowing access to their Social Survey and Labour Force Survey, for providing details of their population projections and for their support of the research more generally.

We also thank PSI for use of their Fourth National Survey of Ethnic Minorities and also the Data Archive at the University of Essex for supplying the data.

We particularly want to thank the members of the project consultation forum who gave us an enormous amount of help and advice and the young people and women who took part in the interviewing.

## Notes

1. The Labour Force Survey defines economic activity as being in paid work or looking for a job and available to start.
2. In May 2001 there were three days of rioting in Oldham, followed by similar disturbances in Burnley in June and Bradford in July. In the weeks leading up to the Oldham Riot the National Front (NF) had been trying to capitalise on an attack on an old white pensioner which the local police had described as a 'racial attack' despite the victim and his family saying this was not true.
3. We could, in theory, have addressed this using an inter-action effect between qualifications and children. This would have shown whether the negative effect of young children was the same for all levels of qualification. However, there were insufficient numbers of women with higher qualifications to allow this.

## References

Afshar, H. (1994) Muslim Women in West Yorkshire, in Afshar, H. and Maynard, M. (eds), *The Dynamics of 'Race' and Gender: some feminist interventions*, London: Taylor and Francis.

Allen, S. and Wolkowitz, C. (1987) *Homeworking: myths and realities*, London: Macmillan.

Blackburn, R., Dale, A. and Jarman, J. (1997) Ethnic differences in attainment in education, occupation and life-style, in Karn, V. (ed.), *Employment, Education and Housing amongst Ethnic Minorities in Britain*, London: HMSO.

Brah, A. (1993) Race and culture in the gendering of labour markets: South Asian young Muslim women and the labour market, *New Community*, 19(3): 441–58.

Brah, A. (1996) *Cartographies of diaspora*, London: Routledge.

Brah, A. and Shaw, S. (1992) *Working Choices: South Asian Women and the Labour Market*, Department of Employment Research Paper, no. 91.

Dale, A. and Egerton, M. (1997) *Highly Educated Women: Evidence from the National Child Development Study*, London: HMSO.

Dale, A., Fieldhouse, F., Shaheen, N. and Kalra, V. (2002) The labour market prospects of Pakistani and Bangladeshi women, *Work, Employment and Society*, 16 (1): 5–25.

Denham, J. (2001) Building Cohesive Communities, Ministerial Group on Public Order.

Kalra, V. (2000) *From Textile Mills to Taxi Ranks: Experiences of Migration, Labour and Social Change*, Ashgate: Aldershot.

Karn, V., Mian, S., Brown, M., Dale, A. (1999) *Minority Ethnic Housing Needs in Manchester: Tradition and Change*, London: Housing Corporation.

Macran, S., Joshi, H. and Dex, S. (1996) 'Employment after childbearing: a survival analysis', *Work, Employment and Society*, 10(2): 273–96.

Modood, T. and Shiner, M. (1994) *Ethnic Minorities and Higher Education*, London: Policy Studies Institute.

Modood, T., Berthoud, R., Lakey, J., Nazroo, J., Smith, P., Virdee, S., Beishon, S. (1997) *Ethnic minorities in Britain – diversity and disadvantage*, London: Policy Studies Institute.

Oldham Independent Review Report (2001) Oldham: Oldham Metropolitan Borough Council.

Oldham Metropolitan Borough Council (1997) *Population Projections for Oldham: report to the Chief Executive's Policy Unit*, Oldham: Oldham Metropolitan Borough Council.

ONS (1966) *Social Focus on Ethnic Minorities*, Table 36, London: The Stationery Office.

Peach, C. (ed.) (1966) *The ethnic minority populations of Great Britain (Vol 2), Ethnicity in the 1991 Census*. ONS, HMSO, London.

Phizacklea, A. and Wolkowitz, C. (1993) *Homeworking Women: gender, racism and class at work*, London: Sage.

Sly, F., Thair, T. and Risdon, A. 'Trends in the Labour Market Participation of Ethnic Groups', Labour Market Trends, December 1999.

# 13

# Care Workers and Work–Life Balance: The Example of Domiciliary Careworkers[1]

*Clare Ungerson and Sue Yeandle*

## Introduction: challenging the dichotomy between 'work' and 'life'

In much of the literature, and in most popular discussion, the term 'work–life balance' is used to imply the need for individuals, employers and policy-makers to act to achieve an optimum state, in which each person can achieve a state of equilibrium between two time-consuming and competitive activities: on the one hand, paid work and, on the other, a 'life' that contains a wide variety of activities, but, by definition, is *not* paid work. Although this equilibrium can involve different allocations of time and effort to 'work' and 'life' by different people, and indeed by the same people at different life stages, the concept implies a dichotomy between 'work' for wages or for financial gain, and 'life' in which the rewards of activities, effort and commitments are non-monetary.

It is no accident that this concept came into prominent use in the late 20th century, an historical point at which two critical changes coincided. First, a legal infrastructure became established which gave women formal rights with men to equal participation in most public activities, notably in employment; and second, working hours, after decreasing for over a century, began to increase, to be delivered in more varied patterns, and to include increasing amounts of unpaid overtime (Harkness, 1999; Kodz *et al.*, 1998; TUC, 1998). Work–life balance thus became a popular issue because 'paid work' came to compete with 'life' in two ways, first, in terms of time. Changes in 'working hours' mean that paid work consumes increasing amounts of many individuals' working days (and nights), often encroaching on evenings and weekends, time associated throughout the mid-20th century with family activities and commitments. At the same time, the way time is consumed in paid work means that many individuals, particularly mothers and other carers, find it very difficult to combine paid work with the time needed to care. Their strategies for doing so include deliberately reducing their working hours or choosing part-time employment, taking paid and unpaid leaves, using (where they are available) state-funded and allocated services that act as surrogate carers, or purchasing substitute care on the commercial market (Yeandle *et al.*, 2003).

Second, 'paid work' can encroach on 'life' in other and more symbolic ways, suborning so much attention that the conventional activities of 'life' – eating, sleeping, maintaining intimate relationships, shopping, leisure – become increasingly problematic as the time available for these activities is squeezed, and the pleasure normally experienced as part of these activities evaporates in a miasma of paid work related 'stress' (The Work Foundation, 2002).

It has long been recognised that the activities of the 'life' side of the equation are very various – and others have challenged the use of the term, in some cases preferring 'the reconciliation of work and family life', a phrase used in many European Union documents and policies, or 'work-family integration' (Fletcher and Rapoport, 1996). Yeandle has written elsewhere (Yeandle, 2001) about 'three sorts of time' (work time, care time and personal time).

Figure 13.1 outlines these three forms of time for individuals engaged in paid work. It also presents the relationship between the private individual and policy in the public domain, whether that is social policy or the 'family-friendly' policies of their employer. Is there an infrastructure of services in place that supports heavy demands on 'care time', are there family-friendly employment policies which accommodate the pressures of 'work time'? If this portfolio of support fails or is inadequate the diagram also outlines the personal and social damage should personal time be squeezed too hard (stress, exhaustion, depression, ill-health, and poor relationships). Also implied by the diagram is the notion that these forms of time are in competition with each other. Thus, if we take the concept of 'life' in 'work–life' balance to mean the way in which individuals spend their time, then 'life' includes *both* 'care time' and 'personal time'. In particular, parents, especially mothers, and carers of frail elderly and other disabled people, find that their 'life' can be taken over by the obligation and their willingness to service the needs of their children and their dependent kin, friends and neighbours. Once the activities of 'life' are unpacked they can also be seen to be gendered. It is for this reason that these servicing activities within families and households undertaken informally by unpaid family and household members were claimed by second wave feminists as exploitative of women and are frequently and increasingly conventionally named as 'unpaid work' (Himmelweit, 1995). 'Work–life balance' could in this sense be renamed as 'Paid/Unpaid work balance'. However, we prefer to work with the notion of 'work–life balance' in order to sustain the idea that 'life' consists of both 'care time' and 'personal time'. As we shall see in the data that follows, even when individuals appear to have ample time for 'life', 'care time' may well impinge on or completely engulf time for autonomy and the practice of personal identity.

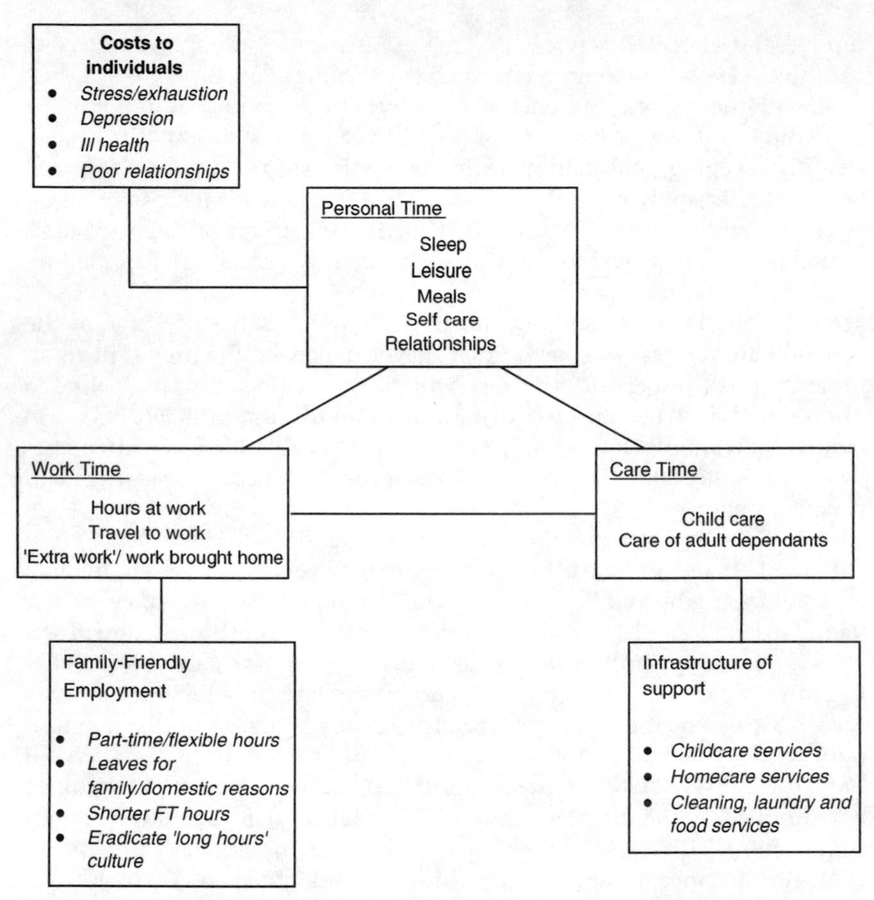


*Figure 13.1* Time dimensions for individuals within and beyond the household
*Note*: Figure originally developed in Yeandle, S. (2001), 'Three sorts of time', in Wilson, J. (ed.), *Women in the New Economy: a regional perspective*, London: The Smith Institute, pp. 41–6.

One irony of conceptualising a dichotomy between work time on the one hand, and care time and personal time on the other, is that in many respects the actual tasks carried out in work time and in care time are very similar. Housework, personal care, cooking for others, are all activities which are available as commodities within a market and can be purchased. Individual and household practices (and at times conscious decisions) about whether these activities are purchased as commodities or provided unpaid by individuals within households depends on numerous factors. Thus the dominant culture concerning the nature of marriage and motherhood, intra-familial negotiations around these cultural concerns within families (Finch and Mason, 1993), the availability of household and kin networks, income levels, desire for leisure time – all are factors that help determine the particular configuration of these tasks within individual households. Moreover, some of these tasks, particularly those which involve the care of children, disabled persons or the frail elderly are supported by developed welfare states, such that services are provided that either substitute for or complement unpaid caring activities. In these cases, social service employees, childcare workers, care assistants, and home care workers, are employed by the state (or, in some cases, the voluntary sector) to provide caring and childcare support services, either on a collective basis or directly to individual households. The precise configuration of state/family provided services depends on the politics of care – not least construed around questions of work–life balance – and on the availability of state funded or subsidised surrogate services in particular localities and at particular times.

Into this nexus of the 'work–life' balance and dichotomy – named by Glucksmann as the 'total social organisation of labour' (Glucksmann, 1995) – has come a relatively new and policy-driven phenomenon. This is the introduction, by many welfare states, of schemes which allow elderly and disabled people to receive cash instead of services, in the expectation that they will use these monies to pay (and employ) their carers directly. In the cases we have studied, elderly care users are being given the effective demand to enter the labour market for care, and to purchase their own care labour, thus relieving both their kin network and the state from providing them with some or all of the care they need. An additional complicating factor is that some of these schemes considered here allow elderly care users to pay their relatives to care for them – and so, in a sense, they become the direct employers of members of their own household or kin network. In these circumstances, the 'work–life balance' of those who care becomes extremely complex: if relatives who have previously cared for their elderly kin out of love or obligation but for no pay move into a situation of carrying out *precisely the same activities* for pay, then their 'work–life balance' is profoundly altered. Their 'life' has become their 'work'. The dichotomy between 'work' and 'life' no longer holds. The boundary between these two forms of activity no longer exists. And, as we shall see later, the dissolution of this boundary has implications for the division between care time and personal time.

In order to understand the way in which the various arrangements for care emerge once the dichotomy no longer holds, we have developed a conceptually based and schematic diagram that uses the idea that, instead of a boundary between paid care and unpaid care, there now exists a spectrum along which these various arrangements can be placed. This spectrum is the horizontal axis in Figure 13.2. On the left of the spectrum are the care relationships where recruitment of caring labour is almost entirely through the operation of obligation and affect played out through kin

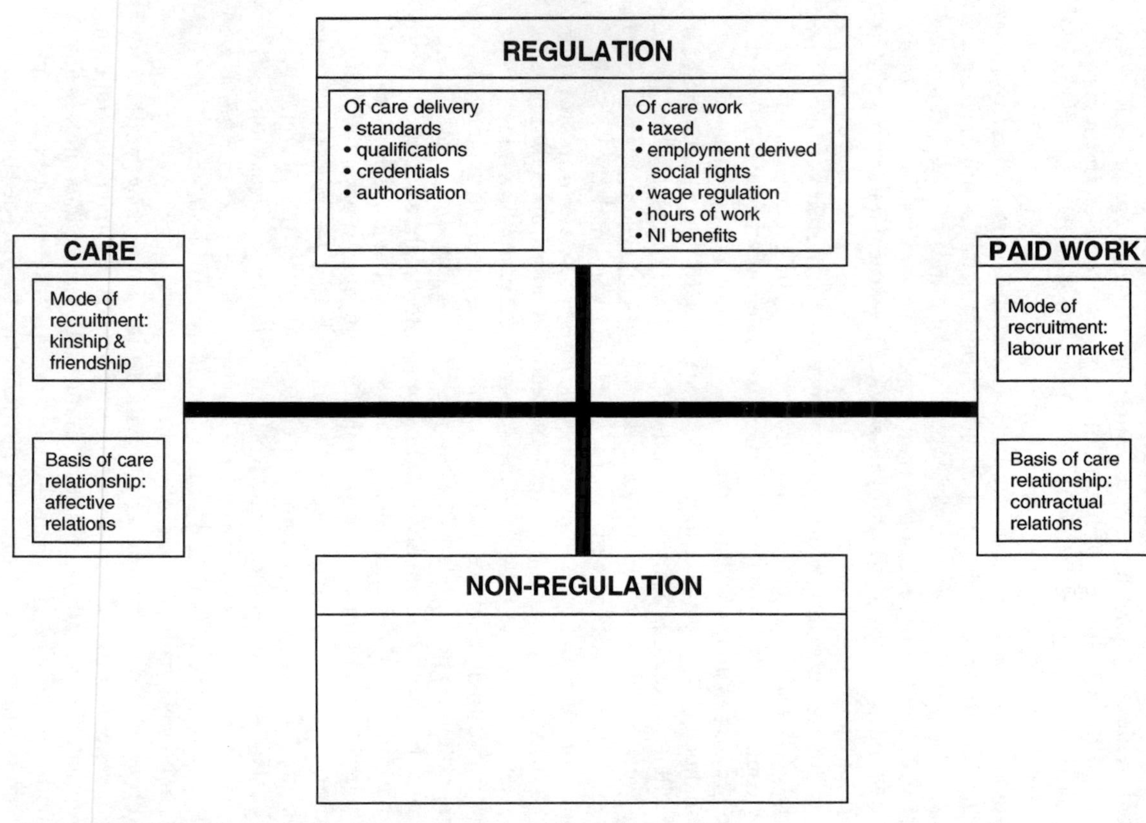


*Figure 13.2* Unpaid care and paid care: the cross of 'routed wages'

relations. These relationships are almost always unpaid (although, as we shall see later, they can, under special circumstances, be paid). On the right of the spectrum are the paid care relationships, where recruitment is normally through the conventional labour market, and careworkers are paid in the conventional form of a wage. The horizontal axis is particularly useful in understanding the way in which 'cash for care' schemes operate when they allow (or indeed specifically encourage) elderly care users to pay their relatives. This axis is cross cut by a vertical axis which refers to the second feature of many of these schemes – namely, whether the scheme regulates the care relationship, such that it ensures that the careworkers' social rights are covered, they receive paid leaves for sickness and holidays etc, and whether it oversees the recruitment of careworkers and ensures, for example, that they have qualifications to care, and that they have been subject to police checks.

In the paper that follows we use this schema to identify the particular features of some of the 'cash for care' schemes that were explored in the cross national study. In each of these examples we look at the way in which 'work–life balance' of the careworker/givers is differentially impacted by the type of 'cash for care' scheme within which they operate.

## The five country study: methods and types of scheme

The five countries under scrutiny in this project were Austria, France, Italy, the Netherlands, and the UK, each of which, as we shall see in Figure 13.3, can be placed in different segments of the schematic diagram outlined in Figure 13.2 and described above. The data collected in this project has been largely exploratory. We were concerned to investigate the employer/employee relationship in depth, and to develop an understanding of how and whether the presence of the cash nexus alters the care relationship, such that it emerges as a hybrid of work and care (Ungerson, 1999). In addition, the cross-national framework allowed us to look at the expected differential impact of the five funding regimes, and to explore the impact on differently organised labour markets. The methods adopted were appropriate to these aims and contexts. In each of the five countries the research teams interviewed ten elderly care users who were in receipt of monies through a 'cash for care' scheme. In three of the countries – Austria, the Netherlands and the UK – the sample was found through the agency or agencies involved in either allocating the monies or acting as a support for care users. In France the sample was found through an agency providing careworkers, and in Italy through local Church organisations who directed the researchers to frail elderly care users. In no sense then can the samples be said to be representative, but the qualitative data generated provided considerable insight into the meaning of 'cash for care' schemes for the elderly care users themselves. Once contacted and interviewed, the elderly

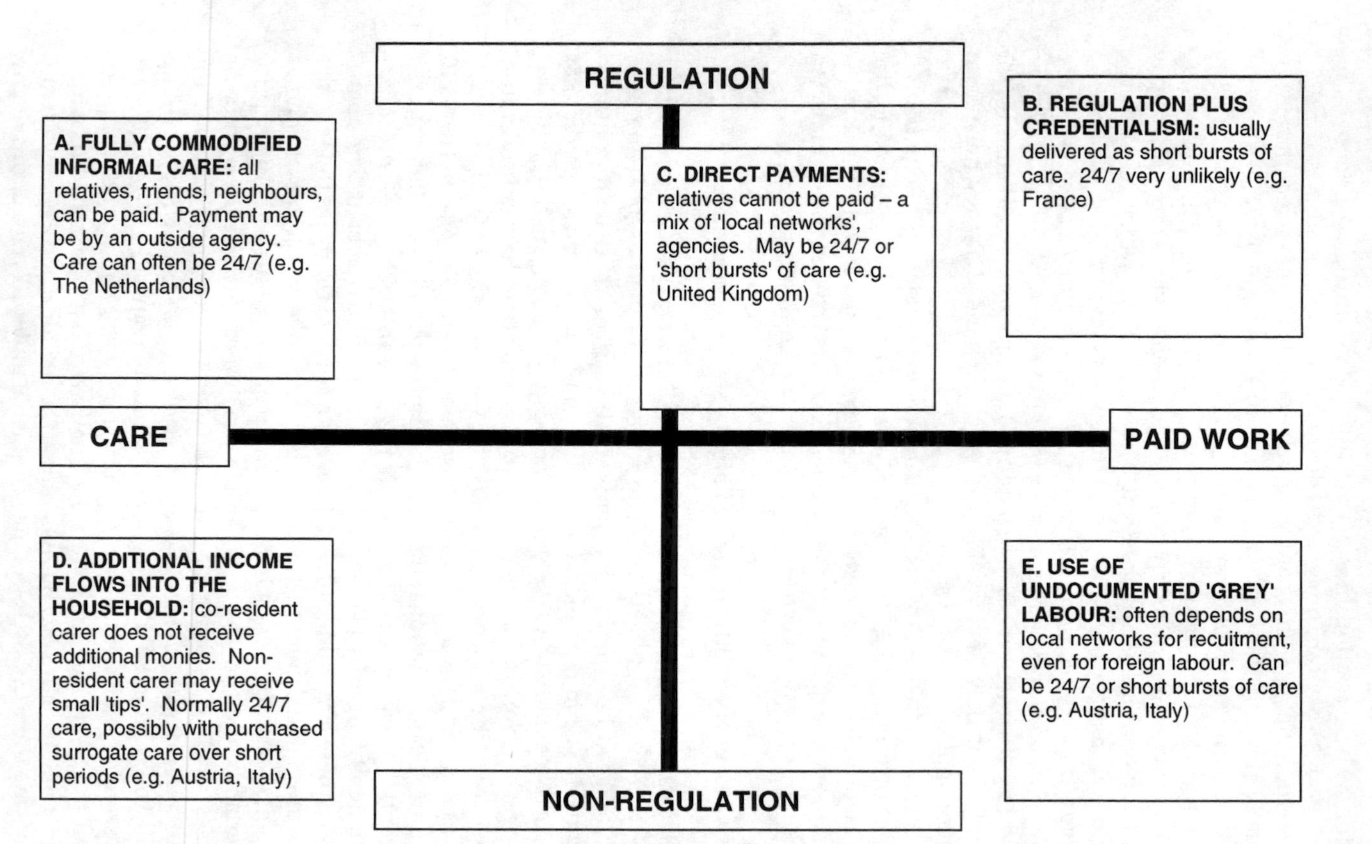


*Figure 13.3* Schemes for organising 'routed wages': type of payment, time availability and national examples

care users were invited to provide the names and contact addresses of their caregivers and the majority of interviews with caregiver/workers were conducted within these caring dyads. However, it became clear during the studies in Italy and Austria that there were interesting migratory and global features of the care labour market, and in both these studies some purposive sampling, using snowballing methods, was used to find additional migrant careworkers. In each of the five countries approximately twenty caregiver/workers were interviewed using qualitative interview methods. The research teams had collaborated in devising the interview schedules for both elderly care users and caregiver/workers, and the interviewers, who all spoke excellent English, had actively participated in these meetings, thus ensuring that each of the research teams fully understood the aims and objectives of the study.

Figure 13.3 uses the original schema to describe the position of the five different 'cash for care' schemes. In the top left hand quarter lies the type of 'cash for care' scheme we have named as 'Fully commodified informal care'. In this five country study there were two examples of this type of 'cash for care' scheme where elderly care users are allowed, and indeed encouraged, to pay their relatives to care for them. In the Netherlands, the scheme is run by the government in conjunction with the Social Insurance Bank which pays the caregiver/workers directly into their bank accounts; in Austria, alongside a very different government funded benefit for elderly care users, a major Catholic charity – Caritas – works with the city of Salzburg to fund a scheme whereby relatives are paid to care. Both schemes are heavily regulated, and the rights of 'workers' are carefully protected through contractual agreements. In the Dutch case in particular, the number of hours which the 'worker' should provide, even if they are co-resident relatives, is carefully specified within the contract.

In the top right hand quarter are schemes such as those that prevail in France. Here elderly care users are given benefits which, again, they are encouraged to use to purchase care work, and they can, if they wish, pay any relative (apart from their spouse) to care. However, the French system is also designed to develop employment opportunities particularly in areas of the labour market where there is a risk, because the work takes place in the private domain, that its sheer invisibility will allow for the development of unofficial 'grey' labour outside the tax and social security systems. One of the purposes of the French scheme is to pre-empt the possibility of grey market development, through the use of officially recognised agencies which allocate qualified and credentialised careworkers to multiple care users within a visible, recognised labour market.

Located in the middle of the horizontal axis, and lower down the vertical regulation/non regulation axis lies the UK example of 'Direct Payments'. This is a system, introduced for non-elderly disabled people in 1996, and extended to elderly care users in 2000, which allows them to opt for cash in the form of a 'direct payment' rather than the receipt of social services, and to employ their own caring labour directly. Low take-up of this option (about 2000 elderly care users in contrast to the approximately 1m French care users) means that the development of agencies to supply carers in response to this increase in effective demand has, so far in the UK, been limited. More often, UK care users themselves find their labour – typically unqualified, low paid careworkers drawn from their own neighbourhood and extant networks, with a scattering of agency workers who are also almost always unqualified and hence low paid. While efforts are made to regulate this labour, this is minimally undertaken, and means only that relatives cannot be paid and that care users have to produce invoices and evidence that their employees are covered for national insurance in order to obtain the Direct Payment from their local Social Services Department.

Below the horizontal axis and into the non-regulated segment of Figure 13.3 lie the two further examples of the Italian and Austrian allowances to care users. Here the state is insouciant about the ultimate destination of these payments, and there are no conditions, apart from levels of disability and, in the Italian case, means tests, attached to receipt of these benefits. However, they are large enough to allow for the effective demand of very cheap labour and, as we shall see, in the Italian case an unofficial labour market containing largely international migrant labour exists which is available to care for very low pay rates. In both schemes, it is also the case that many households regard the benefit as simply a form of income maintenance and the cash remains within the household.

## When 'life' becomes 'work': the payment and employment of relatives to care

The payment of relatives to care is a feature of the Dutch 'personal budget scheme' and of the charity, Caritas, in Austria (for a fuller description of these schemes, see Ungerson (2004)). The discussion that follows uses mainly Austrian data to illustrate the impact on the work–life balance of those who care. Most, but not all, of the paid relatives in Austria had experienced, as had the Dutch sample, a change in status from unpaid to paid carer as a result of the introduction of the scheme. For them, 'life' had literally been transformed into 'work'. For many of them, the particular appeal of the transfer of their caring activities from unpaid to paid work was the shift in their own self-perception and the perception of others: once 'life' had become 'work' they were more complete citizens:

> You can only say that I simply felt as if I had been promoted. Society also saw it totally differently then. Suddenly it was: 'Aha, you're doing a job'. Although I didn't do anything differently than before, it was suddenly seen as self-evident. But if you then say that you're working for

> Caritas, people say to you: 'Wow, you're working now'. When actually nothing has changed, apart from now going to a discussion group and presentations. In principle it's the same. [...] As soon as you're in employment and can say to the doctor that you have your own health insurance, it appears that you're a better type of person. From the point of view of society, this type of employment is very good for women. (*Case 16, Austrian woman carer paid through Caritas, caring for her mother-in-law*)

This respondent was unusual in reporting the precise way in which others, within the public domain, regarded her transition from unpaid to paid worker. For our other Austrian respondents, paid through the Caritas scheme, it was the way their interior lives and the care relationship had developed once they were paid that was the more important. For example, one carer said, when asked about how she experienced 'this type of work', that it was:

> Absolutely fantastic. We understand each other very well. *Previously we scarcely knew each other. The other person was always somewhere else.* It's quite different now. She is sweet, grateful and easy to look after. (*Case 7, Austrian woman carer paid through Caritas, caring for her mother*), our italics

The transformation of 'life' into 'work' had meant that the opportunity costs of taking up unpaid care had been reduced, thus allowing this carer to successfully substitute her own paid kin care for her previous paid employment as a school teacher. Here a major benefit of being paid to care had been the development of a stronger bond between mother and daughter.

Not all relatives paid by the Caritas scheme reported such positive outcomes as far as their work–life balance was concerned. Many of them reported that as the boundaries between 'work' and 'life' had been dissolved, they now experienced particular difficulties in establishing their own privacy, space, and time for themselves. Precisely because it was now paid, 'care time' had encroached on 'personal time'. For example, one woman, caring for her mother and paid to do so by Caritas, had opted to take on this work because it fitted particularly well with her other caring responsibilities for her son:

> The plus side is that I can always be with my son, because he is ill an amazing amount, just as I was as a child. I don't have to get into trouble with an employer because I'm automatically at home. Of course I'm employed in the sense that I'm earning money and my son is insured. If I was employed in a firm, I wouldn't always be able to take time off. My son was sick twice in January – no employer would have given me time

> off. Then I would lose my job. That's the only plus side. (*Case 15, Austrian woman carer paid through Caritas, caring for her mother*)

In that sense, then, she had resolved her personal 'work–life' balance by taking on the paid care of her mother. But, due to the lack of boundaries between the 'work' she undertook for her mother and her own 'life' away from the people she cared for, she had difficulties in leading a properly adult life:

> The minus side is that I never have any free time. I can't go out in the evenings if I want to. I couldn't actually do that, because I don't want to push my son onto someone else – but I don't go out that much any more. I can go out once a month, and then I have to be home by 3 a.m. because I've got to work to a prescribed time. I'll be 39 this year but I have to be home by 3 a.m.

These kinds of difficulties in leading a life of one's own are frequently reported by informal unpaid carers (Ungerson, 1987). But in this study, where unpaid care has been transformed into paid care, the carers felt additionally obligated, through the payment of a wage and the existence of a contract, to conform to the conventions of paid work – namely, punctuality, reliability and consistency – at the cost of their own autonomy.

Thus, when 'life' becomes 'work' there are complex outcomes. On the one hand, paid care by relatives can constitute a transformative form of citizenship. It constitutes the recognition and remuneration of previously invisible unpaid caring work, and some caregivers/workers, as a result, experience an upsurge in self-esteem and the respect accorded them by others. However, by dissolving entirely the boundary between 'work' and 'life' the activities of 'life' that are *not* concerned with the care of dependants, but rather, are concerned with autonomy and identity, come directly under threat. Unless both 'employer' and 'employee' in these paid kin care relationships are aware of that threat, and are able to negotiate a suitable solution, paid care by kin can, in just the same way as unpaid care, become burdensome and a trap. 'Work–life balance' can transform into 'work-nolife' stasis.

## Where cash payments to users are low

In the examples discussed above, caregiver/workers were in receipt of reasonable amounts of money. Indeed, as one of the Austrian respondents employed by Caritas remarked, 'I earn more than I did in the factory' (Case 15). But some 'cash for care' schemes pay monies to care users with no conditions attached. This is the case with the Italian system of allowances to care users, and the government paid system of allowances payable to disabled Austrians. In this study we found elderly care users who spent this money on a wide range of commodities: basic living costs, medicines, small payments to neighbours for discrete services such as cleaning and shopping, as well as the employment of caring labour. In both Austria and Italy frail elderly people eked out their allowances by finding very cheap labour to help them with the activities of daily living on a twenty four hour basis. By tapping into a low wage care labour market, available in both countries – in Milan through global migration of undocumented workers, and in Vienna through the recruitment of cross-border workers from Hungary and Slovenia – and by offering, in addition to a low wage, payment in kind in the form of accommodation and basic subsistence, elderly care users were able to negotiate *both* relatively low expenditure on personal care and to achieve 24/7 care. In contrast, in France, in a context where payments to care users are partially designed to assist the development of an official labour market for care work, and where there has been rapid growth in credentialism for a strict occupational hierarchy of care work, relatively low payments mean that elderly care users can generally only employ well-qualified careworkers for very short bursts of time. As the discussion that follows indicates, the result is that the 'work–life balance' of the careworkers involved emerges very differently.

We have previously described the way in which, when relatives are paid to care, the boundaries between 'work' and aspects of 'life' dissolve such that there is a risk of loss of the aspects of life that constitute autonomy in the private sphere. The evidence of this study, particularly of the migrant workers in the Italian city of Milan, is that, especially where the workers live with their employers, their 'work' becomes their 'life'. Similar results have been reported by Anderson (2000) particularly in relation to domestic work in Athens. The boundaries between their own lives and those of their elderly employers dissolve: their emotional lives, their own time, their personal space, all become very closely entangled with those of their employers. For example, in this study we found a Spanish woman who had very recently quarrelled with and left her employer of 26 years. Although she did not live with her employer it was clear that her life and that of her employer had become so bound together that she described her employer as 'like a sister'. They had quarrelled over the careworker's time and the fact that she wished to spend time with her own grandson:

> At a certain point we didn't understand each other. This all happened because she became jealous of my little grandchild. One time I said that I could not come to her house for a week because I had to take care of my grandson, and she got very angry. We quarrelled, and I decided to go. Now I feel great remorse in having done so, because I really am very fond of her. (*Spanish careworker, working in Milan*)

Another migrant worker reported the pressure that her employers exerted on her, such that she had made an open ended commitment to remain in the job, and was unable, even when unwell, to claim her own time and space:

> The son and daughter-in-law tell me, 'We cannot change over to another person. You must stay here as long as mother survives'. I have committed myself...I got ill, but I live here, so I stay and work as usual.

Problems surrounding privacy and personal time were frequently reported by these migrant workers to the extent that they felt they had lost all personal autonomy. A Peruvian living with her elderly employer described her difficulties:

> When she watches television in the afternoon, seeing that she ... doesn't need me, I want to take the opportunity to write a letter to my family, but she does not want that. She wants me to stay always by her side, and watch television seated next to her, so if she sees me going away, she says 'Where are you? What are you doing? I pay you to stay with me and keep me company. I don't pay you to wander about the house.' However, she has got to understand that *she has not bought me* with that little salary she pays me. (our italics)

Not surprisingly, in these circumstances, where 'work' has become 'life', boundaries have dissolved and balance has been lost, such workers long for what they consider to be the aspects of a 'normal' job, with boundaries once more firmly in place:

> Living in this lady's house helps us enormously. However, it is not like living in your own house...you never have a moment free as you do when you're at home, not even when you're sleeping. It is not a normal job. A normal job is when you know what time you start and what time you finish. (*Migrant careworker in Milan*)

Other global migrants had left their own dependants (their children) in their countries of origin, where they were cared for by grandparents. Again, for these workers, an idealised work–life balance was referred to, where boundaries between 'work' and 'life' had been put back in place:

> I would like to have my children here and living with me within five years, working in a rest home during the day and going home to them in the evening. (*Migrant careworker in Milan*)

The elderly care users in this situation were clearly getting an excellent deal – for relatively low cost they were in receipt of good enough care delivered over 24/7. But there were very high costs to the workers. For them, the separate entities of 'work' and 'life' had entirely disappeared; in reaction, they sought a nostalgic past and optimistic future where the work–life dichotomy could be reinstated, and all the activities of 'life', including the care of their own dependants, reconstituted.

In France, where relatively low payments combined with an official labour market for care which promoted the use of qualified relatively well paid workers, the care solution for elderly care users was rather different. They recruited through a local care agency and were attended by careworkers (most of whom were qualified with a basic French care diploma) who delivered services to large numbers of elderly people during their working day. The net result was that these careworkers, despite having a qualification which encouraged holistic care, were constantly rushed, and found their time for their own 'life' constrained by their sense that they were obligated to spend more time with and for their multiple clients:

> One lady called me for bread. I told her, 'I am sorry but I am going out.' I was going to a wedding. She said 'Can't you spare five minutes?' She started to shout. I said, 'I am sorry, you knew I was not going to come today, I have to go to a wedding which has been planned for a long time – I am going to the hairdresser.' She said, 'If you have time to go to the hairdresser you have time to get my bread.' What did I do? I went and got her bread. (*Case 4, Rennes agency worker, France*)

However, despite these senses of obligation and the fact of often working beyond their contracted and paid for hours, these careworkers were also able, unlike the live-in migrant workers in Italy, to put boundaries around their 'work' and to protect their own 'lives'. This same careworker, after explaining how difficult she found it to say 'no' to her clients, commented:

> Sometimes I think I do my work, I put in my hours, now I am at home, finished, I put the answering machine on.

The main difficulty for these workers was that the agency for which they worked was delivering a service seven days a week, and in order to do so was compelled to ask workers to work at times when they would in fact prefer to be in their own homes:

> I have been working for the ADMR for three years and I have noticed that the longer I am there, the more they ask me to work on Saturdays and Sundays. It is not clear. People think that there is a 24 hour service, 7 days a week. They do not understand that we, I refer to all of us in general, have our own family life and we also would like to stay at home on Saturdays and Sundays.

Thus these workers were operating within a 'work–life' dichotomy: for them the boundaries were not so much dissolved as *disputed*. The disputes took place between themselves and their multiple employers – first, with their individual clients who could exert emotional power over them; and second with their employing agency which could operate the rather more material levers of remuneration and continued employment. Moreover, in terms of time, these workers were trained to work with the body times of their elderly clients, but simultaneously, were subject to the much faster bureaucratic and organisational time exigencies of their employing agency. One of these paid careworkers described this conflict graphically:

> I asked, 'Until what time are we to work in the evening?' I was told, 'Usually you should be home by 7.30 at the latest'. Yes, but when I have both clients. Like this evening: I have Mr. M. first. Friday is griddle cake night, the night on which he eats best. So the griddle cakes have to be heated up, the egg has to be placed on top and everything. I don't know where he puts it all! He eats 3 of them! But it makes him happy. On Friday he treats himself. You cannot do it in 5 minutes! Afterwards there is the washing up, and then he has to be undressed. As I have shopping to do this evening I will take $^{1}/_{4}$ of an hour to go to the nearest grocers, it's more expensive but what can you do? On Fridays, instead of $^{1}/_{4}$ of an hour it takes a good $^{3}/_{4}$ of an hour, plus $^{1}/_{4}$ of an hour for shopping, that makes 1 hour.

## Conclusion

This paper has shown some of the very complex ways in which the boundaries between paid and unpaid care work are shifting under the influence of changing social policies. There are risks and benefits for both care users and for those supplying caring labour within these policy frameworks. For any individual, the most desirable work–life balance changes over time, as personal circumstances and the needs of dependants change. In writing this chapter, our aim is not to indicate the 'right' solution to the care dilemmas faced by elderly people, their families and those charged with providing welfare services, still less to prescribe the best way forward. In developing cash for care systems and in implementing policy in this field, however, all parties need to be aware of the unintended consequences which may flow from the changes made.

Thus any empowering of care users within these systems inevitably comes at the cost of taking on the responsibilities of an employer – including an employer's responsibility for the fair and reasonable treatment of their employees. Today's employers are expected to respond favourably to their employees' needs to balance work and life, and care users may need support in adopting good practice in the way they employ their careworkers. This may be a particularly sensitive issue when careworkers are also kin who have previously been unpaid caregivers.

Furthermore, as this chapter has indicated, some European states have taken significant steps to regulate and accredit domiciliary careworkers in recent years. These developments, designed both to protect those to whom care is given and to create better jobs and career pathways for careworkers, also have certain unintended consequences. The French examples cited here suggest that it is important to consider their impact on careworkers' own work–life balance, alongside other benefits. The Italian examples of how these systems can involve grey labour also alert us to the social risks to unprotected workers whose status is vulnerable – although their preference for this type of work over more risky alternatives, such as sex work or illegal factory employment, needs also to be recognised.

Finally, examining our data through the lens of the concept of work–life balance has illuminated a number of important features of 'cash for care' systems. This data problematises a simple work–life dichotomy, and heightens awareness of the complex ways in which paid employment impinges on other areas of life.

## Note

1. The data presented here is taken from the ESRC project L212252080: Shifting Boundaries of Paid and Unpaid Work: Cross National Perspectives, co-directed by Clare Ungerson and Sue Yeandle. We are very grateful to our colleagues in the five countries who collected the data, as follows: *Austria*: August Oesterle and Elisabeth Hammer, Vienna University of Economics and Business Administration; *France*: Claude Martin and Blanche Le Bihan, ENSP, Rennes; *Italy*: Cristiano Gori, Barbara da Roit and Michela Barbot, Istituto per la recerca sociale, Milan; *Netherlands*: Marja Pijl and Clarie Ramakers, University of Nijmegen; *United Kingdom*: Sue Yeandle and Bernadette Stiell, Sheffield Hallam University.

## References

Anderson, B. (2000) *Doing the dirty work?: the global politics of domestic labour*, London: Zed Books.

Finch, J. and Mason, J. (1993) *Negotiating Family Responsibilities*, London: Routledge.

Fletcher, J.K. and Rapoport, R. (1996) 'Work-Family Issues as a Catalyst for Organizational Change', in Lewis, S. and Lewis, J. (eds), *The Work-Family Challenge: Rethinking Employment*, London: Sage.

Glucksmann, M. (1995), 'Why "work"? Gender and the "total social organisation of labour"', *Gender, Work and Organisation*, vol. 2, no. 2, pp. 63–75.

Harkness, S. (1999) 'The 24-hour Economy', *Employment Audit No. 11*, London: Employment Policy Institute.

Himmelweit, S. (1995), 'The Discovery of "Unpaid Work": The Social Consequences of the Expansion of "Work"', *Feminist Economics*, vol. 1, no. 2, pp. 1–19.

Kodz, J., Kersley, B., Strebler, M.T. and O'Regan, S. (1998) *Breaking the Long Hours Culture*, IES Report No. 352, London: Institute for Employment Studies.

The Work Foundation (2002) *Working Capital*, London: The Work Foundation.

TUC (1998) *The Time of Our Lives: A TUC Report on Working Hours and Flexibility*, London: TUC.

Ungerson, C. (1987) *Policy is Personal: sex, gender and informal care*, London: Tavistock.

Ungerson, C. (1999) Personal assistants and disabled people: an examination of a hybrid form of work and care, *Work, Employment and Society*, vol. 13, no. 4, pp. 583–600.

Yeandle, S. (2001) 'Three Sorts of Time' in Wilson, J. (ed.) *Women in the New Economy: a regional perspective*, pp. 41–6, London: The Smith Institute.

Yeandle, S., Phillips, J., Scheibl, F., Wigfield, A. and Wise, S. (2003) *Line Managers and Family-friendly Employment: Roles and Perspectives*, Bristol: The Policy Press.

# Author Index

# Subject Index